11th
BLUE
BOOK®
Dolls & Values

photographs
by Howard Foulke

Published by Hobby House Press, Inc.
Grantsville, Maryland 21502

Other Titles by Author:
Blue Book of Dolls & Values®
2nd Blue Book of Dolls & Values®
3rd Blue Book of Dolls & Values®
4th Blue Book of Dolls & Values®
5th Blue Book of Dolls & Values®
6th Blue Book of Dolls & Values®
7th Blue Book of Dolls & Values®
8th Blue Book of Dolls & Values®
9th Blue Book of Dolls & Values®
10th Blue Book of Dolls & Values®
Focusing on Effanbee Composition Dolls
Focusing on Treasury of Mme. Alexander Dolls
Focusing on Gebrüder Heubach Dolls
Kestner: King of Dollmakers
Simon & Halbig Dolls: The Artful Aspect
Doll Classics
Focusing on Dolls

COVER(left to right): 32in (81cm) Circle Dot Bru Bébé. *H & J Foulke, Inc.* 13in (33cm) Circle Dot Bru Bébé, all original. *Richard Wright Antiques.* Gebrüder Heubach Pouty Character. *H & J Foulke, Inc.*

TITLE PAGE: 26in (66cm) Simon & Halbig 1250 child. *H & J Foulke, Inc.* (For further information see page 332.)
BACK COVER: (top) *Barbie* #3, original swimsuit. *Courtesy of McMasters Doll Auctions.* (For further information see page 80.) (bottom) 14in (36cm) *Amy. H & J Foulke, Inc.* (For further information see page 26.)

ADDITIONAL COPIES AVAILABLE @ $17.95 plus $4.75
FROM
HOBBY HOUSE PRESS, INC.
GRANTSVILLE, MD 21536
1-800-554-1447

Doll collecting continues to increase in popularity every year. The great number of collectors entering the field has given rise to larger and more frequent doll shows, more dealers in dolls, more books on dolls, thicker doll magazines and more doll conventions and seminars, as well as an overwhelming offering of new dolls by mass-production companies and individual artists. This explosion has also increased the demand for old dolls and discontinued collector's dolls, causing prices to rise as more collectors vie for the same dolls.

With the average old doll representing a purchase of at least several hundred dollars, today's collectors must be as well informed as possible about the dolls they are considering as additions to their collections. Since the first *Blue Book of Dolls & Values* was published in 1974, our objectives have remained the same:

- To present a book that will help collectors to identify and learn more about dolls.
- To provide retail prices as a guide for buyers and sellers of dolls.

Since every edition of the *Blue Book* has sold more copies than the previous one, we can only conclude that these objectives are in line with the needs of the doll lovers, collectors, dealers and appraisers who keep buying the latest editions of our book.

The dolls presented in this book are listed alphabetically by maker, material or the trade name of the individual doll. An extensive index has been provided to help in locating a specific doll.

Of course, in a book this size, not every doll ever made can be discussed, but we have tried to include a broad spectrum of dolls that are available, desirable, interesting and popular, and even some that are rare.

For each doll we have provided historical information, a description of the doll, a copy of the mark or label, the retail selling price and a photograph or picture reference to a previous edition of the *Blue Book* as there is not enough space to show a photograph of each doll in each edition.

The price for a doll listed in this price guide is the retail value of a doll fulfilling all of the criteria discussed in the following chapter if it is purchased from a dealer.

In some cases the doll sizes given are the only ones known to have been made, but in the cases of most of the French and German bisque, china, papier-mâché and wood dolls, sizes priced are chosen at random and listed sizes must not be interpreted as definitive. It is impossible to list every doll in every possible size, especially for dolls that range from 6 to 42 inches (15 to 106cm). The user will need to call a little common sense into play to interpolate a price for an unlisted size.

The historical information given for some of the dolls would have been much more difficult to compile were it not for the original research already published by Dorothy S., Elizabeth A. and Evelyn J. Coleman; Johana G. Anderton; and Jürgen and Marianne Cieslik.

The data for retail prices was gathered during 1992 and 1993 from antique shops and shows, auctions, doll

4

shops and shows, advertisements in collectors' periodicals, lists from doll dealers, and purchases and sales reported by both collectors and dealers. This information, along with our own valuations and judgments, was computed into the range of prices shown in this book. When we could not find a sufficient number of dolls to be sure of giving a reliable range, we marked those prices with two asterisks ("**").

In setting a price for each doll, we use a range to allow for the variables of originality, quality and condition that must be reflected in the price. As collectors become more sophisticated in their purchases, fine examples of a doll, especially those which are all original or with period clothing, can bring a premium of up to 50% more than prices quoted for ordinary examples. Sometimes a doll will bring a premium price because it is particularly cute, sweet, pretty or visually appealing, making an outstanding presentation. There is no way to factor this appeal into a price guide.

The international market has been an important factor in the change of domestic doll prices during the past few years. International interest has added a whole new dimension to the American doll market as increasing awareness of antique dolls in Germany, France, Switzerland, Holland, Denmark and other countries is causing a great exodus and a depletion of our supply of antique dolls.

Of particular interest in the international arena are German bisque character children, German bisque babies by Kestner, Kämmer & Reinhardt, and Hertel, Schwab & Co., German bisque closed-mouth shoulder heads, German bisque "dolly" faces (particularly small sizes) by Kestner, Kämmer & Reinhardt, and Handwerck, Käthe Kruse dolls and German celluloid dolls. This interest has caused continued price increases in these categories. The Japanese collectors who were pushing up the prices of antique French dolls have pulled out of the market, causing prices for these dolls to fall.

All prices given for antique dolls are for those of good quality and condition, but showing normal wear, and appropriately dressed in new or old clothing, unless other specifications are given in the description accompanying that particular doll. Bisque or china heads should not be cracked, broken or repaired, but may have slight making imperfections such as speckling, surface lines, darkened mold lines and uneven coloring. Bodies may have repairs or be nicely repainted, but should be old and appropriate to the head. A doll with old dress, shoes and wig will generally be valued at higher than quoted prices because these items are in scarce supply and can easily cost more than $65 each if purchased separately.

9in (23cm) Gebr. Heubach googly 8995, very rare. (For further information see page 186.)
H & J Foulke, Inc.

Prices given for modern dolls are for those in overall good to excellent condition with original hair and clothing, except as noted. Composition may be lightly crazed, but should be colorful. Hard plastic and vinyl must be perfect, with hair in original set and crisp, original clothes. A never-played-with doll in original box with labels would bring a premium price.

The users of this book must keep in mind that no price guide is the final word. It cannot provide an absolute answer as to what to pay. This book should be used only as an aid in purchasing a doll. The final decision must be yours, for only you are on the scene, actually examining the specific doll in ques-

tion. No book can take the place of actual field experience. Doll popularity can cycle; prices can fluctuate; regional variations can occur. Before you buy, do a lot of looking. Ask questions. Most dealers and collectors are glad to talk about their dolls and pleased to share their information with you.

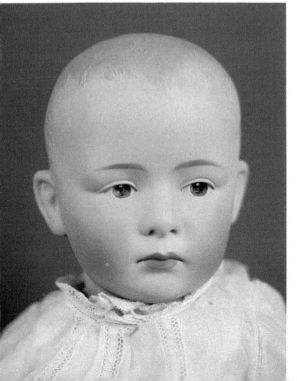

Above: 18in (46cm) Alt, Beck & Gottschalck 1358 character girl. (For further information see page 52.) *H & J Foulke, Inc.*

Left: 19in (48cm) Gebr. Heubach 7602 character boy. (For further information see page 202.) *H & J Foulke, Inc.*

Acknowledgements

For their encouragement and support, we again wish to thank our friends, customers, fellow dealers and fans, as well as doll collectors around the world. Special thanks to:

Those who allowed us to use photographs of their dolls or who provided special information for use in this edition are indispensable: Nancy A. Smith, Jim Fernando, Richard Wright, Richard Saxman, Jane Mann, Peggy Bealfield of Doodlebug Dolls, Joyce Watson of McMasters Doll Auctions, Esther & Seymour Schwartz, Vern & Cathy Kiefer, Kay & Wayne Jensen, Carole Jean Zvonar, Leslie & Norman Hurford, Jackie Kaner, Mary Barnes Kelley, Ruth Noden, Ursula Mertz, Joanna Ott, Miriam Blankman, Yvonne Baird, Gayle Elan, June Beckett, Margaret Cousins, Virginia Ann Heyerdahl, Anna May Case, Christine Lorman, Becky & Jay Lowe, Don Pinegar, Cookie Wershbale, Ruth West, George Humphrey, Joan & Larry Kindler, June & Norman Verro, Geri Gentile, Betty Lunz, Richard W. Withington, Inc., and H & J Foulke, Inc.

Those who shared their doll collections but wished to remain anonymous are greatly appreciated.

The Colemans, who allowed some marks to be reproduced from their book, *The Collector's Encyclopedia of Dolls.*

Gary and Mary Ruddell of Hobby House Press, Inc., with whom we have worked for more than 20 years.

Howard, for his beautiful photographs.

All of these people helped make this book possible.

Jan Foulke
June 1993

In Memoriam
Friends who were always willing to share their dolls. They are missed.
Barbara Fernando
Ralph Griffith
Joe Jackson
Frances Walker

Out-of-print editions of the **Blue Books of Dolls & Values** have become collectors' items. Out-of-print books can be found at dolls shows or auctions. We sometimes have books available for purchase. Write us in care of the publisher. The following prices are for clean books with light wear on covers and corners.

Blue Book of Dolls & Values®	**$135**
2nd Blue Book of Dolls & Values®	**110**
3rd Blue Book of Dolls & Values®	**75**
4th Blue Book of Dolls & Values®	**75**
5th Blue Book of Dolls & Values®	**35**
6th Blue Book of Dolls & Values®	**30**

Investing in Dolls

With the price of the average old doll representing a purchase of at least several hundred dollars in today's doll market, the assembling of a doll collection becomes rather costly. Actually, very few people buy dolls strictly as an investment; most collectors buy a doll because they like it. It has appeal to them for some reason: perhaps as an object of artistic beauty, perhaps because it evokes some kind of sentiment, perhaps because it fills some need that they feel or speaks to something inside them. It is this personal feeling toward the doll which makes it of value to the collector.

However, most collectors expect to at least break even when they eventually sell their dolls. Unfortunately, there is no guarantee that any particular doll will appreciate consistently year after year; however, the track record for old or antique dolls is fairly good. If you are thinking of the future sale of your collection, be wary of buying expensive new or reproduction dolls. They have no track record and little resale value. Collectible dolls of the last 30 years are a risky market. Alexander dolls are a case in point. After many years of doubling their value the minute they were carried from the toy store shelves, dolls of the 1960s and 1980s have slid in price so that many are now bringing only 25 - 50% of their cost to collectors.

Because most collectors have only limited funds for purchasing dolls, they must be sure they are spending their dollars to the best advantage. There are many factors to consider when buying a doll, and this chapter will give some suggestions about what to look for and what to consider. Probably the primary tenet is that a collector who is not particularly well-informed about a doll should not consider purchasing it unless he or she has confidence in the person selling the doll.

MARKS

Fortunately for collectors, most of the antique bisque, some of the papier-mâché, cloth and other types of antique dolls are marked or labeled. Marks and labels give the buyer confidence because they identify the trade name, the maker, the country of origin, the style or mold number, or perhaps even the patent date.

Most composition and modern dolls are marked with the maker's name and sometimes also the trade name of the doll and the date. Some dolls have tags sewn on or into their clothing to identify them; many still retain original hang tags.

Of course, many dolls are unmarked, but after you have seen quite a few dolls, you begin to notice their individual characteristics and can often determine what a doll possibly is. When you have had some experience buying dolls, you begin to recognize an unusual face or an especially fine quality doll. Then there should be no hesitation about buying a doll marked only with a mold number or no mark at all. The doll has to speak for itself, and the price must be based upon the collector's frame of doll reference. That is, one must relate the face and quality to those of a known doll maker and make price judgments from that point.

Top left: 19in (48cm) English wood, so-called Queen Anne, with "fork" hands. (For further information see page 355.) *Private Collection.*

Top right: 17¾in (45cm) signed Pierotti wax doll, all original. (For further information see page 351.) *Private Collection.*

Left: 25in (64cm) Rochard lady with Stanhope "jewelled" shoulder plate. (For further information see page 170.) *Private Collection.*

QUALITY

The mark does not tell everything about a doll. Two examples from the same mold could look entirely different and carry vastly different prices because of the quality of the work done on the doll, which can vary from head to head, even with dolls made from the same mold by one firm. To command top price, a bisque doll should have lovely bisque, decoration, eyes and hair. Before purchasing a doll, the collector should determine whether the example is the best available of that type.

Top left: 15in (38cm) Alexander *Princess Elizabeth*, all original. (For further information see page 20.) *H & J Foulke, Inc.*

Top right: 28in (71cm) Steiner *Bébé Le Parisien*. (For further information see page 339.) *Jan Foulke Collection.*

Right: 16in (41cm) Lenci *Laura*, all original. (For further information see page 268.) *H & J Foulke, Inc.*

Even the molding of one head can be much sharper with more delineation of such details as dimples or locks of hair. The molding detail is especially important to notice when purchasing dolls with character faces or molded hair.

The quality of the bisque should be smooth; dolls with bisque which is pimply, peppered with tiny black specks or unevenly colored or which has noticeable firing lines on the face would be second choices at a lower price. However, collectors must keep in mind that porcelain factories sold many heads with small manufacturing defects because companies were in business for profit and were producing expendable play items, not works of art. Small manufacturing defects do not devalue a doll. It is perfectly acceptable to have light speckling, light surface lines, firing lines in inconspicuous places, darkened mold lines, a few black specks or cheek rubs. The absolutely perfect bisque head is a rarity.

Since doll heads are hand-painted, the artistry of the decoration should be examined. The tinting of the complexion should be subdued and even, not harsh and splotchy. Artistic skill should be evident in the portrayal of the expression on the face and in details such as the lips, eyebrows and eyelashes, and particularly in the eyes, which should show highlights and shading when they are painted. On a doll with molded hair, individual brush marks to give the hair a more realistic look would be a desirable detail.

If a doll has a wig, the hair should be appropriate if not old. Dynel or synthetic wigs are not appropriate for antique dolls; a human hair or good quality mohair wig should be used. If a doll has glass eyes, they should be old with natural color and threading in the irises to give a lifelike appearance.

If a doll does not meet all of these standards, it should be priced lower than one that does. Furthermore, an especially fine example will bring a premium over an ordinary but nice model.

CONDITION

Another important factor when pricing a doll is the condition. A bisque doll with a crack on the face or extensive professional repair involving the face would sell for one-quarter or less

than a doll with only normal wear. An inconspicuous hairline would decrease the value somewhat, but in a rare doll it would not be as great a detriment as in a common doll. As the so-called better dolls are becoming more difficult to find, a hairline is more acceptable to collectors if there is a price adjustment. The same is true for a doll which has a spectacular face — a hairline would be less important to price in that doll than in one with an ordinary face.

Sometimes a head will have a factory flaw which occurred in the making, such as a firing crack, scratch, piece of kiln debris, dark specks, small bubbles, a ridge not smoothed out or light surface lines. Since the factory was producing toys for a profit and not creating works of art, heads with slight flaws were not all discarded, especially if flaws were inconspicuous or could be covered. If factory defects are not detracting, they have little or no effect on the value of a doll.

It is to be expected that an old doll will show some wear. Perhaps there is a rub on the nose or cheek, a few small "wig pulls" or maybe a chipped earring hole; a Schoenhut doll or a Käthe Kruse may have some scuffs; an old papier-mâché may have a few age cracks; a china head may show wear on the hair; an old composition body may have scuffed toes or missing fingers. This wear is to be expected and does not necessarily affect the value of a doll. However, a doll in exceptional condition will bring more than "book" price.

Unless an antique doll is rare or you particularly want that specific doll, do not pay top price for a doll which needs extensive work: restringing, setting eyes, repairing fingers, replacing body parts, new wig or dressing. All of these repairs add up to a considerable sum at the doll hospital, possibly making the total cost of the doll more than it is really worth.

Composition dolls in perfect condition are becoming harder to find. Because their material is so susceptible to the atmosphere, their condition can deteriorate literally overnight. Even in excellent condition, a composition doll nearly always has some fine crazing or slight fading. It is very difficult to find a composition doll in mint condition and even harder to be sure that it will stay that way. However, in order for a composition doll to bring "book" price, there should be a minimum of crazing, very good coloring, original uncombed hair and original clothes in very good condition. Pay less for a doll that does not have original clothes and hair or that is all original but shows extensive play wear. Pay even less for one with heavy crazing and cracking or other damages. For composition dolls that are all original, unplayed with, in original boxes and with little or no crazing, allow a premium of about 50% over "book" price.

Hard plastic and vinyl dolls must be in excellent condition if they are at "book" price. The hair should be perfect in the original set: clothes should be completely original, fresh and unfaded. Skin tones should be natural with good cheek color. Add a premium of 25-50% for mint dolls never removed from their original boxes.

BODY

In order to command top price, an old doll must have the original or an appropriate old body in good condition. If a doll does not have the correct type of body, the buyer ends up not with a complete doll but with parts that may not be worth as much as one whole doll. As dolls are becoming more difficult to find, more are turning up with "put together" bodies. Many dolls are now entering the market from old collections assembled years ago. Some of these contain dolls which were "put together" before there was much information available about correct heads and bodies. Therefore, the body should be checked to make sure it is appropriate to the head, and all parts of the body should be checked to make sure that they are appropriate to each other. A body with mixed parts from several makers or types of bodies is not worth as much as one with correct parts.

Minor damage or repair to an old body does not affect the value of an antique doll. An original body carefully repaired, recovered or even, if necessary, completely repainted is preferable to a new one. An antique head on a new body would be worth only the value of its parts, whatever the price of the head and new body, not the the full price of an antique doll. A rule of thumb is that an antique head is generally worth about 40-50% of the price of the complete doll. A very rare head could be worth up to 80%.

If there is a choice of body types for the same bisque head, a good quality ball-jointed composition body is more desirable than a crudely made five-piece body or stick-type body with only pieces of turned wood for upper arms and legs. Collectors prefer jointed composition bodies over kid ones for dolly-faced dolls, and pay more for the same face on a composition body.

Occasionally the body adds value to the doll. In the case of bisque heads, a small doll with a completely jointed body, a French fashion-type with a wood-jointed body, a *Tête Jumeau* head

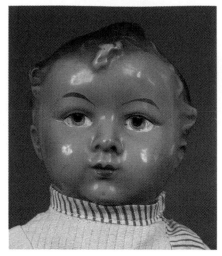

Top left: 36in (91cm) *Jumeau Triste*. (For further information see page 221.) *Private Collection.*

Top right: 16in (41cm) Effanbee **Billy Boy**, all original. (For further information see page 155.) *H & J Foulke, Inc.*

Bottom Left: 16in (41cm) Schoenhut pouty with molded hair. (For further information see page 326.) *H & J Foulke, Inc.*

on an adult body or a character baby head on a jointed toddler-type body would all be higher in price because of their special bodies.

As for the later modern dolls, a composition doll on the wrong body or with a body that is cracked, peeling and in poor condition would have a greatly reduced value. The same is true of a vinyl doll with replaced parts, body stains or chewed-off fingers.

CLOTHING

It is becoming increasingly difficult to find dolls in old clothing because, as the years go by, fabrics continue to deteriorate. Consequently, collectors are paying more than "book" price for an antique doll if it has appropriate old clothes, shoes and hair. Even faded,

Top left: 18in (46cm) parian bisque *Grape Lady*. (For further information see page 299.) *Richard Wright Antiques.*

Top right: 19in (48cm) parian lady with glass eyes. (For further information see page 299.) *H & J Foulke, Inc.*

Right: 16in (41cm) Farnell's *King George VI*, all original. (For further information see page 270.) *H & J Foulke, Inc.*

somewhat worn, or carefully mended original or appropriate old clothes are preferable to new ones. As collectors become more sophisticated and selective, they realize the value of old doll clothing and accessories. Some dealers are now specializing in these areas. Good old leather doll shoes will bring more than $75 per pair; a lovely Victorian white-work doll dress can easily cost $75; an old dress for a French fashion lady, $300. Good old doll wigs can bring from $25 to $250.

However, when clothing must be replaced and appropriate old clothing cannot be obtained, new clothes should be authentically styled for the age of the doll and constructed of fabrics that would have been available when the doll was produced. There are many reference books and catalog reprints showing dolls in original clothing, and doll supply companies offer patterns for dressing old dolls.

To bring top price, a modern doll must have original clothes. It is usually fairly simple to determine whether or not the clothing is original and factory made. Some makers even placed tags in the doll's clothing. Replaced clothing greatly reduces the price of modern dolls. Without the original clothing, it is often impossible to identify a modern doll because so many were made using the same face mold.

TOTAL ORIGINALITY

Today totally original dolls are becoming rare. It is often difficult to determine whether the head and body and all other parts of a doll, including wig, eyes and clothes, have always been together. Many parts of a doll may have been changed and clothing and accessories could have been added over the years. Many dolls labeled "all original" are simply wearing contemporary clothing and wigs. Some collectors and dealers are "embellishing" more expensive dolls by taking original clothing and wigs from cheaper dolls to further enhance the value of the more costly ones. Dolls with trunks of clothing and in boxed sets are particularly vulnerable to this type of raiding.

Collectors should examine clothes and accessories carefully before they pay ultra-high prices for such ensembles. Of course, when these ensembles are genuine, they are the ultimate in doll collecting.

AGE

The oldest dolls do not necessarily command the highest prices. A lovely old china head with exquisite decoration and very unusual hairdo would bring a price of several thousand dollars, but not as much as a 20th century German bisque character child, one of which set the current world's record doll price of nearly $170,000. Many desirable composition dolls of the 1930s and *Barbie*® dolls of the 1960s are selling at prices higher than older bisque dolls of 1890 to 1920. So, in determining price, the age of the doll may or may not be significant.

SIZE

The size of a doll is usually taken into account when determining a price. Generally, the size and price for a certain doll are related: a smaller size is lower, a larger size is higher. However, there are a few exceptions. The 11in (28cm) *Shirley Temple*, and tiny German dolly-faced dolls on fully-jointed bodies are examples of small dolls that bring higher prices than their larger counterparts.

AVAILABILITY

The price of a doll is directly related to its availability in most cases. The harder a doll is to find, the higher will be its price. Each year brings more new doll collectors than newly discovered, desirable old dolls; hence, the supply of old dolls is diminished. As long as the demand for certain antique and collectible dolls is greater than the supply, prices will rise. This explains the great increase in prices of less common dolls, such as the K & R and other German character children, early china heads and papier-mâchés, composition personality dolls, Sasha dolls and some Alexander dolls that were made for only a limited period of time. Dolls that are fairly common, primarily the German dolly-faces and the later china head dolls made over a long period of production, show a more gentle increase in price.

POPULARITY

There are fads in dolls just as in clothes, food and other aspects of life. Dolls that have recently risen in price because of their popularity include the early Jumeaus, all-bisques, German character children, *Patsy* family dolls, small dolly-faces with jointed bodies, *Shirley Temples*, large composition babies, early *Barbie*® dolls, composition personality dolls and hard plastic dolls. Some dolls are popular enough to tempt collectors to pay prices higher than the availability factor warrants. Although *Shirley Temples*, *Tête Jumeaus*, *Bye-Los*, *Hildas*, K & R 117, and some plastic Alexander dolls are not rare, the high prices they bring are due to their popularity.

DESIRABILITY

Some very rare dolls do not bring a high price because they are not particularly desirable. There are not many collectors looking for them. Falling into this category are the dolls with shoulder heads made of rubber or rawhide. While an especially outstanding example will bring a high price, most examples bring very low prices in relationship to their rarity.

UNIQUENESS

Sometimes the uniqueness of a doll makes price determination very diffi-

cult. If a collector has never seen a doll exactly like it before, and it is not cited in a price guide or even shown in any books, deciding what to pay can be a problem. In this case, the buyer has to use all available knowledge as a frame of reference for the unknown doll. Perhaps a doll marked "A.M. 2000" or "S & H 1289" has been found, and the asking price is 25% higher than for the more commonly found numbers by that maker. Or perhaps a black *Kamkins* is offered for twice the price of a white one, or a French fashion lady with original wardrobe is offered at 60% more than a redressed one. In cases such as these, a collector must use his or her own judgment to determine what the doll is worth.

VISUAL APPEAL

Perhaps the most elusive aspect in pricing a doll is its visual appeal. Sometimes, particularly at auction, we have seen dolls bring well over their "book" value simply because of their look. Often this is nothing more than the handiwork of someone who had the ability to choose just the right wig, clothing and accessories to enhance the doll's visual appeal and make it look particularly cute, stunning, beautiful or otherwise especially outstanding.

Sometimes, though, the visual appeal comes from the face of the doll itself. It may be the way the teeth are put in, the placement of the eyes, the tinting on the face or the sharpness of the molding. Or it may not be any of these specific things; it may just be what some collectors refer to as the "presence" of the doll, an elusive indefinable quality which makes it the best example known!

Selling A Doll

So many times we are asked, "How do I go about selling a doll?," that it seems a few paragraphs on the topic are in order. The first logical step is to look through the *Blue Book* to identify the doll and to ascertain a retail price. Work from there to decide what you might ask for your doll. It is very difficult for a private person to get a retail price for a doll.

Be realistic about the condition. If you have a marked 18in (46cm) *Shirley Temple* doll with combed hair, no clothing, faded face with crazing and a piece off of her nose, do not expect to get book price of $600 for her because that would be a retail price for an excellent doll, all original, in pristine unplayed-with condition if purchased from a dealer. Your very used doll is probably worth only $50 to $75 because it will have to be purchased by someone who wants to restore it.

If you have an antique doll with a perfect bisque head but no wig, no clothes and unstrung, but with all of its body parts, you can probably expect to get about half of its retail value depending upon how desirable the particular doll is. If your doll has a perfect bisque head with original wig, clothing and shoes, you can probably get up to 75% of its retail value.

As to actually selling the doll, there are several possibilities. Possibly the easiest is to advertise in your local paper. You may not think there are any doll collectors in your area, but there probably are. You might also check your local paper to see if anyone is advertising to purchase dolls; many

dealers and collectors do so. Check the paper to find out about antique shows in your area. If anyone has dolls, ask if they would be interested in buying your doll. Also, you could inquire at antique shops in your area for dealers who specialize in dolls. You will probably get a higher price from a specialist than a general antique dealer because the former are more familiar with the market for specific dolls. A roster of doll specialists is available from The National Antique Doll Dealers Association, Inc., P.O. Box 143, Wellesley Hills, MA 02181.

You could consign your doll to an auction. If it is a common doll, it will probably do quite well at a local sale. If it is a more rare doll, consider sending it to one of the auction houses that specializes in selling dolls; most of them will accept one doll if it is a good one, and they will probably get the best price for you. It would probably be worth your while to purchase a doll magazine from your local book store, doll shop or newsstand; most doll magazines include ads from auction houses, doll shows and leading dealers. You could advertise in doll magazines, but you might have to ship the doll and guarantee return privileges if the buyer does not like it.

If you cannot find your doll in the *Blue Book*, it might be a good idea to have it professionally appraised. This will involve your paying a fee to have the doll evaluated. We provide this service and can be contacted through the publisher. Many museums and auction houses also appraise dolls.

Alabama Indestructible Doll

FACTS

Ella Smith Doll Co., Roanoke, Ala., U.S.A. 1900 - 1925. All-cloth. 11½ - 27in (29 - 69cm); 38in (96cm) black one known.

Mark: On torso or leg, sometimes both:

PAT. NOV. 9, 1912
NO. 2
ELLA SMITH DOLL CO.

or

"MRS. S. S. SMITH
Manufacturer and Dealer to
The Alabama Indestructible Doll
Roanoke, Ala.
PATENTED Sept. 26, 1905"
(also 1907 on some)

Alabama Baby: All-cloth painted with oils, tab-jointed shoulders and hips, flat derriere for sitting; painted hair (or rarely a wig), molded face with painted facial features; applied ears (a few with molded ears); painted stockings and shoes (a few with bare feet); appropriate clothes; all in good condition, some wear acceptable.

14 - 16in (36 - 41cm)	**$1400 - 1600**
22 - 24in (56 - 61cm)	**2100 - 2500**
Black:	
14 - 19in (36 - 48cm)	**6600****
Wigged 24in (61cm)	**3500****

**Not enough price samples to compute a reliable range.

Below: Wigged *Alabama Baby*. *Nancy A. Smith Collection.*

Madame Alexander

FACTS

Alexander Doll Co. Inc., New York, N.Y., U.S.A. 1923 - on, but as early as 1912 the Alexander sisters were designing doll clothes and dressing dolls commercially. **Mark:** Dolls themselves marked in various ways, usually "ALEXANDER." Clothing has a white cloth label with blue lettering sewn into a seam which says "MADAME ALEXANDER" and usually the name of the specific doll. Cloth and other early dolls are unmarked and identifiable only by the clothing label.

Little Shaver: 1942. Yarn hair. Very good condition.

10 - 12in (25 - 31cm)	**$275 - 325**
20in (51cm)	**475 - 525**

Kamkins-type (hard felt face). Very good condition.

20in (51cm)	**$500 - 600**

16in (41cm) *Oliver Twist. H & J Foulke, Inc.*

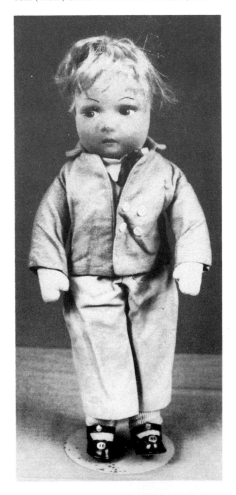

CLOTH

Cloth Character Dolls: Ca. 1933 through the 1930s. All-cloth with one-piece arms and legs sewn on; mohair wig, molded mask face of felt or flocked fabric, painted eyes to the side, original tagged clothes. Produced characters from *Little Women*, Charles Dickens, Longfellow and other literary works, as well as storybook characters.

16in (41cm) only:

Fair	**$200 - 250**
Good	**350 - 400**
Mint	**650 - 700**

20in (51cm) Alice:

Fair	**200 - 250**
Good	**350 - 400**
Mint	**650 - 700**

Bunny Belle:
13in (33cm) mint, at auction **$700**
Cloth Baby: Ca. 1936. (For photograph see *7th Blue Book*, page 20.)
17in (43cm) Very good   **$375 - 425**
Cloth Dionne Quintuplet: Ca. 1935. (For photograph see *6th Blue Book*, page 18.)
17in (43cm) Very good   **$700 - 800**
Susie Q. & Bobby Q.: Ca. 1938. (For photograph see *6th Blue Book*, page 19.)
12 - 16in (31 - 41cm) Very good
$525 - 575

Madame Alexander continued

Children: Ca. 1935 to mid 1940s. All-composition with one-piece head and body on smaller ones and separate head on larger ones, jointed shoulders and hips; mohair wig, painted eyes; original tagged clothes; all in excellent condition.

7 - 9in (18 - 23cm)

Foreign Countries	$ 150 - 200
Storybook Characters	200 - 250
Special Outfits	250 up

Birthday Dolls, complete set at auctions.

Mint in boxes	4100

Little Colonel: 1935.

13in (33cm)	500 - 600

Unnamed Girl: Dimples, sleep eyes. Ca. 1935. 13in (33cm) 250 - 300

Nurse: Ca. 1935.

13in (33cm)	400 - 450

Betty: Ca. 1935. Painted or sleep eyes, wigged or molded hair.

13in (33cm)	250 - 300
16in (41cm)	400 - 425

Topsy Turvy: Ca. 1936.

7½in (19cm)	185 - 210

8in (20cm) *Dionne Quintuplet Annette*, all original. *H & J Foulke, Inc.*

COMPOSITION

Dionne Quintuplets: 1935. All-composition with swivel head, jointed hips and shoulders, toddler or bent-limb legs (some babies have cloth bodies with composition lower limbs); wigs or molded hair, sleep or painted eyes; original tagged clothing, all in excellent condition.

7 - 8in (18 - 20cm)	$ 250 - 275
Matched set	1500
10in (25cm) baby	325 - 350
11 - 12in (28 - 31cm) toddler	375 - 425
14in (36cm) toddler	475 - 525
16in (41cm) baby with cloth body	400 - 450
23 - 24in (58 - 61cm) baby with cloth body	500 - 600
Pins, each	90 - 100

Each Quint has her own color for clothing:
Yvonne - pink
Annette - yellow
Cecile - green
Emelie - lavender
Marie - blue

13in (33cm) *Nurse*, all original. *H & J Foulke, Inc.*

Madame Alexander Composition continued

Marionettes: 1935. Character faces.
10 - 12in (25 - 30cm)

Tony Sarg	**$150 - 250**
Disney	**300 - 400**

Snow White set including seven dwarfs, hunter, prince, wicked queen, witch and *Snow White*, excellent, at auction **$3500**

Babies: 1936 - on. "Little Genius," "Baby McGuffey," "Precious," "Butch," "Bitsey." Composition head, hands and legs, cloth bodies; molded hair or wigged, sleep eyes, open or closed mouth; original tagged clothes; all in excellent condition.

11 - 12in (28 - 31cm)	**$ 200 - 250**
16 - 18in (41 - 46cm)	**350 - 400**
24in (61cm)	**450 - 500**

Pinky, 16 - 18in (41 - 46cm) **$400 - 450**

Princess Elizabeth Face: All-composition, jointed at neck, shoulders and hips; mohair or human hair wig, sleeping eyes, open mouth; original tagged clothes; all in excellent condition.

Mark: On head:
   "PRINCESS ELIZABETH
   ALEXANDER DOLL CO."

Clothing tagged with individual name of doll.

Princess Elizabeth, 1937. (See photograph on page 9.)

13in (33cm) **Betty** face	**$275 - 325**
16 - 18in (41 - 46cm)	**375 - 425**
22 - 24in (56 - 61cm)	**500 - 600**
27in (69cm)	**700 - 750**

McGuffey Ana, 1937, braids. (For photograph see *9th Blue Book*, page 27.)

9in (23cm) painted eyes, **Wendy** face	**$300 - 350**
11in (28cm) closed mouth	**350 - 400**
15 - 16in (38 - 41cm)	**450 - 500**
20 - 22in (51 - 56cm)	**550 - 650**

27in (69cm) *Princess Elizabeth*, all original. *H & J Foulke, Inc.*

Above left: 13in (33cm) *Flora McFlimsey*, all original. *Elizabeth Ann Foulke Collection.*

Above right: 11in (28cm) *Scarlett*, all original. *H & J Foulke, Inc.*

Left: 14in (36cm) *Sleeping Beauty*, all original. *H & J Foulke, Inc.*

(See following page for further information on dolls pictured on this page.)

Madame Alexander Composition continued

Snow White, 1937, closed mouth, black hair. (For photograph see *6th Blue Book*, page 23.)

13in (33cm)	**$375 - 425**
16 - 18in (41 - 46cm)	**500 - 600**

Flora McFlimsey, 1938, red hair, freckles. (For photograph see preceding page.)

15in (38cm)	**$650 - 700**

Kate Greenaway, 1938

16 - 18in (41 - 46cm)	**$550 - 600**

Wendy Ann Face: All-composition, jointed at neck, shoulders and hips; human hair or mohair wig, sleeping eyes, closed mouth; original tagged clothes; all in excellent condition.

Wendy Ann, 1936. (For photograph see *9th Blue Book*, page 28.)

9in (23cm) painted eyes	**$250 - 300**
14in (36cm) swivel waist	**350 - 400**
21in (53cm)	**550 - 650**

Scarlet O'Hara, 1937, black hair, blue or green eyes. (For photograph see preceding page.)

11in (28cm)	**$425 - 475**
14in (36cm)	**525 - 575**
18in (46cm)	**700 - 800**
21in (53cm)	**900 - 1000**

Note: Sometimes the name is spelled "Scarlet"; other times "Scarlett."

Bride & Bridesmaids, 1940. (For photograph see *9th Blue Book*, page 28.)

14in (36cm)	**$250 - 300**
18in (46cm)	**375 - 425**

Portraits, 1940s

21in (53cm)	**$900 up**

Carmen (Miranda), 1942. (For photograph see *7th Blue Book*, page 30.) (black hair):

9in (23cm) painted eyes	**$225 - 250**
14 - 15in (36 - 38cm)	**325 - 375**

Fairy Princess or **Fairy Queen**, 1942. (For photograph see *8th Blue Book*, page 28.)

18in (46cm)	**$450 - 500**

Armed Forces Dolls, 1942. (For photograph see *7th Blue Book*, page 29.) WAAC, WAVE, WAAF, Soldier, Marine

14in (36cm)	**$500 - 600**

Miss America, 1939

14in (36cm)	**$550 - 650**

Sleeping Beauty, Ca. 1941. (For photograph see preceding page.)

14in (36cm)	**$290 - 340**

Special Face Dolls:
Dr. Dafoe, 1936. (The Quintuplets' doctor)

14in (36cm)	**$ 800 - 900**

Jane Withers, 1937. (For photograph see *5th Blue Book*, page 11.)

13in (33cm) closed mouth	**$700 - 800**
15 - 16in (38 - 41cm)	**800 - 900**
21in (53cm)	**1000 - 1200**

Sonja Henie, 1939. (For photograph see *10th Blue Book*, page 39.) 14in (36cm) can be found on **Wendy-Ann** body with swivel waist.

14in (36cm)	**$ 375 - 425**
18in (46cm)	**500 - 600**
21in (53cm)	**575 - 675**

Jeannie Walker, 1941. (For photograph see *10th Blue Book*, page 39.)

13 - 14in (33 - 36cm)	**$ 425 - 475**

Baby Jane, 1935

16in (41cm)	**800 - 900**

Special Girl, 1942

22in (56cm)	**450 - 550**

Margaret Face: All-composition, jointed at neck, shoulders and hips; human hair, mohair, or floss wig, sleeping eyes, closed mouth; original tagged clothes; all in excellent condition.

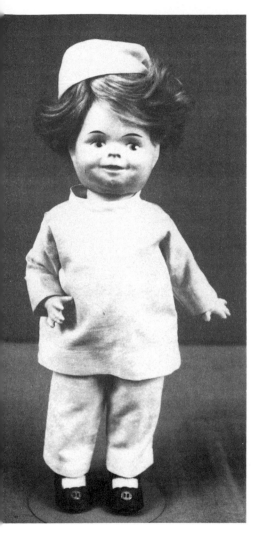

Margaret O'Brien, 1946. (For photograph see *9th Blue Book*, page 30.)
(dark braided wig):

14in (36cm)	**$525 - 575**
18in (46cm)	**675 - 775**

Karen Ballerina, 1946. (For photograph see *8th Blue Book*, page 29.)
(blonde wig in coiled braids):

18in (46cm)	**$550 - 650**

Alice-in-Wonderland, 1947

14in (36cm)	**$350 - 400**
18in (46cm)	**450 - 550**

14in (36cm) *Dr. Dafoe*, all original. *H & J Foulke, Inc.* (For further information see preceding page.)

Right: 18in (46cm) *Alice-in-Wonderland*, all original.

Madame Alexander Hard Plastic

HARD PLASTIC
Margaret Face: 1948 - on. All-hard plastic, jointed at neck, shoulders and hips; lovely wig, sleep eyes, closed mouth; original tagged clothes; all in excellent condition.

Babs, 1948 - 1949*	
14in (36cm)	**$375 - 425**
Bride, 1952	
18in (46cm)	**375 - 425**
Cinderella, 1950*	
14in (36cm)	**575 - 625**
Cynthia (black), 1952 - 1953	
14in (36cm)	**600 - 650**
Fairy Queen, 1947 - 1948*	
14in (36cm)	**325 - 375**
Glamour Girls, 1953*	
18in (46cm)	**750 - 850**
Godey Ladies, 1950*	
14in (36cm)	**750 - 850**
Margaret O'Brien, 1948*	
14in (36cm)	**625 - 675**
Margaret Rose, 1948 - 1953*	
14in (36cm)	**325 - 375**
Margot Ballerina, 1953	
18in (46cm)	**425 - 475**
Mary Martin, 1950	
14in (36cm)	**600 - 700**
Nina Ballerina, 1949-1951	
14in (36cm)	**350 - 400**
18in (46cm)	**425 - 475**
Prince Charming, 1950	
14in (36cm)	**550 - 600**
Prince Philip, Ca. 1950*	
18in (46cm)	**600 - 650**
Queen Elizabeth, 1953	
18in (46cm)	**700 - 800**

Snow White, 1952	
14in (36cm)	**500 - 550**
Story Princess, 1954 - 1956	
14in (36cm)	**350 - 400**
Wendy-Ann, 1947 - 1948	
18in (46cm)	**450 - 500**
Wendy Bride, 1950*	
14in (36cm)	**350 - 400**
Wendy (from **Peter Pan** set), 1953	
14in (36cm)	**450 - 500**

*For photographs see *Treasury of Mme. Alexander Dolls.*

18in (46cm) *Glamour Girl*, all original. *H & J Foulke, Inc.*

Maggie Face: 1948 - 1956. All hard plastic, jointed at neck, shoulders and hips; good quality wig, sleep eyes, closed mouth, original tagged clothes; all in excellent condition.

Alice in Wonderland, 1950 - 1951*
  17in (43cm)   **$450 - 500**
Annabelle, 1952*
  15in (38cm)   **375 - 425**
Ballerina, Ca. 1950
  15in (38cm)   **350 - 400**
Glamour Girls, 1953*
  18in (46cm)   **750 - 850**
Godey Man, 1950*
  14in (36cm)   **750 - 850**
John Powers Models
  14in (36cm)   **800 - 900**
Kathy, 1951*
  14in (36cm)   **400 - 450**

Maggie, 1948 - 1953*
  14in (36cm)   **325 - 375**
  17in (43cm)   **425 - 475**
Me and My Shadow, 1954
  18in (46cm)   **750 - 850**
Peter Pan, 1953*
  15in (38cm)   **450 - 500**
Polly Pigtails, 1949
  14in (36cm)   **350 - 400**
Rosamund Bridesmaid, 1953*
  15in (38cm)   **350 - 400**

*For photographs see *Treasury of Mme. Alexander Dolls.*

14in (36cm) **Kathy**, all original. *H & J Foulke, Inc.*

14in (36cm) **Amy**, rare model with braids, all original. *H & J Foulke, Inc.* (For further information see following page.)

Madame Alexander Hard Plastic continued

Little Women: 1948 - 1956. All hard plastic, jointed at neck, shoulders and hips; synthetic wig, sleep eyes, closed mouth, original tagged clothes; all in excellent condition. Some models have jointed knees.
"Maggie" face: "Jo" and "Beth"
"Margaret" face: "Amy," "Marme" and "Meg"
14 - 15in (36 - 38cm)
Floss hair, 1948 - 1950 **$350 - 400 each**
Amy, loop curls. (See preceding page for photograph.) **400 - 425**
Dynel hair **275 - 300 each**
Little Men, 1952 **800 up each**

Babies: 1948 - 1951. Hard plastic head, hands and legs; cloth body; synthetic wig, sleep eyes, closed mouth; original tagged clothes; excellent condition.
"Baby Genius":
12in (31cm) **$200 - 225**
16 - 18in (41 - 46cm) **275 - 325**

Cissy: 1955 - 1959. Head, torso and jointed legs of hard plastic, jointed vinyl arms; synthetic wig, sleep eyes, closed mouth, pierced ears; original tagged clothes; all in excellent condition with perfect hair and rosy cheeks.
21in (53cm)

Street clothes	**$375 - 425**
Gowns	**475 up***
Elaborate fashion gowns	**700 up***
Queen	**700 - 800**
Bride	**375 - 475**

*Depending upon costume.

Left: *Cissy Queen Elizabeth*, all original. *H & J Foulke, Inc.*

Below: *Alexander-Kins Ballerina*, bent knees, all original. *H & J Foulke, Inc.*

Madame Alexander Hard Plastic continued

Winnie and Binnie: 1953 - 1955. All-hard plastic, walking body, later with jointed knees and vinyl arms; lovely wig, sleep eyes, closed mouth; original tagged clothes; all in excellent condition.

15in (38cm)	**$275 - 325**
18in (46cm)	**325 - 375**
Mary Ellen,	
31in (79cm)	**450 - 550**

Alexander-Kins: 1953 - to present. All hard plastic, jointed at neck, shoulders and hips; synthetic wig, sleep eyes, closed mouth; original clothes; all in excellent condition.
7½ - 8in (19 - 20cm)
1953, straight leg non-walker
1954 - 1955, straight-leg walker
1956 - 1964, bent-knee walker
1965 - 1972, bent knee
1973 - current, straight leg

Wendy, basic (panties, shoes and socks), through 1972	**$ 200 - 225**
Wendy, in dresses, 1953 - 1972	**350 up**
Wendy Ballerina, pink, 1965 - 1972	**250 - 300**
Wendy Bride, 1956 - 1972	**350**
Quizkin, 1953	**450 - 550**
Little Women, set of 5, 1956 - 1964	**1000 - 1200**

Wendy in Special Outfits:

Billy or Bobby	**$ 450**
Parlor Maid	**800 up**
Prince Charles	**800 up**
Princess Ann	**800 up**
My Shadow	**1000**
Cherry Twin, each	**500**
Little Minister	**800 up**
Groom, 1956 - 1972	**450**

Lissy: 1956 - 1958. All-hard plastic, jointed at neck, shoulders, hips, elbows and knees; synthetic wig, sleep eyes, closed mouth; original clothes; all in excellent condition.

12in (31cm)	**$ 300 - 400**
Kelly, 1959*	**400 - 500**

12in (31cm) *Lissy*, all original. *H & J Foulke, Inc.*

Little Women, 1957 - 1967	**200 - 250**
Southern Belle, 1963*	**1000 up**
McGuffey Ana, 1963*	**1000 up**
Laurie, 1967*	**400 - 450**
Pamela, 1962 - 1963*	**650**

*For photographs see *Treasury of Mme. Alexander Dolls*, pages 74 - 78.

Madame Alexander Hard Plastic continued

Elise: 1957 - 1964. All-hard plastic with vinyl arms, completely jointed; synthetic wig, sleep eyes, closed mouth; original tagged clothes; all in excellent condition.
16½ - 17in (42 - 43cm)

Street clothes	**$ 300 - 350**
Gowns	**375 up**
Bride, Ballerina	**350 - 375**
Elaborate fashion gowns	**500 up**
Sleeping Beauty	**450 - 550**

Cissette: 1957 - 1963. All hard-plastic, jointed at neck, shoulders, hips and knees; synthetic wig, sleep eyes, closed mouth, pierced ears; original tagged clothes; all in excellent condition. (For photographs see *Treasury of Mme. Alexander Dolls*, pages 79 - 84.)
Mark: None on doll
On dress tag: "Cissette"

10in (25cm) **Cissette**	**$ 225 up**
Basic **Cissette**, mint and boxed	
	200 - 225

Portrettes, 1968 - 1973	**500 - 600**
Gibson Girl	**1000 up**
Gold Rush	**1000 up**
Jacqueline, 1962	**475 - 575**
Portrettes, 1986 to present	**50 - 100**

Shari Lewis: 1959. All-hard plastic with slim fashion body; auburn hair, brown eyes, closed mouth; original tagged clothes; all in excellent condition. (For photographs see *5th Blue Book*, page 17.)

14in (36cm)	**$350 - 375**
21in (53cm)	**450 - 475**

Maggie Mixup: 1960 - 1961. All-hard plastic, fully-jointed; red straight hair, green eyes, closed mouth, freckles; original tagged clothes; all in excellent condition. (For photograph see *6th Blue Book*, page 32.)

16½ - 17in (42 - 43cm)	**$ 350 - 400**
8in (20cm)	**450 - 550**
8in (20cm) angel	**1000 up**
Little Lady	**400 - 500**
Scottish, 1956 - 1964	**275 - 325**

Left: 16in (41cm) *Elise*, all original. *Virginia Ann Heyerdahl Collection.*

Opposite page: 21in (53cm) *Portrait Scarlett,* #2210, 1978, all original. *H & J Foulke, Inc.* (For further information see page 31.)

Madame Alexander Vinyl Dolls

VINYL

Kelly Face: 1958 - on. Vinyl character face with rooted hair, vinyl arms, hard plastic torso and legs, jointed waist; original tagged clothes; all in excellent condition. (For photograph see *9th Blue Book*, page 37.)

Kelly, 1958 - 1959, 15in (38m)
$225 - 250

Pollyana, 1960 - 1961 15in (38cm)
225 - 250

Marybel, 1959 - 1965 15in (38cm), in case 275

Edith, 1958 - 1959, 15in (38cm)
225 - 250

Elise, 1962, 15in (38cm) 250 - 300

Jacqueline: 1961 - 1962. Vinyl and hard plastic; rooted dark hair, sleep eyes, closed mouth; original tagged clothes; all in excellent condition.

21in (53cm) $700 - 750

Portrait Dolls, 1965 to present 100 up

Caroline: 1961 - 1962. Hard plastic and vinyl; rooted blonde hair, smiling character face; original tagged clothes; in excellent condition.

15in (38cm) $250 - 300
Riding Habit 300 - 350

Janie: 1964 - 1966. Vinyl and hard plastic with rooted hair, impish face, pigeon-toed and knock-kneed; original tagged clothes; all in excellent condition.

12in (31cm) $225 - 250
Lucinda, 1969 - 1970 250 - 275
Rozy, 1969 275 - 300
Suzy, 1970 275 - 300

Smarty: 1962 - 1963. Hard plastic and vinyl, smiling character face with rooted hair, knock-kneed and pigeon-toed; original tagged clothes; in excellent condition.

12in (31cm) $200
Katie (black), 1965 350 - 400
Brother 225

Polly Face: 1965. All-vinyl with rooted hair, jointed at neck, shoulders and hips; original tagged clothes; all in excellent condition.

17in (43cm):
Polly $225 - 250
Leslie (black) 300 - 400

Mary Ann Face: 1965 to present. Vinyl head and arms, hard plastic torso and legs; appropriate synthetic wig, sleep eyes; original clothes; all in excellent condition.

14in (35cm) only:
Easter Girl, 1968 $1000 - 1200
Scarlett #1495, flowered gown, 1968
500
Disney Snow White, to 1977 (See photograph on page 32.)
400

Discontinued Dolls
1965 - 1982 100 - 200
1982 - 1992 50 - 90

Babies: 1960s to present. Vinyl head, arms and legs, cloth body; sleeping eyes, appropriate synthetic hair; original tagged clothes; all in excellent condition.

Baby Lynn, 20in (51cm) $ 100
Mary Cassatt Baby, 20in (51cm)
100 - 125
Black Pussy Cat, 20in (51cm)
75 - 100

Sound of Music: Hard plastic and vinyl with appropriate synthetic wigs and sleep eyes; original tagged clothes; all in excellent conditon.

Small set, 1965 - 1970.

8in (20cm) **Friedrich**	**$200**
8in (20cm) **Gretl**	200
8in (20cm) **Marta**	200
10in (25cm) **Brigitta**	200
12in (31cm) **Maria**	275
10in (25cm) **Louisa**	325
10in (25cm) **Liesl**	275

Large set*, 1971 - 1973.

11in (28cm) **Friedrich**	**$225**
11in (28cm) **Gretl**	200
11in (28cm) **Marta**	200
14in (36cm) **Brigitta**	200
17in (43cm) **Maria**	275
14in (36cm) **Louisa**	250
14in (36cm) **Liesl**	250
11in (28cm) **Kurt** (sailor)	350

*Allow considerably more for sailor outfits.

Coco: 1966. Vinyl and hard plastic, rooted blonde hair, jointed waist, right leg bent slightly at knee; original tagged clothes; all in excellent condition. This face was also used for the 1966 portrait dolls.

21in (53cm)	**$1800 - 2000**
1966 **Portrait Dolls**	**1800 - 2000**

11in (28cm) **Kurt**, sailor outfit, all original. *H & J Foulke, Inc.*

Opposite Page: 14in (35cm) *Disney Snow White*, all original. *H & J Foulke, Inc.* (For further information see page 30.)

12in (31cm) *Scarlett and Rhett*, 1981 - 1985, all original *Romantic Couple*. *H & J Foulke, Inc.* (For further information see following page.)

Madame Alexander Vinyl Dolls continued

Elise: 1966 to present. Vinyl face, rooted hair; original tagged clothes; all in excellent condition.
17in (43cm)

Elise	**$125 - 175***
Marlo, 1967	**400 - 500**
Maggie, 1972 - 1973	**200 - 250**

*Discontinued styles only.

Peter Pan Set: 1969. Vinyl and hard plastic with appropriate wigs and sleep eyes; original tagged clothes; all in excellent condition.

14in (36cm)	**Peter Pan**	**$200 - 225**
14in (36cm)	**Wendy**	**200 - 225**
12in (31cm)	**Michael**	**250**
10in (25cm)	**Tinker Bell**	**250 - 300**

Nancy Drew Face: 1967 - 1992. Vinyl head and arms, hard plastic torso and legs; appropriate synthetic wig, sleep eyes; original tagged clothes; all in excellent condition.
12in (31cm) only:

Nancy Drew, 1967	**$200**
Renoir Child, 1967	**150 - 200**
Pamela with wigs, 1962 - 1963	**350 - 400**
Romantic Couples	**75 - 100 pair**

First Ladies: 1976 - 1989. Hard plastic and vinyl with rooted synthetic hair individually styled and sleep eyes; original tagged clothes; in mint condition. **"Martha"** and **"Mary Ann"** faces.
14in (36cm)   **$60 - 90**

17in (43cm) *Elise* #1750, 1966, all original.

FACTS

Henri Alexandre, Paris, France, 1888 - 1892; Tourrel 1892 - 1895; Jules Steiner and successors 1895 - 1901. Bisque head, jointed composition body.
Designer: Henri Alexandre.
Trademark: Bébé Phénix.

Approximate Size Chart:
*81 = 10in (25cm)
*84 = 12in (31cm)
*85 = 14in (36cm)
*88 = 17in (43cm)
*90 = 18in (46cm)
*92 = 19 - 21in (48 - 53cm)
*93 = 22in (56cm)
*94 = 23 - 24in (58 - 61cm)
*95 = 23 - 25in (58 - 64cm)

H.A. Bébé: 1889 - 1891. Perfect bisque socket head, closed mouth, paperweight eyes, pierced ears, good wig; jointed composition and wood body; lovely clothes; all in good condition.
Mark: H ⋊ A

12in (31cm)	$2400 - 2500
15 - 17in (38 - 43cm)	3300 - 3600
22 - 24in (56 - 61cm)	4500 - 5000

17 - 19in (43 - 48cm)
        $5500 - 6500**

Open Mouth:
17 - 19in (43 - 48cm)	$2000 - 2200

Bébé Phénix: 1889 - 1900. Perfect bisque head, closed mouth, paperweight eyes, pierced ears, good wig; composition body sometimes with one-piece arms and legs; well dressed; all in good condition. (For photographs see *10th Blue Book*, page 17.)
Mark: Red Stamp Incised

PHÉNIX
★ 95

**Not enough price samples to compute a reliable range.

17in (43cm) H.A. Bébé *Private Collection.*

All-Bisque Dolls (So-Called French)

FACTS

Various French and/or German firms.
Ca. 1880 - on. All-bisque. Various small
sizes, under 12in (31cm).
Mark: None, sometimes numbers.

All-Bisque French Doll: Jointed at shoulders and hips, swivel neck, slender arms and legs; good wig, glass eyes, closed mouth; molded shoes or boots and stockings; appropriately dressed; all in good condition, with proper parts.

5in (13cm)	**$1000 - 1100***
6in (15cm)	**1500 - 1800***
With bare feet,	
5in (13cm)	**1150 - 1250***
6in (15cm)	**1700 - 1900***
With jointed elbows and knees,	
5½in (14cm)	**2700 - 3000****
With jointed elbows,	
5½in (14cm)	**2300 - 2600****
Painted eyes,	
4 - 4½in (10 - 12cm) all original	
	700 - 800

*Allow extra for original clothes.
**Not enough price samples to compute a reliable range.

6in (15cm) French all-bisque, all original. *H & J Foulke, Inc.*

All-Bisque Dolls*(German)

Various unidentified firms. Ca. 1880 - on. Bisque. Various small sizes, most under 12in (31cm).

Mark: Some with "Germany" and/or numbers; some with paper labels on stomachs.

*See also Amberg; Alt, Beck & Gottschalck; Kestner; Kling; Simon & Halbig; Hertel, Schwab & Co.; Bähr & Pröschild; Limbach.

Below left: 3¾in (9cm) early girl with molded cap. *H & J Foulke, Inc.*

Below right: 5¼in (13cm) boy with molded shift. *H & J Foulke, Inc.*

All-Bisque with molded clothes: Ca. 1890 - on. Many by Hertwig & Co. Jointed at shoulders (sometimes hips), molded and painted clothes or underwear; molded and painted hair, sometimes with molded hat, painted eyes, closed mouth; molded shoes and socks (if in underwear often barefoot); good quality work; all in good condition, with proper parts.

Children:

3¼in (8cm)	$ 95 - 110
4 - 5in (10 - 13cm)	135 - 160
6 - 7in (15 - 18cm)	200 - 250

Punch, Judy and other white bisque characters,

3 - 4in (8 - 10cm)	95 - 110

All-Bisque Dolls (German) continued

Acrobat, fine quality and decoration,
4in (10cm)   **300 - 350**

All-Bisque Slender Dolls: Ca. 1880 - on. Jointed usually by wire or pegging at shoulders and hips, stationary neck, slender arms and legs; good wig, glass eyes, closed mouth; molded shoes or boots and stockings; dressed or undressed; many in regional costumes; all in good condition, with proper parts.

3in (8cm)	**$225 - 250**
3¾ - 4in (9 - 10cm)	**185 - 210**
5 - 6in (13 - 15cm)	**300 - 350**
Swivel neck:	
4in (10cm)	**375 - 425**
5½in - 6in (14 - 15cm)	**525 - 575**
4in (10cm) 10a or 39/11	**225 - 250**
5½in (14cm) 13a	**325 - 350**
Black or Mulatto:	
4 - 4½in (10 - 12cm)	**325 - 375**
Swivel neck:	
4in (10cm)	**400 - 450**

All-Bisque with painted eyes: Ca. 1880 - 1910. Jointed at shoulders, stiff or jointed hips, stationary neck; molded and painted hair or mohair wig, painted eyes, closed mouth; molded and painted shoes and stockings; fine quality work; dressed or undressed; all in good condition, with proper parts.

1¼in (3cm) crocheted clothes		
	$ 65 -	75
1½ - 2in (4 - 5cm)	75 -	85
4 - 5in (10 - 13cm)	175 -	200
6 - 7in (15 - 18cm)	225 -	275
Swivel neck:		
2½in (6cm) all original	**150**	
4 - 5in (10 - 13cm)	225 -	275
Early round face, (bootines):		
4 - 5in (10 - 13cm)	200 -	250
6 - 6½in (15 - 16cm)	300 -	350
Early face, molded hat, swivel neck:		
7in (18cm)	2500 - 2750**	
Black stockings, tan slippers:		
6in (15cm)	350 -	400

Early face, (pink or blue shirred hose):

4½in (12cm)	**175 -**	**200**
6in (15cm)	**350 -**	**375**
8in (20cm)	**550 -**	**575**
Early face (molded hair):		
3¾in - 4½in (9 - 11cm)	**160 -**	**185**
6 - 7in (15 - 18cm)	**275 -**	**325**
Molded hat:		
3¾in (9cm)	**275 -**	**300**

**Not enough price samples to compute a reliable range.

4in (10cm) Slender all-bisque, all original. *H & J Foulke, Inc.*

6½in (16cm) 160 all-bisque with sleep eyes.
H & J Foulke, Inc.

Below: 7in (18cm) early style all-bisque.
H & J Foulke, Inc.

All-Bisque with glass eyes: Ca. 1890 -
1910. Very good quality bisque, jointed at
shoulders, stiff or jointed hips; good wig,
glass eyes, closed mouth (sometimes open);
molded and painted shoes and stockings;
dressed or undressed; all in good condition,
with proper parts. Very good quality.

3in (8cm)	$ 275 - 325*
4½ - 5in (11 - 13cm)	275 - 325*
6in (15cm)	350 - 375*
7in (18cm)	400 - 450*
8in (20cm)	500 - 550*
9in (23cm)	700 - 800
10in (25cm)	900 -1000
12in (31cm)	1300 -1400

Early style model, stiff hips, shirred hose
or bootines:

3in (8cm)	275 - 325
4½in (11cm)	275 - 325
6in (15cm)	425 - 475
8½in (21cm)	800 - 900

*Allow $25 - 75 extra for yellow boots or un-
usual footwear and/or especially fine quality.

All-Bisque Dolls (German) continued

All-bisque with swivel neck and glass eyes: Ca. 1880 - 1910. Swivel neck, pegged shoulders and hips; good wig, glass eyes, closed or open mouth; molded and painted shoes or boots and stockings; dressed or undressed; all in good condition, with proper parts. Very good quality.

3¼in (8cm)	$ 350 - 375
4 - 4½in (10 - 12cm)	375 - 425*
5 - 6in (13 - 15cm)	550 - 650*
7in (18cm)	750 - 800*
8in (20cm)	900 - 1000*
9in (23cm)	1100 - 1200*
10in (25cm)	1300 - 1500

Early Kestner or S&H type:

5in (13cm)	900 - 1000
6in (15cm)	1300 - 1500
8in (20cm)	2000 - 2200
10in (25cm)	2800 - 3000
7in (18cm) in trunk with outfits and accessories, at auction	2100

With kneeling legs:

8in (20cm) at auction	4000

With jointed knee:

6½in (16cm)	3000

#102 (So-called: "Wrestler"):

6½in (16cm)	1250 - 1350
8½in (22cm)	1650 - 1850
9½in (24cm)	2000 - 2200
In original store box with clothes and accessories	3600

Bare feet:

5½ - 6in (14 - 15cm)	1650 - 1800
8in (20cm)	2500 - 2600

Round face, bootines:

6in (15cm)	800 - 850
8in (20cm)	1200 - 1300

*Allow $75 extra for yellow boots or unusual footwear.

Left: 8½in (21cm) Kestner all-bisque. *H & J Foulke, Inc.*
Right: 7½in (19cm) Simon & Halbig-type all-bisque. *H & J Foulke, Inc.*

All-Bisque Dolls (German) continued

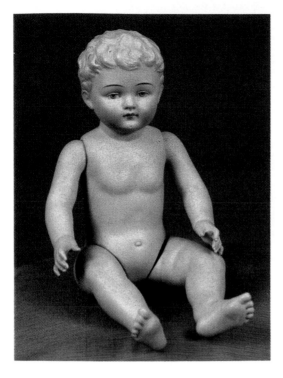

13in (33cm) fine early quality all-bisque baby. *H & J Foulke, Inc.*

Long black or blue stockings (**886** and **890**):
(For photograph see page 330.)
Long black stockings, tan slippers,
7½in (19cm) **$950**

All-Bisque Baby: 1900 - on. Jointed at shoulders and hips with curved arms and legs; molded and painted hair, painted eyes; not dressed; all in good condition, with proper parts.

2½ - 3½in (6 - 9cm)	**$ 75 -**	**95**
4 - 5in (10 - 13cm)	**150 -**	**175**
Fine early quality blonde molded hair:		
3½ - 4½in (9 - 11cm)	**160 -**	**185**
6 - 7in (15 - 18cm)	**250 -**	**300**
9in (23cm)	**600 -**	**700**
13in (33cm)	**900 - 1100**	
5 - 6in (13 - 15cm) immobile		
	150 -	**175**

All-Bisque Character Baby: Ca. 1910. Jointed at shoulders and hips, curved arms and legs; molded hair, painted eyes, character face; undressed; all in good condition, with proper parts. (For photograph see *10th Blue Book*, page 57.)

3½in (9cm)	**$ 95 - 110**
4½ - 5½in (11 - 14cm)	**175 - 225**
7in (18cm)	**275 - 325**
8in (20cm)	**375 - 425**
#830 and others with glass eyes:	
4 - 5in (10 - 13cm)	**275 - 325**
6in (15cm)	**400 - 450**
8in (20cm)	**600 - 650**
Swivel neck, glass eyes:	
6in (15cm)	**450 - 500**
8in (20cm)	**650 - 725**
10in (25cm)	**900 - 975**
Swivel neck, painted eyes:	
5 - 6in (13 - 15cm)	**325 - 375**
8in (20cm)	**475 - 525**
11in (28cm)	**775 - 875**
#260, Molded clothes:	
4in (10cm)	**225 - 250**

All-Bisque Dolls (German) continued

Later All-Bisque with glass eyes: Ca. 1910 on. Many of pretinted pink bisque. Jointed at shoulders and hips; good wig, glass eyes, closed or open mouth; molded and painted black one-strap shoes and stockings; undressed or dressed; all in good condition, with proper parts.

Good smooth bisque:

4 - 5in (10 - 13cm)	**$150 - 185**
6in (15cm)	**225 - 250**
7in (18cm)	**300**

Grainy bisque:

4½in (12cm)	**95**
6in (15cm)	**150**

Below: 5½in (14cm) 208 all-bisque "***Baby Rose***." *H & J Foulke, Inc.*

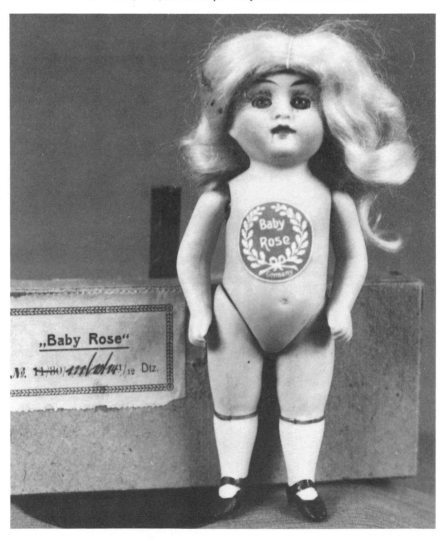

"Baby Rose"

No. 11/80 *mtotw* ½/12 Dtz.

4in (10cm) *Medic* and *Nurse* characters. *H & J Foulke, Inc.*

All-Bisque Character Dolls: 1913 - on. Character faces with well-painted features and molded hair. All in good condition with proper parts.

Pink bisque:

2 - 3in (5 - 8cm)	$ 45 - 50
5in (13cm)	75 - 85
Thumbsucker, 3in (8cm)	200 - 225

Girl with molded hair bow loop,

2½in (6cm)	65
Chubby, 4½in (11cm)	165 - 185
6in (15cm)	250 - 300
HEbee, SHEbee, 6in (15cm)	600
7in (18cm)	700 - 800
Peterkin, 5 - 6in (13 - 15cm)	225 - 250
Little Imp, 5in (13cm)	125 - 150
Medic, 4in (10cm)	95 - 110
Nurse, 4in (10cm)	95 - 110
Sailor Boy, 3½in (9cm)	75 - 85

All-Bisque with character face: Ca. 1915. Jointed at shoulders and hips; smiling character face, closed or open mouth; molded and painted shoes and stockings; dressed or undressed; all in good condition, with proper parts. Very good quality.

#150 open/closed mouth with two painted teeth, dimples. (For photograph see *9th Blue Book*, page 49.)

Glass eyes:

5 - 6in (13 - 15cm)	$ 350 - 450
8 - 9in (20 - 23cm)	700 - 800

Painted eyes:

4½ - 5½in (11 - 14cm)	175 - 225
7in (18cm)	300 - 350

#602 Kestner, swivel neck glass eyes (For photograph see *10th Blue Book*, page 59.)

5½ - 6in (14 - 15cm)	550 - 650

#155, 156, smiling face. (For photograph see *8th Blue Book*, page 48.)

6 - 7in (15 - 18cm)	450 - 550
#168, 7in (18cm)	350
#79 pierced nose, 4½in (11cm)	
	500
#790, 5½ - 6in (14 - 15cm)	450 - 500
#160 Molded hair, 5½ - 6in (14 - 15cm)	
	300 - 350

All-Bisque Dolls (German) continued

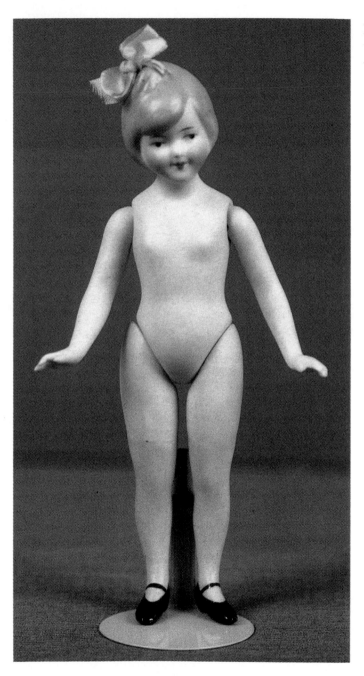

6¼in (16cm) 128 "*Flapper*"; tinted bisque. *H & J Foulke, Inc.*

All-Bisque Dolls (German) continued

Later All-Bisque with painted eyes: Ca. 1920. Many by Hertwig. Some of pretinted bisque. Jointed at shoulders and hips, stationary neck; mohair wig or molded hair, painted eyes, closed mouth; molded and painted one-strap shoes and white stockings; dressed or undressed; all in good condition, with proper parts. (For photograph see *10th Blue Book, page 60.*)

3½in (9cm)	$ 65 - 75
4½ - 5in (12 - 13cm)	90 - 100
6 - 7in (15 - 18cm)	140 - 175
8in (20cm)	225
Swivel neck,	
6½in (16cm)	225 - 250

Left: 3in (7cm) *Snowflake. H & J Foulke, Inc.*

Right: 3¼in (8cm) *Santa* nodder. *H & J Foulke, Inc.* (For further information see following page.)

All-Bisque "Flapper" (tinted bisque): Ca. 1920. Jointed at shoulders and hips; molded bobbed hair with loop for bow, painted features; long yellow stockings, one-strap shoes with heels; undressed or dressed; all in good condition, with proper parts, very good quality.

5in (13cm)	$250 - 300
6 - 7in (15 - 18cm)	350 - 400
Standard quality,	
4in (10cm)	125 - 135

All-Bisque Baby: Ca. 1920. Pink bisque, so-called "Candy Baby," jointed at shoulders and hips, curved arms and legs; painted hair, painted eyes; original factory clothes; all in good condition, with proper parts.

2½ - 3in (6 - 8cm)	$ 70 - 75

All-Bisque Dolls (German) continued

All-Bisque "Flapper:" Ca. 1920. Pink bisque with wire joints at shoulders and hips; molded bobbed hair and painted features; painted shoes and socks; original factory clothes; all in good condition, with proper parts.

3in (8cm)	**$ 65 - 75**
Molded hats	**185 - 210**
Molded bunny ears cap	**300 - 325**
Aviatrix	**200**
Swivel waist, 3½ (9cm)	**350**

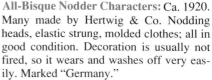

All-Bisque Nodder Characters: Ca. 1920. Many made by Hertwig & Co. Nodding heads, elastic strung, molded clothes; all in good condition. Decoration is usually not fired, so it wears and washes off very easily. Marked "Germany."

3 - 4in (8 - 10cm)	**$ 50 - 60**
Comic characters	**75 up***
Dressed Animals	**125 - 150**
Dressed Teddy Bears	**200**
Santa (For photograph see preceding	
page.)	**175 - 200**
Dutch Girl, 6in (15cm)	**150**

*Depending upon rarity.

All-Bisque Immobiles: Ca. 1920. All-bisque figures with molded clothes, molded hair and painted features. Decoration is not fired, so it wears and washes off very easily. Marked "Germany." (For photographs see *10th Blue Book*, page 19.)

Adults and children,	
1½ - 2¼in (4 - 6cm)	**$ 35 - 45**
Children, 3¼in (8cm)	**45 - 55**
Santa, 3in (8cm)	**125 - 135**
Children with animals on string,	
3in (8cm)	**100 - 125**

Jointed Animals: Ca. 1910 on. All-Bisque animals, wire-jointed shoulders and hips; original crocheted clothes.

Rabbit, 2 - 2¾in (5 - 7cm)	**$ 475 - 525**
Bear, 2 - 2½in (5 - 6cm)	**500**
Bear on all fours,	
3¼in (8cm)	**200 - 225**

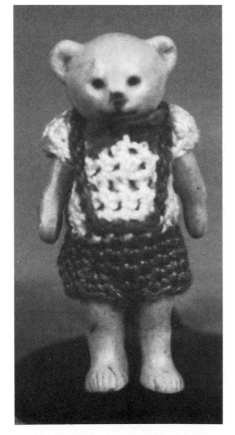

2in (5cm) jointed teddy bear, all original. *H & J Foulke, Inc.*

All-Bisque Dolls (Made in Japan)

FACTS

Various Japanese firms. Ca. 1915 - on.
Bisque. Various small sizes.
Mark: "Made in Japan" or "NIPPON."

Baby:
White, 4in (10cm)	$ 30 - 33
Black, 4 - 5in (10 - 13cm)	55 - 65

Betty Boop-type:
4 - 5in (10 - 13cm)	20 - 25
6 - 7in (15 - 18cm)	32 - 38

Child:
4 - 5in (10 - 13cm)	25 - 28
6 - 7in (15 - 18cm)	35 - 45

Comic Characters,
3 - 4in (8 - 10cm)	25 up*

Stiff Characters:
3 - 4in (8 - 10cm)	$ 5 - 10
6 - 7in (15 - 18cm)	30 - 35
Cho-Cho San, 4½in (12cm)	70 - 80
Nodders, 4in (10cm)	25 - 35
Orientals, 3 - 4in (8 - 10cm)	20 - 25
Queue San, 4in (10cm)	70 - 80
Marked "Nippon" Characters,	
4 - 5in (10 - 13cm)	50 - 60
Three Bears, boxed set	175 - 200
Snow White, boxed set	350 - 450
Black Character Girl, molded hair bow	
loop 4½in (12cm)	35 - 40
Old Woman in Shoe,	
boxed set	135 - 165
Two-face Baby	
(crying and sleeping)	125 - 150
Shirley Temple, 5in (13cm)	85 - 95
Circus Set, boxed, 11 pieces	135 - 165

*Depending upon rarity.

Below: 4in (10cm) Bride and Groom, boxed set.
H & J Foulke, Inc.

Alt, Beck & Gottschalck

FACTS

Alt, Beck & Gottschalck, porcelain factory, Nauendorf near Ohrdruf, Thüringia, Germany. Made heads for many producers including Wagner & Zetzsche. 1854 - on. China and bisque heads for use on composition, kid or cloth bodies; all-bisque or all-china dolls.

China Shoulder Heads: Ca. 1880. Black or blonde-haired china head; old cloth body with china limbs; dressed; all in good condition. Mold numbers such as **784, 1000, 1008, 1028, 1046, 1142, 1210.**

Mark: *1008 ⩞9*

Also ⩞ or *No* in place of *X*

14 - 16in (36 - 41cm)	$300 - 350
21 - 23in (53 - 58cm)	450 - 500

Bisque Shoulder Head: Ca. 1880. Molded hair, painted or glass eyes, closed mouth; cloth body with bisque lower limbs; dressed; all in good condition. Mold numbers, such as 890, 990, 1000, 1008, 1028, 1064, 1142, 1254, 1288, 1304. (For photograph see *10th Blue Book*, page 21.)
Mark: See above.

Painted eyes:
14 - 16in (36 - 41cm)	$350 - 400*
20 - 22in (51 - 56cm)	450 - 500*

Glass eyes:
14 - 16in (36 - 41cm)	$550 - 650*
21in (53cm)	900 - 1000*

#994 molded bonnet, 18in (46cm)	$ 600 - 650
#996 molded white scarf, 16in (41cm)	1600
#998 molded bonnet, 13in (33cm)	450

*Allow extra for unusual or elaborate hairdo or molded hat.

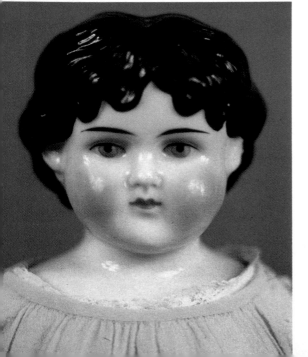

17in (43cm) china shoulder head #1046. *H & J Foulke, Inc.*

22in (56cm) bisque shoulder head #639. *H & J Foulke, Inc.*

12½in (32cm) bisque shoulder header #998. *H & J Foulke, Inc.*

Alt, Beck & Gottschalck continued

24in (61cm) 912 shoulder head.
H & J Foulke, Inc.

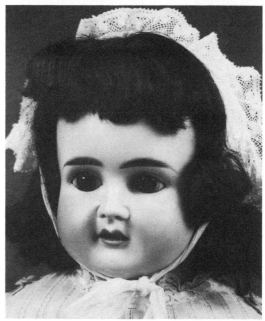

29in (74cm) shoulder head, open
mouth. *H & J Foulke, Inc.*

Bisque Shoulder Head: Ca. 1885 - on. Turned shoulder head, mohair or human hair wig, plaster dome or bald head, glass sleeping or set eyes, closed mouth; kid body with gusseted joints and bisque lower arms, or cloth body with kid lower arms; dressed; all in good condition. Mold numbers, such as **639, 698, 912, 1032, 1123, 1235.**

Mark: 639 ⅏ 6

with DEP after 1888

14 - 16in (36 - 41cm)	$ 725 - 825
19 - 21in (48 - 53cm)	950 - 1150
22 - 24in (56 - 61cm)	1250 - 1450
22 - 24in (56 - 61cm), all original clothing and wig	1800 - 2100

#911, 916, swivel neck. (For photograph see *10th Blue Book*, page 20.)

19 - 22in (48 - 56cm)	2100 - 2300

With open mouth:

Mark:

698 ½ Germany Dep N° 10

15 - 17in (38 - 43cm)	$ 525 - 575
22 - 24in (56 - 61cm)	725 - 775

Child Doll: Perfect bisque head, good wig, sleep eyes, open mouth; ball-jointed body in good condition; appropriate clothes.

Mark:

2 ½
A B & G
Made in Germany

#1362 Sweet Nell: (For photograph see *10th Blue Book*, page 65.)

14 - 17in (36 - 43cm)	$ 425 - 475
20 - 22in (51 - 56cm)	525 - 550
25 - 27in (64 - 69cm)	750 - 850
32 - 33in (81 - 84cm)	1250 - 1350
36in (91cm)	1600 - 1700

#911, closed mouth: (For photograph see *10th Blue Book*, page 20.)

18in (46cm)	2500**

#630, closed mouth:

23in (68cm)	2200 - 2500**

All-Bisque Girl: 1911. Chubby body, loop strung shoulders and hips, inset glass eyes open/closed mouth, painted eyelashes, full mohair or silky wig; molded white stockings, blue garters, black Mary Janes. (For photograph see *9th Blue Book*, page 56.)

Mark:

$$\frac{83}{225}$$
2+

Also **#100, 125** or **150** in place of **225.** Bottom number is centimeter size.

5 - 6in (13 - 15cm)	$ 225 - 250
8in (20cm)	425 - 450

**Not enough price samples to compute a reliable range.

Alt, Beck & Gottschalck continued

Character: 1910 - on. Perfect bisque head, good wig, sleep eyes, open mouth; some with open nostrils; composition body; all in good condition; suitable clothes.

Mark:

Below: 14in (37cm) 1357 character boy. *H & J Foulke, Inc.*

#1322, 1352, 1361:

10 - 12in (25 -31cm)	$ 350 - 400*
16 - 18in (41 - 46cm)	525 - 575*
22 - 23in (56 - 58cm)	850 - 900*

#1357:

16 - 18in (46 - 51cm)	900 - 1000

#1358: (See photograph on page 5.)

18 - 20in (46 - 51cm)	2500**

#1448, smiling, at auction

15in (38cm)	25,000

*Allow $50 extra for flirty eyes or toddler body.
**Not enough price samples to compute a reliable range.

Louis Amberg & Son

FACTS

Louis Amberg & Son, New York, N.Y., U.S.A. 1907 - on (although Amberg had been in the doll business under other names since 1878).

Newborn Babe: 1914, reissued 1924. Designed by Jeno Juszko. Bisque head of an infant with painted hair, sleep eyes, closed or open mouth; soft cloth body with celluloid, rubber or composition hands; appropriate clothes; all in good condition. Mold **886** by Recknagel. Mold **371** with open mouth by Marseille. (For photograph see *10th Blue Book*, page 67.)

Mark:

L · A · & · S ·
371 · 3/0 D · R · G · M ·
Germany

THE ORIGINAL
NEWBORN BABE
(C) Jan. 9th 1914 – No. G. 45520

AMBERG DOLLS
The World Standard

Length:

9 - 10in (23 - 25cm)	**$375 - 425**
13 - 14in (33 - 36cm)	**500 - 600**
17in (43cm)	**700**

Charlie Chaplin: 1915. Composition portrait head with molded and painted hair, painted eyes to the side, closed full mouth, molded mustache; straw-filled cloth body with composition hands; original clothes; all in good condition with wear. (For photograph see *8th Blue Book*, page 57.)
Mark: cloth label on sleeve:

"CHARLIE CHAPLIN DOLL
World's Greatest Comedian
Made exclusively by Louis Amberg
& Son, N.Y.
by Special Arrangement with
Essamay Film Co."

14in (36cm)	**$500 - 600**

Composition Mibs: 1921. Composition shoulder head designed by Hazel Drucker with wistful expression, molded and painted blonde or reddish hair, blue painted eyes, closed mouth; cloth body with composition arms and legs with painted shoes and socks; appropriate old clothes; all in good condition. (For photograph see *10th Blue Book*, page 359.)
Mark: None on doll; paper label only:

"Amberg Dolls
Please Love Me
I'm Mibs"

16in (41cm)	**$850 - 950****

Baby Peggy: 1923. Composition head, arms and legs, cloth body; molded brown bobbed hair, painted eyes, smiling closed mouth; appropriately dressed; all in good condition. (For photograph see page 56.)

20in (51cm)	**$550 - 650****

**Not enough price samples to compute a reliable range.

Louis Amberg & Son continued

3in (8cm) **Mibs**, all original. *H & J Foulke, Inc.*

6in (15cm) girl with molded bow. *H & J Foulke, Inc.*

Baby Peggy: 1924. Perfect bisque head by Armand Marseille with character face; brown bobbed mohair wig, brown sleep eyes, closed mouth; composition or kid body, fully-jointed; dressed or undressed; all in very good condition. (For photographs see *10th Blue Book*, page 69 and following page.)
Mark:

> "19 © 24"
> LA & S NY
> Germany
> —50—
> 982/2"

also:
973 (smiling socket head)
972 (pensive socket head)
983 (smiling shoulder head)
982 (pensive shoulder head)
  18 - 22in (46 - 56cm)   **$2500 - 2850**

All-Bisque Character Children: 1920s. Made by a German porcelain factory. Pink pretinted bisque with molded and painted features, molded hair; jointed at shoulders and hips; molded stockings with blue garters, brown strap shoes, white stockings.
  4in (10cm)   **$125**
  5 - 6in (13 - 15cm)   **160 - 185**
Girl with molded bow,
  6in (15cm)   **275 - 325**
Girl with downward gaze, glass eyes, wig. (For photograph see following page.)
  5½in (14cm)   **425**
Mibs:
  3in (8cm)   **225 - 250**
  4¾in (12cm)   **350 - 375**
Baby Peggy:
  3in (8cm)   **225 - 250**
  5½in (14cm)   **350 - 375**
Coquette:
  5½in (14cm)   **160 - 175**

Vanta Baby: 1927. A tie-in with Vanta baby garments. Composition or bisque head with molded and painted hair, sleep eyes, open mouth with two teeth (closed mouth and painted eyes in all-composition small dolls); muslin body jointed at hips and shoulders, curved composition arms and legs; suitably dressed; all in good condition. (For photograph see page 57.)
Mark: Bisque Head

> Vanta Baby
> L A&S · 3/0 D·R·G·M·
> Germany.

Composition head,
  20in (51cm)   **$ 275 - 325**
Bisque head,
  25in (64cm)   **1100 - 1250**

Sue, Edwina or It: 1928. All-composition with molded and painted hair, painted eyes; jointed neck, shoulders and hips, a large round ball joint at waist; dressed; all in very good condition. (For photograph see *7th Blue Book*, page 59.)
Mark:

> "AMBERG"
> PAT.PEND.
> L.A. & S. © 1928"
14in (36cm)   **$ 425 - 475**

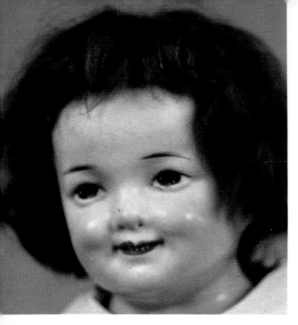

Left:
20in (51cm) composition *Baby Peggy*. *H & J Foulke, Inc.* (For further information see page 53.)

Below:
5¼in (11cm) girl with downward gaze. *H & J Foulke, Inc.* (For further information see page 55.)

Tiny Tots Body Twists: 1928. All-composition with jointed shoulders and a large round ball joint at the waist; molded and painted hair in both boy and girl styles, painted eyes; painted shoes and socks; dressed; all in good condition.

Mark: tag on clothes:

> "An Amberg Doll with
> BODY TWIST
> all its own
> PAT. PEND. SER. NO.
> 32018"

8in (20cm)   **$ 165 - 185**

Louis Amberg & Son continued

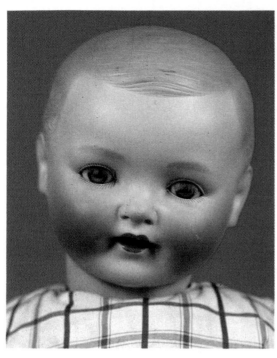

Right: **Vanta Baby** with bisque head. *Richard Wright Antiques.* (For further information see page 55.)

Below: 8in (20cm) Body Twist dolls. *Ruth West.*

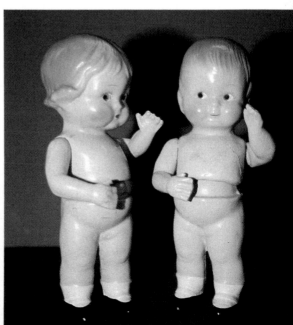

American Character

FACTS

American Character Doll Co., New York, N.Y., U.S.A. 1919 - on. **Trademark:** Petite.

Marked Petite or American Character Mama Dolls: 1923 - on. Composition head, arms and legs, cloth torso; mohair or human hair wig, sleep eyes, closed or open mouth; original clothes; all in good condition. (For photograph see *9th Blue Book*, page 61.)

16 - 18in (41 - 46cm)	**$200 - 250**
24in (61cm)	**300 - 350**

Campbell Kid: 1923. Designed by Grace Drayton; sometimes called *Dolly Dingle*. All composition with swivel head, jointed shoulders and hips; molded and painted hair, eyes to side, watermelon mouth; original clothes; all in good condition. (For photograph see *4th Blue Book*, page 86.)

12in (31cm)	**$500 - 600****

Left:
13in (33cm) *Petite Sally*. *H & J Foulke, Inc.*

Right:
12in (31cm) *Puggy*, all original. *H & J Foulke, Inc.*

Puggy: 1928. All-composition chubby body jointed at neck, shoulders and hips; molded and painted hair, painted eyes to the side, closed mouth, pug nose, frowning face; original clothes; all in good condtion.
Mark:

"A PETITE DOLL"	
12in (31cm)	**$500**

Marked Petite Girl Dolls: 1930s. All-composition jointed at neck, shoulders and hips (some with cloth torsos); human hair or mohair wig, lashed sleeping eyes, closed or open mouth with teeth; original clothes; all in good condition.

16 - 18in (41 - 46cm)	**$250 - 275**
24in (61cm)	**300 - 350**

Sally: 1930. Painted eyes and molded hair or wigged with sleeping eyes.

12in (31cm)	**$200 - 225**
16in (41cm)	**225 - 250**
18in (46cm) **Sally-Joy**	**275 - 300**

**Not enough price samples to compute a reliable range.

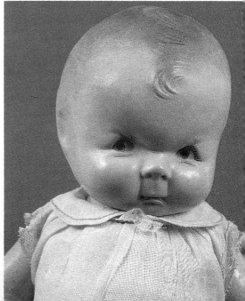

Carol Ann Beery, 1935. "Two-Some Doll" with special crown braid
16½in (42cm)	**$350 - 400****

Toodles: Hard rubber baby, molded hair, sleep eyes; drinks and wets; original clothes; excellent condition.
18½in (47cm)	**$200 - 225**

Tiny Tears: 1950s. Hard plastic head, sleep eyes, tear ducts, molded hair; drinks and wets; rubber or vinyl body; original clothes; excellent condition.
12in (31cm)	**$150**
18in (46cm)	**200**

Sweet Sue: 1953. All-hard plastic or hard plastic and vinyl, some with walking mechanism, some fully-jointed including elbows, knees and ankles; original clothes; all in excellent condition. (For photograph see *10th Blue Book Book*, page 73.)
Marks: "A.C."
                "Amer. Char."
14in (36cm)	**$200 - 225**
18 - 20in (46 - 51cm)	**250 - 300**
24in (61cm)	**325 - 375**

Sweet Sue Sophisticate, vinyl head
20in (51cm)	**$175 - 200**

Toni, vinyl head:
10½in (26cm)	**$110 - 125**
14in (36cm)	**150 - 160**
20in (51cm), boxed with accessories	
	400

Top: *Tiny Tears*, boxed. *H & J Foulke, Inc.*

Bottom: 18½in (47cm) *Toodles*, all original, boxed. *H & J Foulke, Inc.*

American Character continued

Eloise: Ca. 1955. All-cloth with molded face, painted side-glancing eyes, smiling mouth, yellow yarn hair; flexible arms and legs; original clothing; in excellent condition. Designed by Bette Gould from the fictional little girl "Eloise" who lived at the Plaza Hotel in New York City.
Mark: Cardboard tag

21in (53cm)   **$300 - 350**

Betsy McCall: 1957. All-hard plastic with legs jointed at knees; rooted Saran hair on a wig cap, round face with sleep eyes, plastic eyelashes; original clothes; all in excellent condition. (For photograph see *10th Blue Book*, page 74.)
Mark:

8in (20cm)
    Dressed   **$165 - 185**
    Basic (undergarment, shoes and socks)
                                150

Betsy McCall: 1960. All-vinyl with rooted hair, lashed sleep eyes, round face, turned-up mouth; slender arms and legs; original clothes; all in excellent condition.
Mark:

McCALL
19©56
CORP.

14in (36cm)   **$250**
20in (51cm)   **300**
30 - 36in (76 - 91cm)   **450 - 550**

Below: 21in (53cm) **Eloise**, *all original. H & J Foulke, Inc.*

Right:
22in (56cm) **Betsy McCall**, all original. *H & J Foulke, Inc.*

Below:
20in (51cm) **Betsy McCall**, all original. *H & J Foulke, Inc.*

Arranbee

FACTS

Arranbee Doll Co., New York, N.Y., U.S.A. 1922 - 1960.
Mark: "ARRANBEE" or "R & B."

My Dream Baby: 1924. Perfect bisque head with solid dome and painted hair, sleep eyes, closed or open mouth; all-composition or cloth body with composition hands; dressed; all in good condition. Some heads incised "A.M.," "**341**" or "**351**"; some incised "ARRANBEE." See Armand Marseille infant on page 277 for prices.

Storybook Dolls: 1930s. All-composition with swivel neck, jointed arms and legs; molded and painted hair, painted eyes; all original storybook costumes; all in good condition. (For photograph see *10th Blue Book*, page 78.)

9 - 10in (23 - 25cm)	**$150 - 175**
Boxed **Bo-Peep** with lamb	**225 - 250**

Below: 12in (31cm) *Nancy*, all original in wardrobe trunk. *H & J Foulke, Inc.*

Nancy: 1930. All-composition, jointed at neck, shoulders and hips, molded hair, painted eyes and closed mouth; original or appropriate old clothes; all in good condition.

Mark: "ARRANBEE" or "NANCY"

12in (31cm)	**$200 - 225**

16in (41cm) sleep eyes, wig, open mouth
(For photograph see *9th Blue Book*,
page 82.)   **275 - 300**

13in (33cm) Boxed at auction
400

Debu' Teen and Nancy Lee: 1938 - on. All-composition or composition swivel shoulder head and limbs on cloth torso; mohair or human hair wig, sleep eyes, closed mouth, original clothes; all in good condition.

11in (28cm)	**$165 - 185**
14in (36cm)	**225 - 250**
21in (53cm)	**300 - 325**

Skating Doll, 18in (46cm)	**275 - 300**
Brother, 14in (36cm)	**300 - 325**

Little Angel Baby: 1940s. Composition head and lower limbs, cloth torso, molded hair, sleep eyes, closed mouth; original clothes; all in good condition.

16in (41cm)	**$200 - 225**

Boxed and excellent condition
275 - 300

Nanette and Nancy Lee: 1950s. All-hard plastic, jointed at neck, shoulders and hips; synthetic wig, sleep eyes, closed mouth; original clothes; all in excellent condition.

14in (36cm)	**$200 - 225**
17in (43cm)	**275 - 300**

Top: 11in (28cm) *Skater*, all original. *H & J Foulke, Inc.*

Bottom: 16in (41cm) *Little Angel*, all original. *H & J Foulke, Inc.*

Artist Dolls

FACTS

Modern Artist Dolls: 1930s - on. Original dolls which were created as works of art and decorative objects, not intended as playthings.

Armstrong-Hand, Martha, porcelain
babies and children. **$1200 up**

Beckett, Bob & June, carved wood
children. (See photograph page 67.)
300 - 450

Blakeley, Halle, high-fired clay lady dolls.
550 - 750

Brandon, Elizabeth, porcelain children,
Theola, Joshua, Joi Lin. **300 - 500**

Bringloe, Frances, carved wood
American Pioneer Children,
6¼in (16cm) pair. **600**

Bullard, Helen, carved wood.
Holly   **100 - 125**
Hitty   **160 - 195**
American Family Series (16 dolls)
225 - 250 each

Campbell, Astry, porcelain
Ricky & Becky. **850 pair**

Clear, Emma, porcelain, china and bisque
shoulder head dolls. **350 - 500**
Danny   **450**
George & Martha Washington,
depending upon clothes and sharpness
of detail. **400 - 750 pair**
28in(71cm) glass-eyed parian models
1000 - 1100

DeNunez, Marianne,
15in (38cm) Bru Jne. **200 - 225**

Below: *Becky & Ricky* by Astry Campbell.
H & J Foulke, Inc.

Artist Dolls Continued

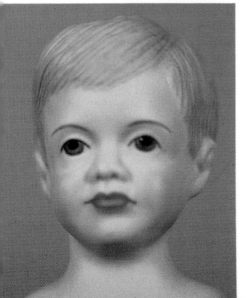

Above:
Group of carved wood dolls by Sherman Smith.
H & J Foulke, Inc.

Left:
Ken-Tuck by Janet Masteller. *H & J Foulke, Inc.*

Artist Dolls continued

Florian, Gertrude, ceramic composition dressed ladies. **$300**

Goodnow, June, bisque Indians 16-17in (41-43cm). **550 - 650**

Heiser, Dorothy, cloth sculpture.
Early dolls **400 - 500**
Queens 10-13in (25-33cm)
1100 - 1500

Kane, Maggie Head, porcelain.
Gypsy Mother **400 - 450**

Oldenburg, Mary Ann, porcelain children. **200 - 250**

Park, Irma, wax-over-porcelain miniatures, depending upon detail.
50 - 100

Redmond, Kathy, elaborately modeled porcelain ladies. **400 - 450**

Sorensen, Lewis, wax.
Father Christmas **1200**
Toymaker **800**

Below:
Gypsy Mother by Maggie Head Kane. *H & J Foulke, Inc.*

Smith, Sherman, carved wood 5 - 6in (13 - 15cm). (See photograph on page 65.) **235**

Sweet, Elizabeth, 18in (46cm)
Amy, 1970. **250**

Thompson, Martha, porcelain.
Princess Caroline, Prince Charles, Princess Ann **900 - 1000 each**
Little Women **1000 each**
Queen Elizabeth & Prince Philip **900 each**
Princess Margaret Rose, Princess Grace **1500 - 2000**
Ike & Mamie Eisenhower **2500 pair**

Thorp, Ellery, porcelain children.
300 - 500

Tuttle, Eunice, miniature porcelain children. **800 - 1100**

Walters, Beverly, porcelain, miniature fashions. **500 up**

Wright, Phyllis, porcelain children.
300 - 450

Wright, John, cloth.
Adult characters **1500 - 2000**
Children **900 - 1100**
Christopher Robin **1300**
Christopher Robin with Winnie the Pooh **1400**
Winnie the Pooh, 1987.
18in (46cm) **750**

Wyffels, Berdine, porcelain.
6in (15cm) girl glass eyes **165**
6in (15cm) girl painted eyes **100**

Zeller, Fawn, porcelain.
One of a Kind Dolls **2000**
Jackie Kennedy, 1959. **900 up**
Polly Piedmont, 1965. **900 up**
Holly, U.S. Historical Society **500 - 600**
Polly II, U.S. Historical Society **150 - 200**

Artist Dolls

U.F.D.C. National & Regional Souvenir Dolls: Created by doll artists in limited editions and distributed to convention attendees as souvenirs. Before 1982, most dolls were given as kits; after 1982, most dolls were fully made up and dressed. Except as noted dolls have porcelain heads, arms and legs; cloth bodies. A few are all porcelain.

Alice in Wonderland: Yolanda Bello, 1990 Ohio Regional. Complete doll.
$165
Alice Roosevelt: Kathy Redmond, 1990 National. Complete doll. **125**
Crystal Faerie: Kazue Moroi & Lita Wilson, 1983 Midwest Regional. Complete. **85**
Father Christmas: (Kit) Beverly Walters, 1980 National. Fully made up.
400 - 500
Janette: Fawn Zeller, 1991 National. Complete doll and pattern portfolio. **300**
Kate: All cloth by Anili, 1986 National. With original box.
165 - 185
Li'l Apple: Faith Wick, 1979 National. Fully made up with romper suit. **50**
Ken-Tuck: (Kit) Janet Masteller, 1972 Regional. Fully made up. (See photograph on page 65.) **65 - 75**
Little Miss Sunshine: (Kit) 1974 Florida Regional. Fully made up. **65 - 75**
Mary: Linda Steele, 1987 National. Fully made up.
100
Miami Miss: (Kit) Fawn Zeller, 1961 National.
Fully made up. **200 - 250**
Dressed. **300 - 350**

Nellie Bly: Muriel Kramer, 1985 Pittsburgh Regional. Complete doll.
85 - 95
Pinky: Linda Cheek, California Regional. Complete doll. **300**
Portrait of a Young Girl: Jeanne Singer, 1986 Rochester Regional. Complete doll.
300
Princess Kimimi: (Kit) 1977 Ohio Regional. Fully made up. **85 - 95**
Rose O'Neill: Lita Wilson, 1982 National. Complete doll. **165 - 200**
Sunshine: Lucille Gerrard, 1983 National. Complete doll. **100**

Bobbi by Bob Beckett. *H & J Foulke, Inc.*

Georgene Averill (Madame Hendren)

FACTS

Averill Mfg. Co. and Georgene Novelties, Inc., New York, N.Y., U.S.A. 1915 - on.
Designer: Georgene Averill (See also Maud Tousey Fangel and Grace Drayton).
Trademarks: Madame Hendren, Georgene Novelties.

Tagged Mme. Hendren Character: Ca. 1915 - on. Composition character face, usually with painted features, molded hair or wig (sometimes yarn); hard-stuffed cloth body with composition hands; original clothes often of felt; included Dutch children, Indians, sailors, cowboys, blacks; all in good condition. (For photograph see *10th Blue Book*, page 80.)

Cloth Label:

Madame Hendren
CHARACTER DOLL
COSTUME PAT. MAY 9th 1916

10 - 14in (25 - 36cm)	**$110 - 135**

Mama & Baby Dolls: Ca. 1918 - on. Composition shoulder head, lower arms and legs, cloth torso with cry box; mohair wig or molded hair, sleep eyes, open mouth with teeth or closed mouth; appropriately dressed; all in good condition. Names such as **Baby Hendren, Baby Georgene** and others. (See photograph on page 70.)

15 - 18in (38 - 46cm)	**$200 - 250**
22 - 24in (56 - 61cm)	**350 - 450**

Dolly Reckord: 1922. Record playing mechanism in torso. Good condition with records.

26in (66cm)	**$500 - 600**

26in (66cm) *Dolly Reckord*.
H & J Foulke, Inc.

Left: 5½in (14cm) all-bisque *Bonnie Babe*. *H & J Foulke, Inc.* (See page 70 for information.)

Below: 15½in (39cm) *Bonnie Babe*, all original with tag. *H & J Foulke, Inc.* (See page 70 for information.)

Georgene Averill (Madame Hendren) continued

Whistling Doll: 1925 - 1929. Composition head with molded hair, side-glancing eyes, mouth pursed to whistle through round opening; composition arms, cloth torso; legs are coiled spring bellows covered with cloth; when head is pushed down or feet are pushed up, the doll whistles. Original or appropriate clothes; all in good condition. (For photographs see *7th Blue Book*, page 198, and *9th Blue Book*, page 84.)

Mark: None.

Original Cardboard Tag:
"I whistle when you dance me on one foot
and then the other.
Patented Feb. 2, 1926
Genuine Madame Hendren Doll."

14 - 15in (36 - 38cm) sailor, cowboy,
(Dan) **$200 - 225**
Black **Rufus** or **Dolly Dingle** 350 - 400**

Bonnie Babe: 1926. Bisque heads by Alt, Beck & Gottschalck; cloth bodies by K & K Toy Co.; distributed by George Borgfeldt, New York. Perfect bisque head with smiling face, molded hair, glass sleep eyes, open mouth with two lower teeth; cloth body with composition arms (sometimes celluloid) and legs often of poor quality; all in good condition. Mold #1386 or 1402. (See photograph on page 69.)

Mark:

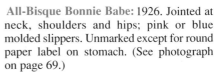

12 - 13in (31 - 33cm)	**$ 950 - 1050**
16 - 18in (41 - 46cm)	**1250 - 1350**
22 - 23in (56 - 58cm)	**1650 - 1750**
15½in (39cm) all original and boxed	**1650**

Composition body,
| 8in (20cm) tall | **1250**** |
Celluloid head:
| 16in (41cm) tall | **550 - 650**** |

All-Bisque Bonnie Babe: 1926. Jointed at neck, shoulders and hips; pink or blue molded slippers. Unmarked except for round paper label on stomach. (See photograph on page 69.)
5in (13cm)	**$ 700 - 750**
7in (18cm)	**950 - 1050**
5in (13cm) original box	**850**

**Not enough price samples to compute a reliable range.

19in (48cm) *Baby Georgene*, all original. *H & J Foulke, Inc.* (For further information see page 68.)

Georgene Averill (Madame Hendren) continued

All-Bisque Sonny: Jointed at neck, shoulders and hips; glass eyes; bare feet.

6½in (16cm)   **$3250****

Rag and Tag: All bisque dog and cat; swivel neck, jointed shoulders and hips, glass eyes; fully marked on back. Rag (890), Tag (891). (For photograph of **Rag**, see *5th Blue Book*, page 52; for photograph of **Tag** see following page.)

5in (13cm)   **$3000****

**Not enough price samples to compute a reliable range.

Body Twists: 1927. All-composition, jointed at neck, shoulders and hips, with a large round ball joint at waist; molded and painted hair, painted eyes, closed mouth; dressed; all in good condition. Advertised as Dimmie and Jimmie.

14½in (37cm)   **$425 - 475**

Sunny Boy and Girl: Ca. 1927. Celluloid "turtle" mark head with molded hair and glass eyes; stuffed body with composition arms and legs; appropriate or original clothes; all in good condition.

15in (38cm)   **$325 - 375**

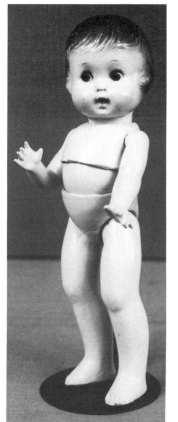

Left: 14½in (37cm) Body Twist *Dimmie* or *Jimmie*. *H & J Foulke, Inc.*

Below: 15in (38cm) *Sunny Boy*. *H & J Foulke, Inc.*

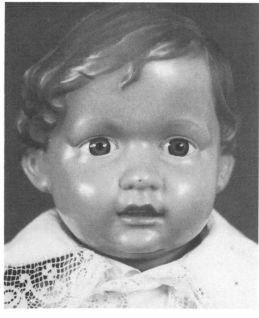

Georgene Averill (Madame Hendren) continued

5in (13cm) All-bisque *Tag* 891. *Richard Wright Antiques.* (See page 71 for information.)

Cloth Dolls: Ca. 1930s - on. Mask face with painted features, yarn hair, painted and/ or real eyelashes; cloth body with movable arms and legs; attractive original clothes; all in excellent condition.

Children or Babies:
12in (31cm)	**$100 - 125**
24 - 26in (61 - 66cm)	**200 - 250**

Topsy & Eva
10in (25cm)	**135 - 150**
International and Costume Dolls:	
12in (31cm)	**75 - 85**
Mint in box with wrist tag	**90 - 110**

Uncle Wiggily or **Nurse Jane,**
18 - 20in (46 - 51cm)	**400 - 500**
Characters, 14in (36cm):	
Little Lulu, Nancy, Sluggo, 1944.	
	500

Tubby Tom, 1951 at auction, mint in box
2000

Alvin, 12in (31cm) at auction, mint in box
2000

Maud Tousey Fangel, 1938. **Snooks, Sweets, Peggy-Ann.** Marked "M.T.F."
12 - 14in (31 - 36cm)	**600 - 650**
17in (43cm)	**750 - 800**

Composition Dolls:
Snookums, 1927. (For photograph see *5th Blue Book*, page 169.)
14in (36cm)	**$300 - 325**

Patsy-Type Girl, 1928. (For photograph see *9th Blue Book*, page 86.)
14in (36cm)	**225 - 250**

Harriet Flanders, 1937. **Little Cherub.** (For photograph see *7th Blue Book*, page 167.)
16in (41cm)	**250 - 275**
Painted eyes, 12in (31cm)	**150 - 165**

Georgene Averill (Madame Hendren) continued

Uncle Wiggily. *Esther*
Schwartz Collection.

15in (38cm) *Maud*
Tousey Fangel girl.
Celina Carroll.

Baby Bo Kaye

FACTS

Composition heads by Cameo Doll Company; bisque heads made in Germany by Alt, Beck & Gottschalck; bodies by K & K Toy Co., New York, N.Y., U.S.A. 1925. Bisque, composition or celluloid head with flange neck; composition or celluloid limbs, cloth body.
Designer: J.L. Kallus.
Distributor: George Borgfeldt Co., N.Y.
Mark: "Copr. by
          J.L. Kallus
          Germany
          1394/30"

Baby Bo Kaye: Perfect bisque head marked as above, molded hair, glass eyes, open mouth with two lower teeth; body as above; dressed; all in good condition.

17 - 19in (43 - 48cm)	**$2800 - 3200**

#1407 (ABG) bisque head, composition body

7½in (19cm)	**1300****
Celluloid head, 16in (41cm)	**650 - 750**

All-Bisque Baby Bo Kaye: Molded hair, glass sleep eyes, open mouth with two teeth; swivel neck, jointed shoulders and hips; molded pink or blue shoes and socks; unmarked.
Mark:

5in (13cm)	**$1250 - 1350**
6in (15cm)	**1600 - 1700**

**Not enough price samples to compute a reliable range.

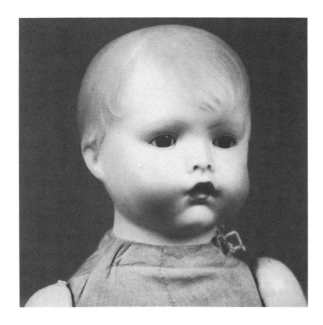

17in (43cm) *Baby Bo Kaye*.
Richard Wright Antiques.

FACTS

E. I. Horsman, New York, N.Y., U.S.A.
Some dolls made for Horsman by Albert
Brückner. 1901 - on. All-cloth. 12 - 30in
(31 - 76cm).
Mark: None.

Babyland Rag: Cloth face with hand-painted features, later with printed features, sometimes mohair wig; cloth body jointed at shoulders and hips; original clothes.

Early hand-painted face:

13 - 15in (33 - 38cm)

very good	$750 - 850*
fair	400 - 500

22in (56cm)

very good	900 - 1000
fair	550 - 600

30in (76cm) very good	2000 - 2200**

Topsy Turvy,

13 - 15in (33 - 38cm) very good	
	700 - 800*

Black,

15in (38cm) fair	650 - 700*
20 - 22in (51 - 56cm) very good	
	1100 - 1300*

Life-like face:

13 - 15in (33 - 38cm)

very good	600 - 650*

Babyland Rag-type (lesser quality):

White, 14in (36cm) good	375 - 475

Topsy Turvy,

14in (36cm) good	450 - 550

Brückner Rag Doll:

Mark: PAT'D. JULY 8ᵀᴴ 1901

Stiffened mask face, cloth body, flexible shoulders and hips; appropriate clothes; all in good condition.

12 - 14in (31 - 36cm)

White	$210 - 235
Black	275 - 300
Topsy Turvy	500 - 550
Dollypop	250**

*Allow more for mint condition doll.
**Not enough price samples to compute a reliable range.

Top right: 15in (38cm) *Dutch Boy* with "Life-like" face, replaced jacket. *H & J Foulke, Inc.*
Left: 15in (38cm) hand-painted brown face. *H & J Foulke, Inc.*

Bähr & Pröschild

FACTS

Bähr & Pröschild, porcelain factory, Ohrdruf, Thüringia, Germany. Made heads for Bruno Schmidt, Heinrich Stier, Kley & Hahn and others. 1871 - on. Bisque heads for use on composition or kid bodies, all-bisque dolls.

Marked Belton-type Child Doll: Ca. 1880. Perfect bisque head, solid domes with flat top having two or three small holes, paperweight eyes, closed mouth with pierced ears; wood and composition jointed body with straight wrists; dressed; all in good condition. Mold numbers in **200** series, usually **204** or **224**.

Mark: 204

11 - 13in (28 - 33cm)	**$1650 - 1850**
16 - 18in (41 - 46cm)	**2200 - 2400**
20 - 22in (51 - 56cm)	**2900 - 3200**
24in (61cm)	**3500 - 3600**

22in (56cm) 224 girl. *H & J Foulke, Inc.*

Marked Child Doll: 1888 - on. Perfect bisque shoulder or socket head, sleeping eyes, open mouth with four or six upper teeth, good human hair or mohair wig; gusseted kid or jointed composition body (many of French-type); dressed; all in good condition. Mold numbers in **200** and **300** series.

Mark: 224
          dep

#204, 239, 273, 275, 277, 289, 297, 325, 340, 379, 394 and other socket heads:

7 - 8in (18 - 20cm),
   five-piece body   **$ 350 - 400**
10in (25cm)   **500 - 600**
14 - 16in (36 - 41cm)
               675 - 725
22 - 24in (56 - 61cm)
             900 - 1000

#224 (dimples):
15 - 17in (38 - 43cm)
             875 - 925
22 - 23in (56 - 58cm)
          1250 - 1350

#246, 309 and other shoulder heads:
16 - 18in (41 - 46cm)
             450 - 500
22 - 24in (56 - 61cm)
             625 - 675

All-Bisque Girl, yellow stockings (Heart mark)
5in (13cm)
             275 - 325

*Allow $500 extra for glass-eyed models.

Top: 29in (74cm) 360 *DEP* girl. *H & J Foulke, Inc.*

Bottom: 25in (64cm) 275 *DEP* girl. *H & J Foulke, Inc.*

Marked B.P. Character Child: Ca. 1910. Perfect bisque socket head, good wig, sleep or painted eyes, closed mouth; toddler or jointed composition body; dressed; all in good condition. Mold #2072, 536 and other child 500 series models made for Kley & Hahn and Bruno Schmidt.

Mark:

15 - 16in (36 - 38cm)	**$3600 - 4000***
19 - 21in (48 - 53cm)	**4500 - 5000***

Marked B.P. Character Baby: Ca. 1910 - on. Perfect bisque socket head, solid dome or good wig, sleep eyes, open mouth; composition bent-limb baby body; dressed; all in good condition. Mold #585, 604, 624, 678, 619, 641 and 587.

Mark:

12 - 14in (31 - 36cm)	**$ 500 - 600**
17 - 19in (43 - 48cm)	**700 - 800**
23 - 25in (58 - 64cm)	**1000 - 1100**
Toddler:	
10 - 12in (25 - 31cm)	**650 - 700**
17 - 19in (43 - 48cm)	**950 - 1050**
28in (71cm)	**2500**

#425, All-bisque baby (For photograph see *10th Blue Book*, page 88.)

5½ - 6in (13 - 15cm)	**225 - 275**

Top: 19in (48cm) 2072 character child. *Richard Wright Antiques.*

Bottom: 12in (31cm) 582 character baby. *H & J Foulke, Inc.*

Barbie®

FACTS

Mattel, Inc., Hawthorne, Calif., U.S.A. 1959 to present. Hard plastic and vinyl. 11½ - 12in (29 - 31cm).
Mark: 1959 - 1962: Barbie TM/Pats. Pend./© MCMLVIII/by/Mattel, Inc.
1963 - 1968: Midge TM/© 1962/ Barbie®/© 1958/by/Mattel, Inc.
1964 - 1966: © 1958/Mattel, Inc./U.S. Patented/U.S. Pat. Pend.
1966 - 1969: © 1966/Mattel, Inc./U.S. Patented/U.S. Pat. Pend./Made in Japan.

First Barbie®: 1959. Vinyl, solid body; very light complexion, white irises, pointed eyebrows, ponytail, black and white striped bathing suit, holes in feet to fit stand, gold hoop earrings; mint condition. (For photograph see *10th Blue Book*, page 325.)
11½in (29cm) boxed   **$3200 - 3700***

Doll only, no box or accessories
Mint	**2600**
Very good	**2000**
Stand	**250**
Shoes	**20**
Hoop earrings	**65**

Second Barbie: 1959 - 1960. Vinyl, solid body; very light complexion, same as above, but no holes in feet, some wore pearl earrings; mint condition. Made 3 months only.
11½in (29cm) boxed   **$3000 - 3500***
Doll only, no box or accessories, very good   **2500**

*Brunette harder to find than blonde.

Barbie® is a registered trademark of Mattel, Inc.

Left:
Barbie #2 in T.M. box. *Ann Helm Collection.*
Right:
Barbie #3 in **Suburban Shopper** dress. *Clare Kline Collection.*

Barbie® continued

Third Barbie: 1960. Vinyl, solid body; very light complexion, same as above, but with blue irises and curved eyebrows; no holes in feet; mint condition.

11½in (29cm) boxed	**$650 - 750**
Doll only	**475 - 500**

Fourth Barbie: 1960. Vinyl; same as #3; but with solid body of flesh-toned vinyl; mint condition.

11½in (29cm) boxed	**$475 - 500**
Doll only	**225 - 250**

Fifth Barbie: 1961. Vinyl; same as #4; ponytail hairdo of firm Saran; mint condition.

11½in (29cm) boxed	**$350**
Doll only	**175**

Right: *Barbie #3*, original swimsuit. *Courtesy of McMasters Doll Auctions.*
Below Left: *Bubble Cut Barbie*, all original in box with wrist tag. *Courtesy of McMasters Doll Auctions.*
Below Right: 1965 *Bendable Leg Barbie*, American Girl hairstyle, original swimsuit and box. *Courtesy of McMasters Doll Auctions.*

Left: *Barbie Mix & Match Set* with *#5 Ponytail Barbie*. *Courtesy of McMasters Doll Auctions.*

See following pages for further information.

1966 *Color Magic Barbie* in box with accessories. *Courtesy of McMasters Doll Auctions.*

1965 *Bendable Leg Midge*, original swimsuit and box. *Courtesy of McMasters Doll Auctions.*

82

Barbie® continued

Bubble Cut Barbie, 1961 on. (See
photograph on page 80.):
  Mint-in-box   **$ 200 - 250**
  Doll only   **95 - 110**

Fashion Queen Barbie, 1963,
  mint-in-box   **300 up**

Miss Barbie, 1964,
  mint-in-box   **400 - 450**

Swirl Ponytail Barbie, 1964,
  Mint-in-box   **350 - 425**
  Doll only   **225**

Bendable Leg Barbie, 1965 & 1966,
  American girl, center part,
  mint-in-box   **700 - 1000**
  Side-part, mint-in-box **2000 - 3000**

Color Magic Barbie, 1966. (See photo-
graph on page 81.):
  Mint-in-box   **1200 up**
  Doll only, mint **600 up**

Twist & Turn Barbie, 1967,
  mint-in-box **300 - 350**

Talking Barbie, 1970,
  mint-in-box **200**

Living Barbie, 1970,
  mint-in-box **200**

Hair Happenin's Barbie, 1971,
  mint-in-box **650**

Montgomery Ward Barbie, 1972,
  mint doll **200 - 250**

Gift Sets **450 - 700 up**

Barbie Mix & Match #5 Ponytail. (See
photograph on page 81.) **800 - 1000**

Little Theatre, 1964 at auction
  4100

Quick Curl Miss America, 1974,
  mint-in-box **60 - 75**

Supersize Barbie:
  Bride, mint-in-box **175**
  Swimsuit, mint-in-box **150**

Outfits*:

Roman Holiday **1500 up**

Gay Parisienne **1500 up**

Easter Parade **1600 up**

Shimmering Magic **600 up**

Here Comes the Bride **600 up**

Pam Am Stewardess **1500 up**

Barbie Baby Sits **200**

Dogs & Duds **200**

Enchanted Evening **250**

1600 Series and Jacqueline
  Kennedy-style outfits **250 up**

*All mint-in-package.

Other Dolls:

Ken #1, 1961, mint-in-box   **$175**
  Bendable legs, mint-in-box   **325**

Midge, 1963, mint-in-box   **350**
  1966 bendable legs, mint-in-box. (See
    photograph on page 81.)   **450**

Allen, 1964 - 1966:
  Mint-in-box   **350**
  Doll only   **150 - 200**

Francie, 1966 - 1967:
  Doll only   **100 - 125**
  Black, 1967, mint-in-package
        700 - 900
  Doll only   **500**
  "No Bangs", 1970, mint-in-box
        1000
  Doll only   **600**
  Hair Happenin's, 1970, mint-in-box
        250

Twiggy, 1967,
  mint-in-box   **250**
Truly Scrumptious, 1969:
  Mint-in-box   **425 - 450**
  Doll only   **250**

Julia, 1969:
  Mint-in-box one-piece uniform
        95 - 110
  Mint-in-box two-piece uniform
        125 - 135
  Talking, mint-in-box
        100

Tutti, 1967 - 1970, mint-in-box
        125

Chris, 1967 - 1970, mint-in-box
        150

Todd, 1967 - 1970, mint-in-box
        125

E. Barrois

FACTS

E. Barrois, doll factory, Paris, France. Heads purchased from an unidentified French or German porcelain factory. 1844 - 1877. Bisque or china head, cloth or kid body (some with wooden arms).
Mark:

$$E . | \text{DÉPOSÉ } B .$$

E.B. Fashion Lady: Perfect bisque shoulder head (may have a swivel neck), glass eyes (may be painted with long painted eyelashes), closed mouth; appropriate wig; kid body, some with jointed wood arms or wood and bisque arms; appropriate clothing. All in good condition.

16 - 18in (41 - 46cm)	**$3000 - 3200***
24in (61cm)	**4200 - 4500***

Socket head and shoulder plate only,
6in (15cm)   **1600**
18in (46cm) kid body, wood upper arms, bisque lower arms, with trunk and original trousseau   **8000**

19in (48cm) Black fashion with rare
swivel neck   **$30,000 up****

*Allow $500 extra for wood or bisque arms.
**Not enough price samples to compute a reliable range.

Above: 24in (61cm) E. 8 Déposé B. *Private Collection.*
Right: 19in (48cm) rare black Barrois fashion with swivel neck. *Jackie Kaner.*

Belton-type (So-called)

FACTS

Various French and German firms such as Bähr & Pröschild. 1875 - on. Bisque socket head, ball-jointed wood and composition body with straight wrists.
Mark: None, except sometimes numbers.

Belton-type Child Doll: Perfect bisque socket head, solid but flat on top with two or three small holes for stringing; paperweight eyes, closed mouth, pierced ears; wood and composition ball-jointed body with straight wrists; dressed; all in good condition.

Fine early quality, French-type face (some mold #137 or #125)

13 - 14in (33 - 36cm)	**$2300 - 2600**
17 - 19in (43 - 48cm)	**2900 - 3100**
22 - 24in (56 - 61cm)	**3500 - 4000**

Standard quality, German-type face:

10 - 12in (25 - 31cm)	**1350 - 1450**
15 - 17in (38 - 43cm)	**1600 - 1800**

Tiny with five-piece body:

8 - 9in (20 - 23cm)	**750 - 850**

#200 Series, see Bähr & Pröschild, page 76.

Black:

12in (31cm)	**$1700**

17½in (44cm) 137 Belton-type.
H & J Foulke, Inc.

C. M. Bergmann

C. M. Bergmann doll factory of Waltershausen, Thüringia, Germany; heads manufactured for this company by Armand Marseille, Simon & Halbig, Alt, Beck & Gottschalck and perhaps others. 1888 - on. Bisque head, composition ball-jointed body.
Distributor: Louis Wolfe & Co., New York, N.Y., U.S.A.
Trademarks: Cinderella Baby (1897), Columbia (1904), My Gold Star (1926).
Mark:

C.M BERGMANN
A - H ½ - M:
Made in Germany

C. M. Bergmann
Waltershausen
Germany
1916
6½ a

Bergmann Child Doll: Ca. 1889 - on. Marked bisque head, composition ball-jointed body, good wig, sleep or set eyes, open mouth; dressed; all in nice condition.
Heads by A.M. and unknown makers:

10in (25cm)	**$ 450**
19 - 21in (48 - 53cm)	**450 - 500**
24 - 25in (61 - 64cm)	**525 - 575**
29 - 30in (74 - 76cm)	**800 - 900**
34 - 35in (86 - 89cm)	**1200 - 1350**
39 - 42in (99 - 111cm)	**2000 - 2200**

Heads by Simon & Halbig:

10in 25(cm)	**$ 500 - 550**
14 - 16in (36 - 41cm)	**425 - 475**
22 - 24in (56 - 61cm)	**575 - 625**
29 - 30in (74 - 76cm)	**1000 - 1100**
33 - 35in (84 - 89cm)	**1350 - 1550**
39in (99cm)	**2200**
Eleonore, 25in (64cm)	**800**

Bergmann/S & H child. *H & J Foulke, Inc.*

Bisque, German

(Unmarked or Unidentified Marks and Unlisted Small Factories)

FACTS

Various German firms. 1860s - on. Bisque head, composition, kid or cloth body.
Mark: Some numbered, some "Germany," some both.

Molded Hair Doll: Ca. 1880. Tinted bisque shoulder head with beautifully molded hair (usually blonde), painted eyes (sometimes glass), closed mouth; original kid or cloth body; bisque lower arms; appropriate clothes; all in good condition.

5 - 7in (13 - 18cm)	$ 125 - 150*
11 - 13in (28 - 33cm)	225 - 250*
15 - 18in (38 - 46cm)	325 - 375*
23 - 25in (38 - 64cm)	550 - 625*

With glass eyes,

10 - 12in (25 - 31cm)	500 - 600
18 - 22in (46 - 56cm)	800 - 900

Unusual hairdo,
18 - 22in (46 - 56cm)
600 up
With glass eyes **1000 up**
With glass eyes and decorated bodice **1200 up**

Dog or Cat Shoulder Heads:
4in (10cm) (See photograph on following page.)
$1600 - 1800**

American Schoolboy:
Cloth or kid body,

10 - 12in (25 - 31cm)	$450 - 500
15 - 17in (38 - 43cm)	600 - 700
20in (51cm)	800 - 900

Composition body,

9 - 11in (23 - 28cm)	500 - 600

Shoulder head only,

6in (15cm)	550

*Allow extra for a fancy hairdo.
**Not enough price samples to compute a reliable range.

17½in (44cm) so-called *American Schoolboy*. *H & J Foulke, Inc.*

Bisque, German continued

Hatted or Bonnet Doll: Ca. 1880 - 1920. Bisque head with painted molded hair and molded fancy bonnet with bows, ribbons, flowers, feathers, and so forth; painted eyes and facial features; original cloth body with bisque arms and legs; good old clothes or nicely dressed; all in good condition.

8 - 9in (20 - 23cm)	**$ 150 - 185***
12 - 15in (31 - 38cm)	
"Marqueritas" stone bisque, (Hertwig & Co.)	**225 - 260***
18 - 22in (46 - 56cm), fine quality (A.B.G.)	**1000 up***
All bisque, 4½in (12cm)	**165 - 185***
7in (18cm)	**225 - 250***

*Allow extra for unusual style.

14in (36cm) bisque bonnet head doll.
H & J Foulke, Inc.

Doll House Doll: 1890 - 1920. Man or lady bisque shoulder head with molded hair, painted eyes; cloth body, bisque lower limbs; original clothes or suitably dressed; all in nice condition.

4½ - 7in (12 - 18cm)	
Victorian man with mustache	**$175 - 225**
Victorian lady	**150 - 175**
Lady with glass eyes and wig	**350 - 400**
Man with mustache, original military uniform	**700 - 750**
Molded hair, glass eyes, Ca. 1870	**400 - 450**
Girl with bangs, Ca. 1880	**125 - 150**
Molded hair, painted eyes, Ca. 1870	**250 - 275**
Chauffeur with molded cap	**250**
Black man	**450 - 550**
Soldier, molded hat, goatee and mustache	**1250**
1920s man or lady	**100 - 125**

4in (10cm) dog shoulder head. *Richard Wright Antiques.* (For further information see preceding page.)

Child Doll with closed mouth: Ca. 1880 - 1890. Perfect bisque head; kid or cloth body, gusseted at hips and knees with good bisque hands or jointed composition body; good wig; nicely dressed; all in good condition.
Kid or cloth body:

12 - 13in (31 - 33cm)	**$ 650 - 750**
17 - 19in (38 - 48cm)	**900 - 1000**
22 - 24in (56 - 61cm)	**1250 - 1450**

German fashion, swivel neck:

16 - 18in (41 - 46cm)	**1200 - 1400***
20 - 21in (51 - 53cm)	**1500 - 1700***

#50:

14in (36cm) all original, at auction	**2200**
18 - 20in (46 - 51cm)	**1500 - 1600**

#132 Bru-type face:

19 - 21in (48 - 53cm)	**2500 - 3000**

#51:

13 - 15in (33 - 38cm)	**1550 - 1750**

Composition body:

11 - 13in (28 - 33cm)	**1450 - 1650**
16 - 19in (41 - 48cm)	**1950 - 2250***
22 - 23in (56 - 58cm)	**2700 - 3000***

Left: 4½in (11cm) German child, all original. *H & J Foulke, Inc.*
Right: 12in (31cm) German child shoulder head, closed mouth. *H & J Foulke, Inc.*

#136:

12 - 15in (31 - 38cm)	**2200 - 2400**
19 - 21in (48 - 53cm)	**2800 - 3200**

#TR803:

14 - 16in (36 - 41cm)	**1550 - 1650**

*Allow extra for French look.

Child Doll with open mouth "Dolly Face": 1888 - on. Perfect bisque head, ball-jointed composition body or kid body with bisque lower arms; good wig, glass eyes, open mouth; dressed; all in good condition. Including dolls marked "G.B.," "G & S," "A.W.," "MOA," "S & Q," and "K" inside "H."

Bisque, German continued

Very good quality:

12in (31cm)	$ 400 - 450
15 - 17in (38 - 43cm)	525 - 600
21 - 23in (53 - 58cm)	700 - 800
28 - 30in (71 - 76cm)	1100 - 1300

#50:

16 - 18in (41 - 46cm)	800 - 900

#444:

23 - 25in (58 - 64cm)	900 - 1000

Standard quality; including name dolls, **Princess, My Girlie, My Dearie** and **Pansy:**

12 - 13in (31 - 33cm)	$ 300 - 350
17 - 19in (43 - 48cm)	400 - 450
23 - 25in (58 - 64cm)	550 - 600
29 - 30in (74 - 76cm)	850 - 950

Tiny child doll: 1890 to World War I. Perfect bisque socket head of good quality, five-piece composition body of good quality with molded and painted shoes and stockings; good wig, set or sleep eyes, open mouth; cute clothes; all in good condition.

Very good quality (Simon & Halbig type):

5 - 6in (13 - 15cm)	$250 - 300
8 - 10in (20 - 25cm)	350 - 400

Fully-jointed body,

7 - 8in (18 - 20cm)	450 - 500

Closed mouth:

4½ - 5½in (12 - 14cm)	300 - 350
8in (20cm)	675 - 775

#39-13, five-piece mediocre body, glass eyes:

5in (13cm)	$200 - 225
painted eyes	90 - 100

Standard quality:

5 - 6in (13 - 15cm)	90 - 100
8 - 10in (20 - 25cm)	135 - 165

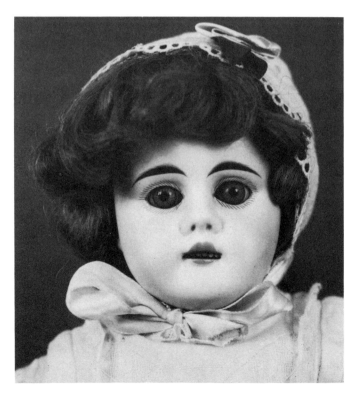

19in (48cm) shoulder head incised "L."
H & J Foulke, Inc.

Character Baby: 1910 - on. Perfect bisque head, good wig or solid dome with painted hair, sleep eyes, open mouth; composition bent-limb baby body; suitably dressed; all in good condition.

8 - 9in (20 - 23cm)	**$250 - 275***
13 - 15in (33 - 38cm)	**450 - 525***
18 - 20in (46 - 51cm)	**550 - 650***
22 - 24in (56 - 61cm)	**750 - 850***

Painted eyes:

7 - 8in (18 - 20cm)	**$225 - 275***
12in (31cm)	**425 - 475***

*Allow more for open/closed mouth, closed mouth or unusual face.

Character Child: 1910 - on. Bisque head with good wig or solid dome head with painted hair, sleep or painted eyes, open or closed mouth, expressive character face; jointed composition body; dressed; all in good condition.

15 - 19in (38 - 48cm)
$1000 up*

*Depending upon individual face.

Infant, unmarked or unidentified maker: 1924 - on. Perfect bisque head with molded and painted hair, glass sleep eyes; cloth body, celluloid or composition hands; dressed; all in good condition.

10 - 12in (25 - 31cm) long	**$ 325 - 375***
15 - 18in (38 - 46cm) long	**525 - 625***

*More depending upon appeal and rarity of face.

25in (64cm) 182 socket head girl.
H & J Foulke, Inc.

Bisque, German continued

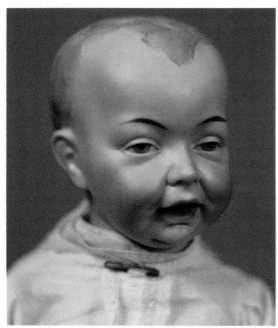

#1764,
11 - 12in (28 - 31cm) long
$ 800 - 900
Gerling Baby:
14in (36cm) long   **600**
  Brown, 14in (36cm)
                      1000
#209SW,
14in (36cm)   **750**

Left: 15in (38cm) Germany 4 character baby. *H & J Foulke, Inc.*

Below: 12in (31cm) 1764 infant.

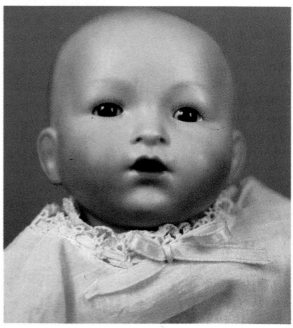

Bisque Japanese (Caucasian Dolls)

FACTS

Various Japanese firms; heads were imported by New York importers, such as Morimura Brothers, Yamato Importing Co. and others. 1915 - on. Bisque head, composition body.
Mark: Morimura Brothers.
Various other marks with Japan or Nippon, such as J.W., F.Y., and others

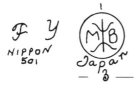

Character Baby: Perfect bisque socket head with solid dome or wig, glass eyes, open mouth with teeth, dimples; composition bent-limb baby body; dressed; all in good condition.

9 - 10in (23 - 25cm)	**$150 - 175***
14 - 15in (36 - 38cm)	**250 - 300***
20 - 22in (51 - 56cm)	**450 - 500***
Hilda look-alike, 19in (48cm)	
	700 - 800*

Child Doll: Perfect bisque head, mohair wig, glass sleep eyes, open mouth; jointed composition or kid body; dressed; all in good condition.

14 - 16in (36 - 41cm)	**$250 - 275***
20 - 22in (51 - 56cm)	**325 - 375***

*Do not pay as much for doll with inferior bisque head.

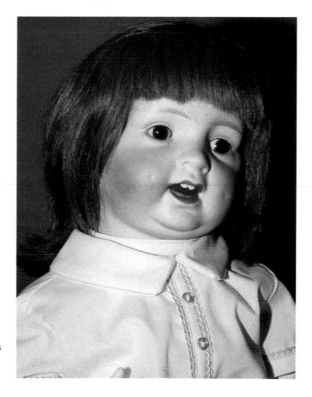

21in (53cm) Morimura Brothers character baby. *George Humphrey.*

Black Dolls*

GERMAN Makers:
A.M.341, 11 - 12in (28 - 31cm), cloth
body $ 400 -   425
  351, 15 - 16in (38 - 41cm),
  compo body   650 -   750
  362, 15in (38cm)
                  700 -   750
  1894, 12 - 14in (31 - 36cm)
                  550 -   650

**Gebr. Heubach 7658, 7657,
7671,** 13in (33cm)
                 1600 - 1800
Belton, 179
  10in (25cm), at auction
                 1900

FRENCH Makers:
Jumeau
  E7J, 17in (43cm) **$ 8500**
  1907, open mouth, 9 - 11in (23 - 28cm)
                 1800 -   2000
  Black characters, 24 - 26in (61 - 66cm)
                 112,000 - 115,000

F.G. Fashion, 14in (36cm)
                 2300 -   2700

SFBJ 226, 16in (41cm)
                 2800 -   3000

Steiner, Figure A, closed mouth,
  11 - 13in (28 - 33cm) **4000 -   5000**

*Also see entries for specific doll makers or material of doll.

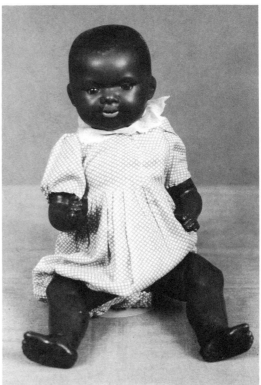

15in (38cm) AM 362. *H & J Foulke, Inc.*

Black Dolls continued

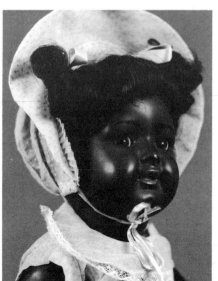

H. Handwerck, 20in (51cm) **$1100 - 1200**

E. Heubach 399, 414, 452,
7½in (19cm) toddler   **375 - 425**
10in (25cm) baby   **400 - 450**

K & R,
7in (18cm) child   **475**

Kestner 134, 13in (33cm)   **900 - 950**

Kuhnlenz 34, 7 - 8in (18-20cm) fully
jointed   **450 - 500**

S PB H Hanna, 7 - 8in (18 - 20cm)
     350 - 400
1909, 15in (38cm)   **550 - 575**

Simon & Halbig 739, 17in (43cm)
     2000 - 2200
1039, 12in (31cm) flirty eye   **1300**
949, 27in (69cm) open mouth
     3400
1358, 19in (49cm)   **7000 - 8000**
1368, 13in (33cm)   **3500 - 4000**
TR809, closed mouth, 17in (43cm)
at auction   **2600**

All-bisque, 4in (10cm) glass eyes
     400

Unmarked, good quality:
Character girl, similar to S & H **1358**,
14in (36cm) at auction   **2200**
Dolly face,
10 - 13in (25 - 33cm), jointed body
     400 - 450
8 - 9in (20 - 23cm), five-piece body
     300 - 325
5in (13cm), closed mouth   **325 - 375**

Top: 10½in (26cm) Steiner, Figure A-3. *Private Collection.*

Bottom: 17in (43cm) K & R 926 composition toddler. *H & J Foulke, Inc.* (For further information on German made black composition dolls, see page 99.)

Black Dolls continued

Opposite Page:
27in (69cm) Black paint over stockinette 1920s rag doll. *Richard Wright Antiques.*

Right:
23in (58cm) Black primitive rag doll. *H & J Foulke, Inc.*

Below Left:
R.A. character girl, very rare. *Richard Wright Collection.*

Below Right:
11in (28cm) Black composition German character. *H & J Foulke, Inc.*

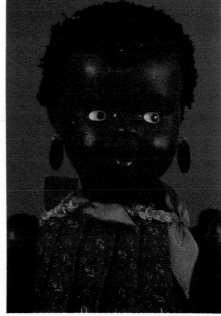

Black Dolls continued

Cloth Black Doll*: 1880s - on. American-made cloth doll with black face, painted, printed or embroidered features; jointed arms and legs; original clothes; all in good condition.

Mammy-type,
18 - 22in (46 - 56cm)   **$ 450 up+**

Stockinette (so-called Beecher-type). (For photograph see *8th Blue Book*, page 98.)
20in (51cm)   **2000 - 2500**

1930s Mammy,
18 - 20in (46 - 51cm)   **250 up+**

WPA, molded cloth face. (For photograph see *7th Blue Book*, page 83.)
22in (56cm)   **1400 - 1500**

Paint over molded stockinette (Chase-type). (For photograph see *9th Blue Book*, page 100.)
18in (46cm)   **2000 - 2500**

Black cloth, embroidered face, 18 - 21in (46 - 53cm)   **1000 up+**

Artist character, Ca. 1920s. Paint over stockinette.
27in (69cm)   **10,000**

Papier-Mâché Black Doll: Ca. 1890. By various German manufacturers. Papier-mâché character face, arms and legs, cloth body; glass eyes; original or appropriate clothes; all in good condition.
12 - 14in (31 - 36cm)   **$ 300 - 350**
18 - 20in (46 - 51cm) character with broad smile   **900 - 1000**

*Also check under manufacturer if known.

+Greatly depending upon appeal.

13½in (34cm) 1910 character. *H & J Foulke, Inc.*

Black Dolls continued

Black Composition Doll: Ca. 1920 - on. German made character doll, all-composition, jointed at neck, shoulders and hips; molded hair or wig, glass eyes (sometimes flirty); appropriate clothes; all in good condition.

11in (28cm)	**$300 - 350**
16 - 18in (41 - 46cm)	**600 - 700***

Black Composition Doll: Ca. 1930. American-made bent-limb baby or mama-type body, jointed at hips, shoulders and perhaps neck; molded hair, painted or sleep eyes; original or appropriate clothes; some have three yarn tufts of hair on either side and on top of the head; all in good condition.

"Topsy" Baby, 10 - 12in (25 - 31cm)
	$125 - 150
Toddler, 18in (46cm)	**275 - 325**

1910 character, 13½in (34cm)
	275 - 300
Patsy-type, 13 - 14in (33 - 36cm)	
	200 - 250

Black Hard Plastic Characters: Ca. 1950. English made by Pedigree and others. All hard plastic, swivel neck, jointed shoulders and hips, sleeping eyes, curly black wig sometimes over molded hair.

16in (41cm)	**$125 - 150**
21in (53cm)	**200 - 225**

*Allow $50 - 75 extra for flirty eyes.

21in (53cm) Pedigree hard plastic toddler. *Kiefer Collection.*

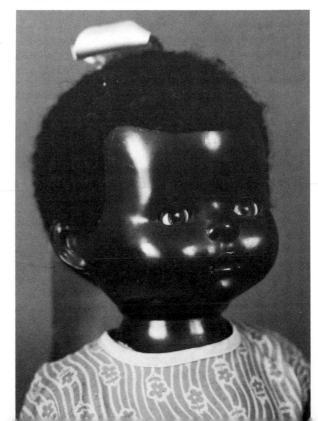

Boudoir Dolls

FACTS

Various French, U.S. and Italian firms. Early 1920s into the 1940s. Heads of composition and other materials; bodies mostly cloth but also of composition and other substances. Many 24 - 36in (61 - 91cm); some smaller.
Mark: Mostly unmarked.

Boudoir Doll: Head of composition, cloth or other material, painted features, mohair wig, composition or cloth stuffed body, unusually long extremities, usually high-heeled shoes; original clothes elaborately designed and trimmed; all in excellent condition.

1920s Art Doll, exceptional quality, silk hair, 28 - 30in (71 - 76cm) **$ 375 - 475**

Standard quality, dressed,
28 - 30in (71 - 76cm) **135 - 165**
undressed **75 - 95**
1940s composition head **85 - 95**

Lenci, 24 - 28in (61 - 71cm) **1800 up**

Smoking Doll, 25in (64cm) **425 - 475**

36in (91cm) Lenci boudoir doll, all original. *Richard Wright Antiques.*

FACTS

Bru Jne. & Cie, Paris, and Montreuil-sous-Bois, France. 1866 - 1899.
Bru Marked Shoes: $500 - 600.

Fashion Lady: 1866 - on. Perfect bisque swivel head on shoulder plate, cork pate, appropriate old wig, closed smiling mouth, paperweight eyes, pierced ears; gusseted kid lady body; original or appropriate old clothes; all in good condition. Incised with letters "A" through "O" in sizes 11in (28cm) to 36in (91cm) tall. (For photograph see *10th Blue Book*, page 28.)

12 - 13in (31 - 33cm)	**$2500 - 2800***
17 - 18in (43 - 46cm)	**3500 - 4000***
20in (51cm)	**4500 - 5000***
Wood body,	
16 - 17in (41 - 43cm)	**6000**

*Allow $500 extra for wood arms.

Fashion Lady: 1866 - on. Perfect bisque swivel head on shoulder plate, cork pate, old mohair wig, closed mouth, paperweight eyes, pierced ears; gusseted or straight kid body; original or appropriate old clothes; all in good condition. Oval face, incised with numbers only. Shoulder plate sometimes marked "B. Jne & Cie." (For photograph see page 102.)

12 - 13in (31 - 33cm)	**$2300 - 2600**
15 - 16in (38 - 41cm)	**3000 - 3200**
20in (51cm)	**4000 - 4500**
Wood body,	
14in (36cm)	**4400 - 4600**

Above: 12in (31cm) Bru fashion lady with painted eyes. *Private Collection.*

Left: 13in (33cm) Breveté Bébé. *Jensen's Antique Dolls.* (For further information see following page.)

Bru continued

15in (38cm) Bru lady incised "B. Jne & Cie." *Private Collection.* (For further information see page 101.)

Marked Breveté Bébé: Ca. 1870s. Perfect bisque swivel head on shoulder plate, cork pate, skin wig, paperweight eyes with shading on upper lid, closed mouth with white space between lips, full cheeks, pierced ears; gusseted kid body pulled high on shoulder plate and straight cut with bisque lower arms (no rivet joints); dressed; all in good condition. (See color photograph on preceding page.)
Mark: Size number only on head.
Oval sticker on body:

or
rectangular sticker like Bébé Bru one, but with words "Bébé Breveté."

Size 5/0 = 10½in (27cm)
Size 2/0 = 14in (36cm)
Size 1 = 16in (41cm)
Size 2 = 18in (46cm)
Size 3 = 19in (48cm)

13 - 15in (33 - 38cm)	**$13,500 - 15,500**
18 - 21in (46 - 53cm)	**18,500 - 22,500**

Jointed wood body "Baby Modele,"
18in (46cm) at auction **23,000****

Marked Crescent or Circle Dot Bébé: Ca. late 1870s. Perfect bisque swivel head on a deep shoulder plate with molded breasts, cork pate, attractive wig, paperweight eyes, closed mouth with slightly parted lips, molded and painted teeth, plump cheeks, pierced ears; gusseted kid body with bisque lower arms (no rivet joints); dressed; all in good condition.
Mark: ⌐ ☉

Sometimes with "BRU Jne"

Approximate size chart:
0 = 11in (28cm)
1 = 12in (31cm)
2 = 13in (33cm)
5 = 17in (43cm)
8 = 22in (56cm)
10 = 26in (66cm)
12 = 30in (76cm)
14 = 35in (89cm)

13 - 14in (33 - 35cm)	**$12,000 - 15,000**
17 - 19in (43 - 48cm)	**19,000 - 21,000**
24in (61cm)	**25,000 - 26,000**
32in (81cm)	**35,000 - 38,000**

**Not enough price samples to compute a reliable average.

Marked Nursing Bru (Bébé Teteur): 1878 - 1898. Perfect bisque head, shoulder plate and lower arms, kid body; upper arms and upper legs of metal covered with kid, lower legs of carved wood, or jointed composition body; attractive wig, lovely glass eyes, open mouth with hole for nipple, mechanism in head sucks up liquid, operates by turning key; nicely clothed; all in good condition. (For photograph see *10th Blue Book*, page 30.)

13 - 15in (33 - 38cm)

Early model	$ 8500 - 9500
Later model	5500 - 6500

Marked Bru Jne Bébé: Ca. 1880s. Perfect bisque swivel head on deep shoulder plate with molded breasts, cork pate, attractive wig, paperweight eyes, closed mouth, pierced ears; gusseted kid body with scalloped edge at shoulder plate, bisque lower arms with lovely hands, kid over wood upper arms, hinged elbow, all kid or wood lower legs (sometimes on a jointed composition body); dressed; all in good condition. (For body photograph see *6th Blue Book*, page 79.)

Mark: "BRU J^{ne}"
Body Label:

11in (28cm) all original	**$16,000**
12 - 13in (31 - 33cm)	**12,000 - 14,000**
15 - 17in (38 - 43cm)	**16,000 - 19,000**
23 - 24in (58 - 61cm)	**23,000 - 25,000**
31in (79cm)	**33,500 - 35,500**
13in (33cm) with original trunk and wardrobe	**21,000**
15in (38cm) composition body	**10,000 - 12,000**

Marked Bru Jne R Bébé: Ca. Early 1890s. Perfect bisque head on a jointed composition body; attractive wig, paperweight eyes, closed mouth, pierced ears; dressed; all in good condition.

Mark: BRU J^{ne} R
11

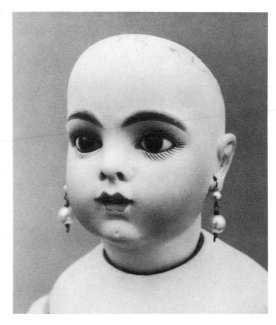

20in (51cm) Bru Jne 7. *H & J Foulke, Inc.*

Bru continued

Body Stamp: "Bebe Bru" with size number
    20 - 22in (51 - 56cm)   **$6000 - 6500**
    20in (51cm) all original, at auction
                                          8300
Open mouth:
    12in (31cm)   **1800 - 2200**
    20 - 21in (51 - 53cm)   **3000 - 4000**
    25in (64cm) "breathing" model at auction
                                            8000

See preceding pages for further information about the dolls shown on pages 104 and 105.

Top right and bottom right: 17in (43cm) Circle Dot Bru Bébé, with wood body. Music box with key wind mechanism inside torso. *Private Collection.*

Bottom left: 32in (81cm) Circle Dot Bru Bébé. *H & J Foulke, Inc.*

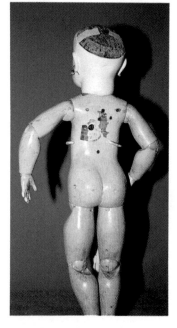

Right:
22in (56cm) Bru Jne 8. *Private Collection.*

Below:
23in (58cm) Bru Jne R 9. *H & J Foulke, Inc.*

Bucherer

FACTS

A. Bucherer, Amriswil, Switzerland. 1921. Composition head, hands and feet, metal ball-jointed body. 8in (20cm) average.
Mark:

"MADE IN
SWITZERLAND
PATENTS
APPLIED FOR"

Bucherer Doll: Composition character head often with molded hat; metal ball-jointed body; original clothes, often felt; all in good condition.

Comic characters: **Mutt, Jeff, Maggie, Jiggs, Katzenjammer Kids,** etc.
$300 up

Regular People: lady, man, fireman, clown, black man, Becassine, baseball player and others. **175 - 225**

Rabbit, mint in box at auction **500**

Bucherer clown, all original. *H & J Foulke, Inc.*

Bye-Lo Baby

FACTS

Bisque heads — J.D. Kestner; Alt, Beck & Gottschalck; Kling & Co.; Hertel, Schwab & Co.; all of Thüringia, Germany.
Composition heads — Cameo Doll Company, New York, N.Y.
Celluloid heads — Karl Standfuss, Saxony, Germany.
Wooden heads (unauthorized) — Schoenhut of Philadelphia, Pa.
All-Bisque Baby — J.D. Kestner.
Cloth Bodies and Assembly — K & K Toy Co., New York, N.Y.
Composition Bodies — König & Wernicke. 1922 - on.
Designer: Grace Storey Putnam.
Distributor: George Borgfeldt, New York, N.Y., U.S.A.

Bisque Head Bye-Lo Baby: Ca. 1923. Perfect bisque head, cloth body with curved legs (sometimes with straight legs), composition or celluloid hands; sleep eyes; dressed. Made in seven sizes, 9 - 20in (23 - 51cm). (May have purple "Bye-Lo Baby" stamp on front of body.) Sometimes Mold **#1373** (ABG).

Mark: © 1923 by
Grace S. Putnam
MADE IN GERMANY

Head circumference:

7½ - 8in (19 - 20cm)	**$ 500 - 525***
9 - 10in (23 - 25cm)	**475 - 500***
12 - 13in (31 - 33cm)	**550 - 600***
15in (38cm)	**900***
17in (43cm)	**1100 - 1300***
18in (46cm)	**1400 - 1600***
Tagged Bye-Lo gown	**50**
Bye-Lo pin	**95**

*Allow extra for original tagged gown and button.

Top: 12in (31cm) bisque head *Bye-Lo Baby*. *H & J Foulke, Inc.*
Bottom: 16in (41cm) bisque head *Fly-Lo Baby*. *Richard Wright Collection.* (For further information see following page.)

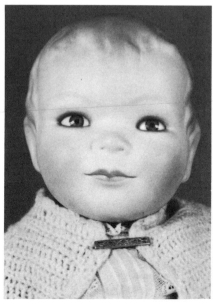

Bye-Lo Baby continued

Baby Aero or **Fly-Lo Baby** bisque head **Mold #1418**. (See photograph on preceding page.)

11in (28cm) at auction **$4250**

Composition head, original costume,
12in (31cm) at auction **800**

Mold #1369 (ABG) socket head on composition body, some marked "K&W."
12 - 13in (30 - 33cm) long **1350 - 1550**

Mold #1415, smiling with painted eyes
13½in (34cm) h.c. **4000****

Composition head, 1924.
12 - 13in (31 - 33cm) h.c. **350 - 375**

Celluloid head,
10in (25cm) h.c. $ **300 - 350****

Painted bisque head, late 1920s.
12 - 13in (31 - 33cm) h.c. **325****

Wooden head, (Schoenhut), 1925.
1500 - 1600

Vinyl head, 1948.
16in (41cm) **150 - 200**

Wax head, 1922. **800 - 900**

**Not enough price samples to compute a reliable range.

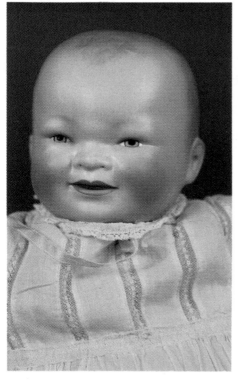

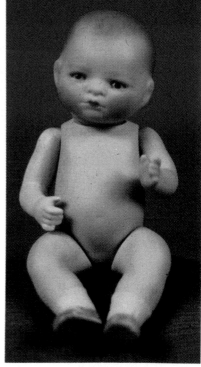

17in (43cm) smiling ***Bye-Lo Baby***, painted eyes. *Richard Wright Antiques.*

6¾in (17cm) all-bisque ***Bye-Lo*** with swivel neck. *H & J Foulke, Inc.*

Marked All-Bisque Bye-Lo Baby: 1925 - on. Sizes 10cm (4in) to 20cm (8in).

Mark: Dark green paper label on front torso often missing; incised on back "20-12" (or other stock and size number).

"Copr. by
G.S. Putnam"

Solid head with molded hair and painted eyes, jointed shoulders and hips,

4 - 5in (10 - 13cm)	$ 275 - 375
6in (15cm)	475 - 525
8in (20cm)	675 - 725

Below: 6in (15cm) all-bisque *Bye-Lo* with wig. *H & J Foulke, Inc.*

Solid head with swivel neck, glass eyes, jointed shoulders and hips,

4 - 5in (10 - 13cm)	$ 550 - 625
6in (15cm)	725 - 825
8in (20cm)	1100 - 1200

Head with wig, glass eyes, jointed shoulders and hips,

4 - 5in (10 - 13cm)	650 - 750
6in (15cm)	850 - 950
8in (20cm)	1250 - 1450

Action **Bye-Lo Baby**, immobile in various positions, painted features,

3in (8cm)	350 - 400
Celluloid 4in (10cm)	150 - 175**

**Not enough price samples to compute a reliable range.

Cameo Doll Company

FACTS

Cameo Doll Company, New York, N.Y.,
U.S.A., later Port Allegany, Pa., U.S.A.
Original owner: Joseph L. Kallus. 1922
- on. Wood-pulp composition and wood.

Below:
Margie with original box. *H & J Foulke, Inc.*

Baby Bo Kaye: 1925. (See page 74.)
Kewpie: 1913. (See page 244.)
Scootles: 1925. Designed by Rose O'Neill.
All-composition, unmarked, jointed at neck,
shoulders and hips; molded hair, blue or
brown painted eyes looking to the side,
closed smiling mouth; not dressed; all in
very good condition.
Mark: Wrist tag only.

7in - 8in (18 - 20cm)	**$ 350 - 400****
12 - 13in (31 - 33cm)	**475 - 500***
15 - 16in (38 - 41cm)	**600 - 650***
20in (51cm)	**800****
Black, 14in (36cm)	**750 - 800****

All-bisque, marked on feet
  5 - 6in (13 - 15cm) Germany

	600 - 700
6 - 7in (15 - 18cm) Japan	**450 - 500**

Vinyl, 14in (36cm) 1973 Maxine's
Ltd. Ed.   **125**

Wood Segmented Characters: Designed by Joseph L. Kallus. Composition head, molded hair, painted features; segmented wood body; undressed; all in very good condition.
Mark: Label with name on chest.

Margie, 1929. 10in (25cm)	**$ 225 - 250**
Pinkie, 1930. 10in (25cm)	**275 - 325**
Joy, 1932. 10in (5cm)	**275 - 325**
15in (38cm)	**375 - 425**
Betty Boop, 1932.	
12in (31cm)	**550 - 650**

With molded bathing suit and composition legs; wearing a cotton print dress,

	650 - 700
Pop-Eye, 1935	**300****
Hotpoint Man, 16in (41cm)	**800****
RCA Radiotron, 16in (41cm)	
	800**

Giggles: 1946. Designed by Rose O'Neill. All-composition, unmarked, jointed at neck, shoulders and hips, molded hair with bun in back, large painted side-glancing eyes, closed mouth; original romper; all in very good condition. (For photograph see *9th Blue Book*, page 113.)
Mark: Paper wrist tag only.
  14in (36cm)   **$ 550 - 650**

*Allow extra for sleep eyes.
**Not enough price samples to compute a reliable range.

Top: *Giggles*, all original. *H & J Foulke, Inc.*

Bottom: *Scootles*, all original. *H & J Foulke, Inc.*

Catterfelder Puppenfabrik

FACTS

Catterfelder Puppenfabrik, Catterfield, Thüringia, Germany. Heads by J.D. Kestner and other porcelain makers. 1902 - on. Bisque head; composition body.
Trademark: My Sunshine.
Mark:

C. P.
2 0 8
45
N

C.P. Child Doll: Ca. 1902 - on. Perfect bisque head, good wig, sleep eyes, open mouth with teeth; composition jointed body; dressed; all in good condition.
#264 (made by Kestner):

17 - 19in (43 - 48cm)	$ 675 - 750
22 - 24in (56 - 61cm)	850 - 950
35 - 36in (89 - 91cm)	2000 - 2500**

19in (48cm) 264 child. *H & J Foulke, Inc.*

C.P. Character Child: Ca. 1910 - on. Perfect bisque character face with wig, painted eyes; composition jointed body; dressed; all in good condition. Sometimes mold **#207** or **#219**.

15 - 16in (38 - 41cm)	$ 3000 - 4000**
#217, 18in (46cm)	9750**
#220, 14in (36cm) glass eyes,	7500**

Rare face character 15in (38cm) at auction
13,000

C.P. Character Baby: Ca. 1910 - on. Perfect bisque character face with wig or molded hair, painted or glass eyes; jointed baby body; dressed; all in good condition.
#200, 201, 208, 209, 262, 263:

15 - 17in (38 - 43cm)	$ 525 - 625
22 - 24in (56 - 61cm)	900 - 1000

**Not enough price samples to compute a reliable range.

20in (51cm) 262 character baby. *Carole Jean Stoessel Zvonar Collection.*

FACTS

Germany: Rheinische Gummi und Celluloid Fabrik Co. (Turtle symbol); Buschow & Beck, *Minerva* trademark (Helmet symbol); E. Maar & Sohn, *Emasco* trademark (3 M symbol); Cellba (Mermaid symbol).
Poland: P.R. Zask (ASK in triangle).
France: Petitcolin (Eagle symbol); Société Nobel Francaise (SNF in diamond); Neumann & Marx (Dragon symbol); Société Industrielle de Celluloid (Sicoine).
United States: Parsons-Jackson Co., Cleveland, Ohio, and other companies.
England: Cascelloid Ltd. (Palitoy). 1895 - 1940s.
All-celluloid or celluloid head with jointed kid, cloth or composition body.
Marks: Various as indicated above: sometimes also in combination with the marks of J. D. Kestner, Kämmer & Reinhardt, Bruno Schmidt, Käthe Kruse and König & Wernicke.

Celluloid Head Child Doll: Ca. 1900 - on. Molded hair or wig, painted or glass eyes, open or closed mouth; cloth or kid body, celluloid or composition arms; dressed; all in good condition. Some with character faces.

Painted eyes:
13 - 15in (33 - 38cm)	**$135 - 160**

Glass eyes:
19 - 22in (48 - 56cm)	**225 - 250**

All-Celluloid Child Doll: Ca. 1900 - on. Jointed at neck, shoulders, and hips; molded hair or wig, painted eyes; dressed; all in good condition.

5in (12cm) googly	**85 - 95**
4in (10cm)	**40 - 50**
7 - 8in (18 - 20cm)	**65 - 75**
10 - 12in (25 - 31cm)	**100 - 125**
14 - 15in (36 - 38cm)	**150 - 175**

Below left: 20in (51cm) French SNF Toddler. *H & J Foulke, Inc.*

Below right: 14in (36cm) German turtle mark girl, all original. *H & J Foulke, Inc.*

Celluloid Dolls continued

Tommy Tucker-type character:
    12 - 14in (31 - 36cm)   **$165 - 185**

Glass Eyes:
    12 - 13in (31 - 33cm)   **165 - 185**
    15 - 16in (38 - 41cm)   **250 - 275**
    18in (46cm)   **350 - 400**

K*R 717 or **728:**
    14 - 16in (36 - 41cm)   **450 - 550**

All-Celluloid Baby: Ca. 1910 - on. Bent-limb baby, molded hair, painted eyes, closed mouth; jointed arms and/or legs; no clothes; all in good condition.
    6 - 8in (15 - 20cm)   **65 - 85**
    10 - 12in (25 - 31cm)   **110 - 135***
    15in (38cm)   **175 - 200***
    21in (53cm)   **250 - 275**

*Allow $25 - 35 extra for glass eyes.

Above: Large Japanese celluloid girl with molded clothes. *H & J Foulke, Inc.*

Left: Cellba celluloid girl with molded braids. *Lesley Hurford Collection. Photograph by Norman Hurford.*

Celluloid Dolls continued

Japanese,
  Molded clothes,
    4in (10cm) $ 30 - 40
    8 - 9in (20 - 23cm)   125 - 135
  Baby, 13in (33cm)   125

Parsons-Jackson Baby,
  11½in (29cm)   165 - 185

Celluloid Head Infant: Ca. 1920s - on.
Celluloid baby head with glass eyes, painted
hair, open or closed mouth; cloth body,
sometimes with celluloid hands; appropriate clothes; all in good condition.
    12 - 15in (31 - 38cm) $135 - 165

Celluloid Socket Head Doll: Ca. 1910 -
on. Wig, glass eyes, sometimes flirty, open
mouth with teeth; ball-jointed or bent-limb
composition body; dressed; all in good condition.
    15 - 18in (38 - 46cm)
                                $300 - 350
    22 - 24in (56 - 61cm)
                                450 - 500

Characters:
K*R 701,
    12 - 13in (31 - 33cm) $900 - 1100**
K*R 717 child,
    16 - 18in (41 - 46cm)   500 - 550
K*R 700,
    14 - 15in (36 - 38cm)   300 - 350
K*R 728,
    12 - 13in (31 - 33cm) baby
                                325 - 350
    14 - 16in (36 - 41cm) toddler
                                450 - 550
F.S. & Co. 1276,
    20in (51cm) baby   500 - 550

**Not enough price samples to compute a reli-
able range

Cellba 12in (31cm) black celluloid
baby. *Kiefer Collection.*

Century Doll Co.

FACTS

Century Doll Co., New York, N.Y., U.S.A.; bisque heads by J.D. Kestner, Germany. 1909 - on. Bisque or composition head, cloth body, composition arms (and legs).
Mark:

Germany
CENTURY DOLL Cº.
200/0½

Marked Century Infant: Ca. 1925. Perfect bisque solid-dome head, molded and painted hair, sleep eyes, open/closed mouth; cloth body, composition hands or limbs; dressed; all in good condition. Some with smiling face are mold #277.
Head circumference:

10 - 11in (25 - 28cm)	**$475 - 525**
13 - 14in (33 - 36cm)	**650 - 750**

Mama doll, bisque shoulder head #281. (For photograph see *Kestner, King of Dollmakers*, page 194.)

21in (53cm)	**$650 - 750****

Child with molded hair #200. (For photograph see *10th Blue Book*, page 132.)

12in (31cm)	**$350****

Marked "Mama" Doll: Ca. 1920s. Composition shoulder head with character face, molded hair, smiling open mouth with two teeth, dimples, tin sleep eyes. Cloth torso with cryer, composition arms and legs; appropriate clothing. All in good condition.

16in (41cm)	**$210 - 235**
23in (58cm)	**350 - 400**

**Not enough price samples to compute a reliable range.

Below left: 19in (48cm) Century baby with bisque head. *H & J Foulke, Inc.*

Below right: 23in (58cm) Century composition Mama doll. *H & J Foulke, Inc.*

Chad Valley

Chad Valley Co. (formerly Johnson Bros., Ltd.), Birmingham, England. 1917 - on. All-cloth.
Mark: Cloth label usually on foot:
"HYGIENIC TOYS
Made in England by
CHAD VALLEY CO. LTD."

Chad Valley Doll: All-cloth, usually felt face and velvet body, jointed neck, shoulders and hips; mohair wig, glass or painted eyes; original clothes; all in excellent condition.

Characters, painted eyes,
10 - 12in (25 - 31cm)	$ 85 - 115

Children, painted eyes,
9in (23cm)	135 - 150
13 - 14in (33 - 36cm)	375 - 425
16 - 18in (41 - 46cm)	550 - 650

Characters, glass eyes,
17 - 20in (43 - 51cm)	1000 - 2000*

Children, glass eyes,
16 - 18in (41 - 46cm)	700 - 775

Royal Children, glass eyes,
16 - 18in (41 - 46cm)	1450 - 1650

Mabel Lucie Attwell, glass inset side-glancing eyes, smiling watermelon mouth. (For photograph see *10th Blue Book*, page 133)
14 - 15in (36 - 38cm)	$ 625 - 700

Dwarfs (Snow White Set),
10in (25cm)	250 - 275 each

* Depending upon rarity.

Above: 9in (23cm) Chad Valley child, all original. *H & J Foulke, Inc.*

Left: 20in (51cm) *Long John Silver*, all original. *Esther Schwartz Collection.*

Martha Chase

Martha Jenks Chase, Pawtucket, R.I., U.S.A. 1889-on. Stockinette and cloth, painted in oils; some fully painted washable models; some designed for hospital training use. 9in (23cm) to life-size.

Designer: Martha Jenks Chase.

Mark: "Chase Stockinet Doll" stamp on left leg or under left arm, paper label on back (usually gone).

PAWTUCKET, R.I
MADE IN U.S.A.

Chase Doll: Head and limbs of stockinette, treated and painted with oils, large painted eyes with thick upper lashes, rough-stroked hair to provide texture, cloth bodies jointed at shoulders, hips, elbows and knees, later ones only at shoulders and hips; some bodies completely treated; showing wear.

Baby,

13 - 15in (33 - 38cm)	$ 575 - 675
17 - 20in (43 - 51cm)	750 - 850
24 - 26in (61 - 66cm)	950 - 1000
16in (41cm), mint with label	
	850 - 900

Child, molded bobbed hair,

12 - 15in (31 - 38cm)	1200 - 1600
20in (51cm)	2000

Lady,

13 - 15in (33 - 38cm)	2200 - 2500

Man,

15 - 16in (38 - 41cm)	3000

Below:
Two views of 16in (41cm) Chase girl with rare hairdo. *Courtesy of Richard Withington, Inc.*

Black, Mammy or child
$10,000 - 11,000
Little Nell, 2 blonde braids
3000
Rare hairdo girl as pictured,
at auction
21,000

George Washington,
26in (66cm) **5000**

Top: 13in (33cm) child with
molded bobbed hair.
H & J Foulke, Inc.

Bottom: 15½in (39cm) man and
lady. *Nancy A. Smith Collection.*

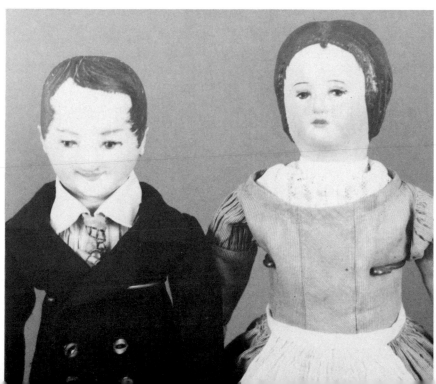

China Heads

(French*)

FACTS

Various French doll firms; some heads sold through French firms may have been made in Germany. 1850s. China head, shapely kid fashion body, some with large china arms.
Mark: None.

(Attributed to England)

FACTS

Unidentified English firm, possibly Rockingham area. Ca. 1840-1860. China shoulder head, lower arms and legs; cloth torso.
Mark: None.

French China Head Doll: China shoulder head, glass or beautifully painted eyes, painted eyelashes, feathered eyebrows, closed mouth, open crown, cork pate, good wig; shapely kid fashion body (may have china arms curved to above elbow); appropriately dressed; all in good condition.

15 - 16in (38 - 41cm)	**$3000 - 3500**
18 - 20in (46 - 51cm)	**4000 - 4500**

Painted short black hair, pink kid body
15in (38cm)	**1400 - 1500**

*For dolls marked "Huret" or "Rohmer," see appropriate entry under those names.

English China Doll: Flesh-tinted shoulder head with bald head (some with molded slit for inserting wig), painted features, closed mouth; human hair wig. Cloth torso and upper arms and legs, china lower limbs with holes to attach them to cloth, bare feet. Appropriately dressed; all in good condition.

19 - 22in (48 - 56cm)	**$2000 - 3000**
without china limbs	**1200**

Below left: 14in (36cm) exceptional French china with glass eyes. *Jackie Kaner.*

Below right: Pink tint china lady with wig. *Richard Wright Antiques.*

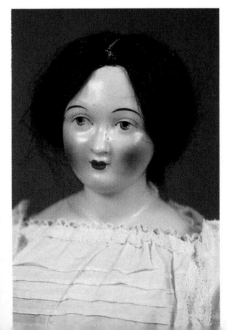

China Heads (German)

Some early dolls by K.P.M., Meissen and Royal Copenhagen (Denmark), but most by unidentified makers. Later dolls by firms such as Kling & Co., Alt, Beck & Gottschalck, Kestner & Co., Hertwig & Co., and others. China head, cloth or kid body, leather arms or china limbs.

Mark: K.P.M., Meissen and Royal Copenhagen usually marked inside the shoulders; later dolls by Kling & Co. and A.B.G. are identifiable by their mold numbers.

1840s Hairstyles: China shoulder head with black molded hair; may have pink tint complexion; old cloth body; (may have china arms); appropriate old clothes; all in good condition.

Hair swept back into bun,
13 - 15in (33 - 38cm)	**$ 1600 - 2200***
18 - 21in (46 - 53cm)	**2500 - 5000***

Fancy braided bun,
22 - 24in (56 - 61cm)	**5000 - 5500**

K.P.M., double side curls, braided bun,
9in (23cm), at auction	**$ 3900**

Brown hair with bun,
16 - 18in (41 - 46cm)	**4000 up***

Young Man, brown hair,
16 - 18in (41 - 46cm)	**2600 - 2800**

Kinderkopf (child head),
15 - 16in (38 - 41cm)	**900 - 1000**

Long Curls:
Falling onto shoulder,
16in (41cm)	**2250****

Above shoulder, brown eyes,
19½in (49cm)	**3100****

Light brown hair, 24in (61cm) at auction
19,000

*Depending upon quality, hairdo and rarity.
**Not enough price samples to compute a reliable range.

Below left: 17in (43cm) brown-haired china man. *Private Collection.*

Below right: 19in (48cm) brown-haired china lady. *Private Collection.*

China Heads (German) continued

16in (41cm) china with Greiner-style hair, brown eyes, all original. *H & J Foulke, Inc.*

26in (66cm) china with covered wagon hairdo. *H & J Foulke, Inc.*

Wood Body, china lower limbs,

5 - 6in (13 - 15cm)	**$1250 - 1450**
11in (28cm)	**3200 - 3400**

1850s Hairstyles: China shoulder head (some with pink tint), molded black hair (except bald), painted eyes; old cloth body with leather or china arms; appropriate old clothes; all in good condition.

Bald head, some with black areas on top, proper wig. Allow extra for original human hair wig in fancy style.

Fine quality:

15 - 17in (38 - 43cm)	**$ 900 - 1000**
22 - 24in (56 - 61cm)	**1400 - 1600**

With glass eyes, fine quality,

20in (51cm)	**2200 - 2400****

Standard quality:

8 - 10in (20 - 25cm)	**$ 300 - 350**
15 - 17in (38 - 43cm)	**575 - 675**
20 - 22in (51 - 56cm)	**775 - 850**

Covered Wagon:

15 - 17in (38 - 43cm)	**550 - 650**
21 - 23in (53 - 58cm)	**900 - 1000**

With brown eyes,

25 - 27in (64 - 69cm)	**1600 - 1900**

Greiner-style, with brown eyes,

14 - 15in (36 - 38cm)	**850 - 950**
19 - 22in (48 - 56cm)	**1500 - 1700**

With glass eyes,

15 - 16in (38 - 41cm)	**3500****
22in (56cm)	**4800****

**Not enough price samples to compute a reliable range.

China Heads (German) continued

27½in (70cm) china head lady of the 1860s, rare brown eyes. *H & J Foulke, Inc.*

China shoulder head with fancy hairdo. *Richard Wright Antiques.*

Waves framing face, brown eyes. (For photograph see *7th Blue Book*, page 114.)

14 - 16in (36 - 41cm)	**$ 750 - 850**
19in (48cm)	**1050 - 1150**
With glass eyes,	
16in (41cm)	**2400 - 2600****

Child or Baby, flange swivel neck; china or papier-mâché shoulder plate and hips, china lower limbs; cloth midsection (may have voice box) and upper limbs. (For photograph see *9th Blue Book*, page 76.)

10in (25cm)	**2500 - 3000****

Alice Hairstyle. (For photograph see *10th Blue Book*, page 99.)

10in (25cm)	**2800 - 3200****

1860s and 1870s Hairstyles: China shoulder head with black molded hair (a few blondes), painted eyes, closed mouth; old cloth body may have leather arms or china lower arms and legs with molded boots; appropriate old clothes; all in good condition.

Plain style with center part (so-called flat top and high brow):

6 - 7 in (15 - 18cm)	**$ 90 - 100**
14 - 16in (36 - 41cm)	**250 - 275**
19 - 22in (48 - 56cm)	**325 - 375**
24 - 26in (61 - 66cm)	**425 - 525**
34 - 35in (86 - 89cm)	**700 - 800**
Molded necklace,	
22 - 24in (56 - 61cm)	**700**
Blonde hair,	
18in (46cm)	**400 - 500**
Brown eyes,	
20 - 22in (51 - 56cm)	**550 - 650**

Mary Todd Lincoln with snood. (For photograph see *8th Blue Book*, page 130.)

18 - 21in (46 - 53cm)	**750 - 850**
Blonde hair, black snood	
20in (51cm)	**1800**

**Not enough price samples to compute a reliable range.

124

For further information on the dolls shown on pages 124 and 125, see preceding and following pages.

21in (53cm) *Morning Glory* china head. *Richard Wright Antiques.*

Adelina Patti china head. *H & J Foulke, Inc.*

23in (58cm) flat-top hairdo china head
with unusual blonde hair.
H & J Foulke, Inc.

22in (56cm) china head lady with
molded snood and long side curls.
Richard Wright Antiques.

China Heads (German) continued

Dolley Madison with molded bow,
  14 - 16in (36 - 41cm) $ **375 - 425**
  21 - 24in (53 - 61cm) **575 - 625**

Adelina Patti (For photograph see page 124.)
  13 - 15in (33 - 38cm) **350 - 450**
  19 - 22in (48 - 56cm) **550 - 650**

Fancy style (only a sampling can be covered because of the wide variety):
Jenny Lind (For photograph see *Doll Classics*, page 130.)
  21 - 24in (53 - 61cm) **1300 - 1400**
Curly Top (For photograph see *7th Blue Book*, page 115.)
  18in (46cm) **900**

Grape Lady (For photograph see *8th Blue Book*, page 130.)
  18in (46cm) **$2000**
Spill Curl (For photograph see *5th Blue Book*, page 98.)
  19 - 22in (48 - 56cm) **800 - 900**
Morning Glory (See photograph on page 124.)
  21in (53cm) **5500 - 6500**

Man or boy. (For photograph see *10th Blue Book*, page 100.)
Fine quality,
  15 - 16in (38 - 41cm) **1100 - 1200**
Standard quality,
  16in (41cm) **500 - 550**

**Not enough price samples to compute a reliable range.

20in (51cm) blonde haired china head of the 1880s.
H & J Foulke, Inc.

China Heads (German) continued

Hair pulled back to low loose bun, molded
  gold beads, 23in (58cm)   **$1650**
Hair pulled back into braided bun,
  18in (46cm)   **1100**
Hair pulled from forehead in row of tight
  small curls, molded hairband,
  22in (56cm)   **1650**

1880s Hairstyles: China shoulder head with
black or blonde molded hair, blue painted
eyes, closed mouth; cloth body with china
arms and legs or kid body; appropriate old
clothes; all in good condition. Many made
by Alt, Beck & Gottschalck (see page 48
for mold numbers) or Kling & Co. (see
page 252 for mold numbers).
  14 - 16in (36 - 41cm)   **300 - 350**
  21 - 23in (53 - 58cm)   **450 - 500**

1890s Hairstyles: China shoulder head with
black or blonde molded wavy hair, blue
painted eyes, closed mouth; old cloth or kid
body with stub, leather, bisque or china
limbs; appropriate clothes; all in good condition.
  7 - 8in (18 - 20cm)   **$ 75 - 85**
  12 - 13in (31 - 33cm)   **125 - 140**
  15 - 17in (38 - 43cm)   **185 - 210**
  21 - 24in (53 - 61cm)   **275 - 325**

Molded poke bonnet,
  13in (33cm)   **185 - 200**
  8in (20cm)   **125 - 135**
Molded "Jewel" necklace,
  22in (56cm)   **300 - 400**

14½in (37cm) china lady with
pierced ears.
H & J Foulke, Inc.

China Heads (German) continued

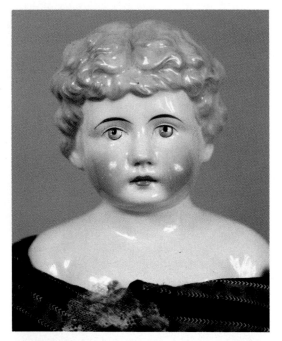

Pet Name: Ca. 1905. Made by Hertwig & Co. for Butler Bros., N.Y. China shoulder head, molded yoke with name in gold; black or blonde painted hair (one-third were blonde), blue painted eyes; old cloth body (some with alphabet or other figures printed on cotton material), china limbs; properly dressed; all in good condition. Used names such as **Agnes, Bertha, Daisy, Dorothy, Edith, Esther, Ethel, Florence, Helen, Mabel, Marion** and **Pauline**.

9 - 10in (23 - 25cm) **$125 - 150**
14 - 16in (36 - 41cm) **225 - 275**
19 - 21in (48 - 53cm) **325 - 375**

Top: Blonde-haired china head of the 1880s. *H & J Foulke, Inc.*

Bottom: 20½in (52cm) blonde-haired china head of the 1880s. *H & J Foulke, Inc.*

Cloth, Printed

9in (23cm) printed cloth girl. *H & J Foulke, Inc.*

16in (41cm) Cocheco girl. *H & J Foulke, Inc.*

FACTS

Various American companies, such as Cocheco Mfg. Co., Lawrence & Co., Arnold Print Works, Art Fabric Mills and Selchow & Righter and Dean's Rag Book Company in England. 1896 - on. All-cloth. 6 - 30in (15 - 76cm)
Mark: Mark could be found on fabric part, which was discarded after cutting.

Cloth, Printed Doll: Face, hair, underclothes, shoes and socks printed on cloth; all in good condition, some soil acceptable. Dolls in printed underwear are sometimes found dressed in old petticoats and frocks. Names such as: **Dolly Dear, Merry Marie, Improved Foot Doll, Standish No Break Doll,** and so on.

7 - 9in (18 - 23cm)	**$ 95 - 125**
16 - 18in (41 - 46cm)	**175 - 200**
22 - 24in (56 - 61cm)	**225 - 250**
Uncut sheet, bright colors, 20in (51cm) doll	**250 - 300**
Brownies: 1892.	
Designed by Palmer Cox; marked on foot.	
8in (20cm)	**90 - 100**
Boys and Girls with printed outer clothes, Ca. 1903.	
12 - 13in (31 - 33cm)	**175 - 200**
17in (43cm)	**240 - 265**
Darkey Doll, made up,	
16in (41cm)	**275 - 325**
Aunt Jemima Family,	
(four dolls)	**90 - 110 each**
Punch & Judy,	**425 - 450 pair**
Soldier, 12in (31cm)	**125 - 135**
Hen and Chicks,	
uncut sheet	**75 - 85**
Gutsell, 16in (41cm) made up with shirt and jacket	
	650 - 750
Tabby Cat	**95 - 100**
Tabby's Kittens	**65**
Ball, uncut	**250 - 275**
Peck 1886 Santa	**225**
Pickaninny	**200**
uncut	**225**
Black Child, Art Fabric,	
18in (46cm)	**300 - 350**
George & Martha Washington	**450 pair**
Pillow-type, printed and hand embroidered,	
1920s - 1930s, 16in (41cm)	**65 - 85**

Cloth, Russian

FACTS

Unknown craftsmen. Ca. 1930.
All-cloth. 10 - 15in (25 - 38cm).
Mark: "Made in Soviet Union"
sometimes with identification of
doll, such as "Ukranian
Woman," "Village Boy,"
"Smolensk District Woman."

Russian Cloth Doll: All-cloth with
stockinette head and hands, molded
face with hand-painted features; au-
thentic regional clothes; all in very
good condition. (See *10th Blue
Book*, page 101 for color photograph.)

11in (28cm) child	**$100 - 110**
15in (38cm)	**150 - 175**

15in (38cm) Russian cloth "Smolensk
District Woman." *H & J Foulke, Inc.*

Dewees Cochran

FACTS

Dewees Cochran, Fenton, Calif., U.S.A.
1940 - on. Latex. 9 - 18in (23 - 46cm).
Designer: Dewees Cochran.
Mark: Signed under arm or behind right ear.

Dewees Cochran Doll: Latex with jointed neck, shoulders and hips; human hair wig, painted eyes, character face; dressed; all in good condition.

15 - 16in (38 - 41cm) Cindy, 1947 - 1948.
$ 800 - 900

Grow-up Dolls: Stormy, Angel, Bunnie, J.J. and Peter Ponsett each at ages 5, 7, 11, 16 and 20, 1952-1956.
$1500 - 1800
Look-Alike Dolls (6 different faces)
1400 - 1600
Baby. 9in (23cm) **1300 - 1500****
Individual Portrait Children
1700 - 2000
Composition American Children (see Effanbee, page 163).

**Not enough price samples to compute a reliable range.

Angel with baby. *Nancy A. Smith Collection.*

Columbian Doll

FACTS

Emma and Marietta Adams. 1891 - 1910 or later. All-cloth. 15 - 29in (38 - 74cm).

Mark: Stamped on back of body.

Before 1900:

"COLUMBIAN DOLL
EMMA E. ADAMS
OSWEGO CENTRE
N.Y."

After 1906:

"THE COLUMBIAN DOLL
MANUFACTURED BY
MARIETTA ADAMS RUTTAN
OSWEGO, N.Y."

Columbian Doll: All-cloth with hair and features hand-painted on a flat face; treated limbs; appropriate clothes; all in good condition, showing wear.

15in (38cm) some repaint **$2500 - 3500**
20 - 22in (51 - 56cm) **5500 - 6500**
20 - 22in (51 - 56cm) fair condition **3000 - 4000**

Below: 15in (38cm) Columbian rag doll. *Richard Wright Antiques.*

Composition (American)

FACTS

Various United States firms, many unidentified. 1912 - on. All-composition
or composition head and cloth body,
some with composition limbs.

Below: 19in (48cm) all-composition character
baby. *H & J Foulke, Inc.*

All-Composition Child Doll: 1912 - 1920.
Various firms, such as Bester Doll Co., New
Era Novelty Co., New Toy Mfg. Co., Superior Doll Mfg. Co., Artcraft Toy Product
Co., Colonial Toy Mfg. Co. Composition
with mohair wig, sleep eyes, open mouth;
ball-jointed composition body; appropriate
clothes; all in good condition. These are
patterned after German bisque head dolls.
(For photograph see *10th Blue Book*, page
163.)

22 - 24in (56 - 61cm)   **$275 - 325**
Character baby, all-composition
19in (48cm)   **250 - 275**

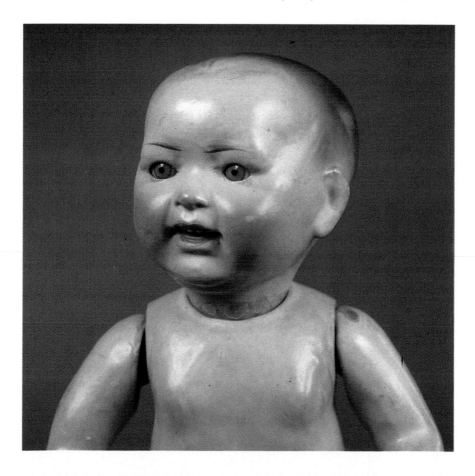

Composition (American) continued

Early Composition Character Head: Ca. 1912. Composition head with molded hair and painted features; hard cloth body with composition hands; appropriate clothes; all in good condition.

12 - 15in (31 - 38cm)	**$150 - 200**
18 - 20in (46 - 51cm)	**250 - 300**
24 - 26in (61 - 66cm)	**350 up**
Two-face toddler,	
14in (36cm)	**275 - 300**

Molded Loop Dolls: Ca. 1930s. All-composition with molded bobbed hair and loop for tying on a ribbon, painted eyes, closed mouth; composition or cloth torso, composition arms and legs; original or appropriate clothing; all in good condition. Quality is generally mediocre.

12 - 15in (31 - 38cm)	**$110 - 135**

Patsy-type Girl: Ca. 1930s. All-composition with molded bobbed hair, sleep or painted eyes, closed mouth; jointed at neck, shoulders and hips; original clothes; all in very good condition, of good quality.

9 - 10in (23 - 25cm)	**$125 - 150**
14 - 16in (36 - 41cm)	**200 - 225**
20in (51cm)	**275 - 300**

Top: 13in (33cm) early composition doll pull toy, all original. *H & J Foulke, Inc.*

Bottom: 16in (41cm) early composition soldier, all original (missing hat). *H & J Foulke, Inc.*

Girl-type Mama Dolls: Ca. 1920 - on. Made by various American companies. Composition head with hair wig, sleep eyes, open mouth with teeth; composition shoulder plate, arms and legs, cloth body; original clothes; all in good condition, of good quality. (See following page for photograph.)

16 - 18in (41 - 46cm)	**$200 - 225**
20 - 22in (51 - 56cm)	**275 - 325**
24 - 26in (61 - 66cm)	**375 - 425**

Composition Baby: Ca. 1930. All-composition or composition head, arms and legs, cloth torso; with molded and painted hair, sleep eyes; appropriate or original clothes; all in very good condition, of good quality. (See photograph on following page.)

12 - 14in (31 - 36cm)	**$150 - 200**
18 - 20in (46 - 51cm)	**250 - 300**
24in (61cm)	**375 - 425**

Dionne-type Doll: Ca. 1935. All-composition with molded hair or wig, sleep or painted eyes, closed or open mouth; jointed at neck, shoulders and hips; original clothes; all in very good condition, of good quality.

7 - 8in (18 - 20cm) baby	**$ 90 - 110**
13in (33cm) toddler	**185 - 210**
18 - 20in (46 - 51cm) toddler	
	275 - 325

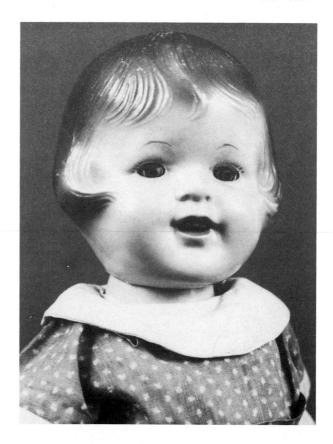

16in (41cm) *Patsy-type* composition girl. *H & J Foulke, Inc.*

136

Right:
13in (33cm) unmarked composition baby. *H & J Foulke, Inc.* (For further information see preceding page.)

Below:
23in (58cm) unmarked composition Mama doll. *H & J Foulke, Inc.* (For further information see preceding page.)

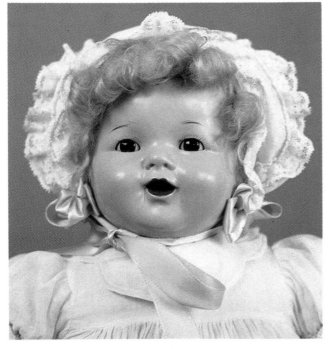

22in (56cm) unmarked composition bride, all original. *H & J Foulke, Inc.*

Composition (American) continued

Alexander-type Girl: Ca. 1935. All-composition, jointed at neck, shoulders and hips; sleeping eyes, mohair wig, closed mouth, dimples. Original or appropriate clothing. All in good condition, of good quality.

13in (33cm)	**$175 - 200**
16 - 18in (41 - 46cm)	**250 - 325**
22in (56cm)	**350 - 400**

Shirley Temple-type Girl: Ca. 1935 - on. All-composition, jointed at neck, shoulders and hips; blonde curly mohair wig, sleep eyes, open smiling mouth with teeth; original clothes; all in very good condition, of good quality.

16 - 18in (41 - 46cm)	**$300 - 350**

Below: 13in (33cm) unmarked composition toddler, all original. *H & J Foulke, Inc.*

Costume Doll: Ca. 1940. All-composition, jointed at neck, shoulders and hips, sleep or painted eyes, mohair wig, closed mouth; original costume; all in good condition.

11in (28cm)
Excellent quality	**$100 - 110**
Standard quality	**65 - 75**

Miscellaneous Specific Dolls:
Royal "Spirit of America"

15in (38cm) with original box and outfits	**300 - 350**
Jackie Robinson	
13½in (34cm)	**600 - 700**
Trudy 3 faces, 1946.	
14in (36cm)	**235 - 265**
Lone Ranger	
16in (41cm)	**350 - 375**
Kewpie-type characters	
12in (31cm)	**80 - 90**
Mountie (Reliable)	
16in (41cm)	**150 - 165**
HEbee, SHEbee	
10½in (27cm)	**500 - 600**

Top: 11in (28cm) unmarked composition doll, all original. *H & J Foulke, Inc.*

Bottom: 14in (36cm) *Trudy*, all original. *H & J Foulke, Inc.*

Composition (American) continued

Buddy Lee
  12in (31cm) all original   **$175 - 225***
Uneeda Rita Hayworth, red mohair wig
  14in (36cm)   **300 - 400****
Hedwig/diAngeli (See *6th Blue Book*, page 175.)
  Elin, Hannah, Lydia, Suzanne
    14in (36cm)   **300 - 350**
  3 Pigs and Wolf boxed set, all original
                                    650
Sterling Doll Co. Sports Dolls
  29in (74cm) all original   **250 - 300**
Paris Doll Co. Peggy
  28in (71cm) walker   **350 - 400**
Monica, 1941 - 1951.
  18in (46cm)   **450 - 550**
Famlee, 1921. Boxed with 3 heads and 4
  costumes   **300 - 350**
Rabbit head doll
  11in (28cm)   **125 - 150**
Santa Claus
  19in (48cm)   **400 - 500**
Pinocchio, Crown Toy, 1939.
  12in (31cm)   **250 - 300**

Puzzy. 1948. H. of P.
  15in (38cm)   **$350 - 400**
Sizzy, 1948. H. of P.
  14in (36cm)   **250 - 300**

*Depending upon costume.
**Not enough price samples to compute a reliable range.

Above: 10½in (26cm) rabbit head
doll. *H & J Foulke, Inc.*

Left: 15in (38cm) *Puzzy*. *H & J
Foulke, Inc.*

Composition (German)

FACTS

Various German firms such as König & Wernicke, Kämmer & Reinhardt and others. Ca. 1925. All-composition or composition head and cloth body. Various sizes.

All-Composition Child Doll: Socket head with good wig, sleep (sometimes flirty) eyes, open mouth with teeth; jointed composition body; appropriate clothes; all in good condition, of excellent quality.

12 - 14in (31 - 36cm)	**$225 - 275**
18 - 20in (46 - 51cm)	**350 - 400**

Character face

18 - 20in (46 - 51cm)	**$400 - 500**

Character Baby: Composition head with good wig, sleep eyes, open mouth with teeth; bent-limb composition baby body or hard-stuffed cloth body; appropriate clothes; all in good condition, of excellent quality.

All-composition baby,

16 - 18in (41 - 46cm)	**$375 - 425**

Cloth body,

14 - 16in (36 - 41cm)	**175 - 225**

All composition toddler,

16 - 18in (41 - 46cm)	**425 - 475**

22in (56cm) "600" German composition girl. *Jensen's Antique Dolls.*

Composition (Japanese)

FACTS

Various Japanese companies. 1920 - on. All-composition.
Mark: None.

Japanese Composition Doll: Composition with molded hair, painted features, swivel or stiff neck, jointed shoulders and hips; dressed or undressed; all in excellent condition.

Dionne Quintuplets
Baby, 7in (18cm)   **$165**
Toddler, 7½in (19cm)   **165**

Choir Boy, 10in (25cm)   **125 - 135**
Toddler, 8in (20cm) all original
                                              110
Shirley Temple, 7½in (19cm)
                                       250 - 300

Below: Japanese composition **Dionne Quintuplet** toddlers, original panties. *H & J Foulke, Inc.*

Composition Shoulder Head
(Patent Washable Dolls)

FACTS

Various German firms, such as Heinrich Stier, J.D. Kestner, F.M. Schilling and C. & O. Dressel. 1880 - 1915. Composition shoulder head, cloth body, composition lower limbs. 10 - 42in (25 - 107cm).
Mark: None.

Composition Shoulder Head: Composition shoulder head with mohair or skin wig, glass eyes, closed or open mouth; cloth body with composition arms and lower legs, sometimes with molded boots; appropriately dressed; all in good condition.

Superior Quality:

12 - 14in (31 - 36cm)	**$ 400 - 450**
16 - 18in (41 - 46cm)	**500 - 550**
22 - 24in (56 - 61cm)	**700 - 800**
30in (76cm)	**1000**

Standard Quality:

11 - 12in (28 - 31cm)	**135 - 165**
14 - 16in (36 - 41cm)	**185 - 215**
22 - 24in (56 - 61cm)	**300 - 350**
30 - 33in (76 - 84cm)	**500 - 600**
38in (97cm)	**700 - 800**
Lady, 13 - 16in (33 - 41cm)	**700 - 800**
Oriental, 12in (31cm)	**225 - 250**

Below: 17½in (44cm) Patent Washable-type composition shoulder head intended for use as a baby. *H & J Foulke, Inc.*

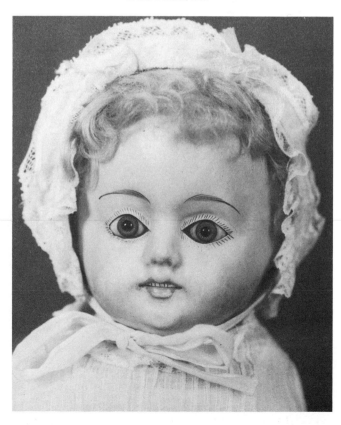

Danel

FACTS

Danel & Cie., Paris & Montreuil-sous-Bois, France. 1889-1895. Bisque socket head, composition body.
Trademarks: Paris Bébé, Bébé Français (also used by Jumeau).

Marked Paris Bébé: 1889. Perfect bisque socket head, good wig, paperweight eyes, closed mouth, pierced ears; composition jointed body; appropriately dressed; all in good condition.
Mark: On Head   TÊTE DÉPOSÉ
PARIS BEBE

On Body

18 - 20in (46 - 51cm)	**$4700 - 5100**
24 - 26in (61 - 66cm)	**5500 - 6000**

Marked B.F.: Ca. 1891. Perfect bisque head, appropriate wig, paperweight eyes, closed mouth, pierced ears; jointed composition body; appropriate clothes; all in good condition.
Mark:

B9F

15 - 17in (38 - 43cm)	**$4000 - 4300**
21 - 23in (53 - 58cm)	**4800 - 5200**
27in (69cm)	**6500 - 7000**

23in (58cm) *Paris Bébé*. *Mary Barnes Kelley Collection.*

D E P* (Open Mouth)

FACTS

Maison Jumeau, Paris, France (heads possibly by Simon & Halbig, Grafenhain, Thüringia, Germany). Late 1890s. Bisque socket head, French jointed composition body (sometimes marked Jumeau). About 11 - 35in (28 - 89cm).

Mark: "DEP" and size number (up to 16 or so); sometimes stamped in red "Tete Jumeau"; body sometimes with Jumeau stamp or sticker.

*For closed mouth **DEP**, see page 168.

DEP: Perfect bisque socket head, human hair wig, sleep eyes, painted lower eyelashes only, upper hair eyelashes (sometimes gone), deeply molded eye sockets, open mouth, pierced ears; jointed French composition body; lovely clothes; all in good condition.

11 - 12in (28 - 31cm)	$ 650 - 750
14 - 16in (36 - 41cm)	800 - 900
19 - 21in (48 - 53cm)	1100 - 1200
24 - 26in (61 - 66cm)	1600 - 1800
29 - 30in (74 - 76cm)	2400 - 2700
35in (89cm)	3200 - 3500

*The letters DEP appear in the mark of many dolls, but the particular dolls priced here have only "DEP" and a size number (unless they happen to have the red stamp "Tete Jumeau"). The face is characterized by deeply molded eye sockets and no painted upper eyelashes.

20in (51cm) *DEP* Jumeau. *H & J Foulke, Inc.*

146

Door of Hope

FACTS

Door of Hope Mission, China; heads by carvers from Ning-Po. 1901 - on. Wooden heads; cloth bodies, some with carved wooden hands. Usually under 13in (33cm).
Mark: Sometimes "Made in China" label.

Door of Hope: Carved wooden head with painted and/or carved hair, carved features; cloth body, some with stubby arms, some with carved hands; original handmade clothes, exact costuming for different classes of Chinese people; all in excellent condition. 25 dolls in the series.

Adult, 11 - 13in (28 - 33cm)	**$ 500 - 600***
Child, 7 - 8in (18 - 20cm)	**550 - 650**
Mother and Baby, 11in (28cm)	**700 - 800**
Manchu Lady,	**1100 - 1200**
Kindergarten Girl, 6in (15cm)	**600 - 675**
Woman with carved flowers in hair,	**700**

*Allow extra for **Bride**, **Policeman** and **Priest**.

Door of Hope lady, all original. *H & J Foulke, Inc.*

Grace G. Drayton

FACTS

Various companies. 1909 - on. All-cloth, or composition and cloth combination, or all-composition. Various sizes.
Designer: Grace G. Drayton.
Mark: Usually a cloth label or a stamp:

Puppy Pippin: 1911. Horsman Co., New York, N.Y., U.S.A. Composition head with puppy dog face, plush body with jointed legs; all in good condition. Cloth label. (For photograph see *7th Blue Book*, page 135.)

8in (20cm) sitting   **$400 - 450****

Campbell Kid: (See page 207.)

**Not enough price samples to compute a reliable range.

14in (36cm) composition girl signed "G.G. Drayton." *H & J Foulke, Inc.*

Printed on cloth ***Dolly Dingle*** with embroidered accents. *H & J Foulke, Inc.*

Grace G. Drayton continued

Peek-a-Boo: 1913 - 1915. Horsman Co., New York, N.Y., U.S.A. Composition head, arms, legs and lower torso, cloth upper torso; character face with molded hair, painted eyes to the side, watermelon mouth; dressed in striped bathing suit, polka dot dress or ribbons only; cloth label on outfit; all in good condition. (For photograph see *7th Blue Book*, page 136.)

7½in (19cm)   **$140 - 160**

Hug-Me-Tight: 1916. Colonial Toy Mfg. Co., New York, N.Y., U.S.A. Mother Goose characters and others in one piece, printed on cloth; all in good condition. (For photograph see *8th Blue Book*, page 149.)

11in (28cm)   **$225 - 250****

Captain Kiddo,
6¼in (16cm)   **$200**

Chocolate Drop: 1923. Averill Manufacturing Co., New York, N.Y., U.S.A. Brown cloth doll with movable arms and legs; painted features, three yarn pigtails; appropriate clothes; all in good condition.

Stamped on front torso and paper label. (For photograph see *6th Blue Book*, page 120.)

11in (28cm)   **$425 - 475**
16in (41cm)   **600 - 650****

Dolly Dingle: 1923. Averill Manufacturing Co., New York, N.Y., U.S.A. Cloth doll with painted features and movable arms and legs; appropriate clothes; all in good condition. Stamped on front torso and paper label:

            DOLLY DINGLE
            COPYRIGHT BY
            G.G. DRAYTON

11in (28cm)   **$375 - 425**
16in (41cm)   **550 - 600****
10in (25cm) double face   **750****

Composition Child: Composition shoulder head, arms and legs, cloth torso; molded bobbed hair, watermelon mouth, painted eyes, round nose; original or appropriate clothes; in fair condition.

Mark: $9 \cdot 9 \cdot Drayton$

14in (36cm)   **$400 - 450****

Kitty-Puss: All-cloth with painted cat face, flexible arms and legs, tail; original clothing; all in good condition. (For photograph see *9th Blue Book*, page 145.)
Mark: Cardboard tag
                         $400**

September Morn: All-bisque, molded hair, painted features; jointed shoulders and hips.
6in (15cm) at auction
                         $2250

**Not enough price samples to compute a reliable range.

11in (28cm) *Dolly Dingle*. H & J Foulke, Inc.

Dressel

FACTS

Cuno & Otto Dressel verlager & doll factory of Sonneberg, Thüringia, Germany. Heads by Armand Marseille, Simon & Halbig, Ernst Heubach, Gebrüder Heubach. 1700 - on. Composition wax over or bisque head, kid, cloth body or ball-jointed composition body.
Trademarks: Fifth Ave. Dolls (1903), Jutta (1907), Bambina (1909), Poppy Dolls (1912), Holz-Masse (1875).

Marked Holz-Masse Heads: 1875 - on. Composition shoulder head, molded hair or sometimes mohair wig, usually painted eyes, sometimes pierced ears; cloth body with composition arms and legs with molded boots; old clothes; all in good condition. (For photograph see page 297.)
Mark:

Molded hair:
13 - 15in (33 - 38cm)	$250 - 300
23 - 25in (58 - 64cm)	500 - 600

Wigged with glass eyes:
(Patent Washable)
14 - 16in (36 - 41cm)	185 - 215
22 - 24in (56 - 61cm)	300 - 350

Dressel character as *Father Christmas*. *Richard Wright Antiques*.

20in (51cm) C.O.D. Character Baby. *H & J Foulke, Inc.* (For further information see page 151.)

Dressel continued

Child Doll: 1893 - on. Perfect bisque head, original jointed kid or composition body; good wig, glass eyes, open mouth; suitable clothes; all in good condition. (For photograph see *10th Blue Book*, page 106.)
Mark:

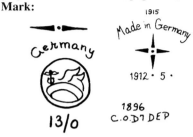

Composition body:

16 - 18in (41 - 46cm)	$ 350 - 400
23 - 24in (58 - 61cm)	500 - 525
32in (81cm)	900 - 950
38in (96cm)	1900 - 2100

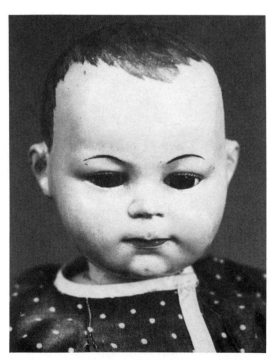

#93, 1896 Kid body,

19 - 22in (48 - 56cm)	$450 - 500

Character-type face, similar to **K*R 117n:**

22 - 24in (56 - 61cm)	800 - 900

Portrait Series: 1896. Perfect bisque heads with portrait faces, glass eyes, some with molded mustaches and goatees; composition body; original clothes; all in good condition. Some marked "S" or "D" with a number.

13in (33cm) Uncle Sam	$1200 - 1500
15in (38cm) Admiral Dewey and	
Officers	1200 - 1600
8in (20cm) Old Rip	600 - 700
10in (25cm) Farmer	700 - 800
10in (25cm) Buffalo Bill	750

Marked Jutta Child: Ca. 1906-1921. Perfect bisque socket head, good wig, sleep eyes, open mouth, pierced ears; ball-jointed composition body; dressed; all in good condition. Head made by Simon & Halbig. (For photograph see *10th Blue Book*, page 179.)
Mold **1348** or **1349**
Mark:

13 - 15in (33 - 38cm)	
	$ 600 - 625
17 - 19in (43 - 48cm)	
	650 - 675
24 - 26in (61 - 66cm)	
	850 - 950
31 - 32in (78 - 81cm)	
	1500 - 1600
38 - 39in (96 - 99cm)	
	2600 - 3100

19in (48cm) Dressel Art Doll with composition head. *H & J Foulke, Inc.*

Character Child: 1909 - on. Perfect bisque socket head, ball-jointed composition body; mohair wig, painted eyes, closed mouth; suitable clothes; all in good condition. Glazed inside of head. (For photograph see *10th Blue Book*, page 179.)

Mark:

C.O.D.
A/2

10 - 12in (25 - 31cm)	**$1650 - 1850****
16 - 18in (41 - 46cm)	**2600 - 2900****

Composition head,	
19in (48cm)	**2600 - 3000****

Marked C.O.D. Character Baby: Ca. 1910 - on. Perfect bisque character face with marked wig or molded hair, painted or glass eyes; jointed baby body; dressed; all in good condition. (See photograph on page 149.)

12 - 13in (31 - 33cm)	
	$350 - 375
16 - 18in (41 - 46cm)	
	450 - 500
22 - 24in (56 - 61cm)	
	675 - 775

**Not enough price samples to compute a reliable range.

Marked Jutta Character Baby: Ca. 1910 - 1922. Perfect bisque socket head, good wig, sleep eyes, open mouth; bent-limb composition baby body; dressed; all in good condition.

Simon & Halbig:

16 - 18in (41 - 46cm)	**$ 650 - 750**
23 - 24in (58 - 61cm)	**1300 - 1500**

Other Makers: (Armand Marseille, E. Heubach)

16 - 18in (41 - 46cm)	**$450 - 500**
23 - 24in (58 - 61cm)	**700 - 800**

Mark: Heubach 6½ Koppelsdorf
Jutta - Baby
Dressel
Germany
1922
10½

⬭
Jutta
1914
8

Toddler:

7 - 8in (18 - 20cm)	**550 - 650**
16 - 18in (41 - 46cm)	**900 - 1100**
22in (56cm)	**1500**

11in (28cm) *Jutta* 1914 character baby. *H & J Foulke, Inc.*

Dressel continued

Lady Doll: Ca. 1920s. Bisque socket head with young lady face, good wig, sleep eyes, closed mouth; jointed composition body in adult form with molded bust, slim waist and long arms and legs, feet modeled to wear high-heeled shoes; all in good condition.

Mark:

1469
C O. Dressel
Germany
2.

#1469
14in (36cm)

Naked	$2000 - 2300
Original clothes	3000 - 4200
Composition head	
14in (36cm)	750 - 850

Above:
14in (36cm) dressed lady with composition head, all original. *H & J Foulke, Inc.*

Left:
14in (36cm) 1469 lady. *H & J Foulke, Inc.*

E. D. Bébé

Marked E. D. Bébé: Perfect bisque head, wood and composition jointed body; good wig, beautiful blown glass eyes, pierced ears; nicely dressed; good condition. Often found on a marked Jumeau body.

Closed mouth:
16 - 18in (41 - 46cm)	**$3000 - 3200***
23 - 25in (58 - 64cm)	**3600 - 4000***
30in (76cm)	**4800 - 5200***

Open mouth:
14 - 15in (36 - 38cm)	**1500 - 1700***
23 - 25in (58 - 64cm)	**2400 - 2700***

*For a pretty face.

27in (69cm) E 11 D child. *H & J Foulke, Inc.*

Eden Bébé

FACTS

Fleischmann & Bloedel, doll factory, of Fürth, Bavaria, and Paris, France. Founded in Bavaria in 1873. Also in Paris by 1890, then on into S.F.B.J. in 1899. Bisque head, composition jointed body.
Trademark: Eden Bébé (1890), Bébé Triomphe (1898).
Mark: "EDEN BEBE, PARIS"

23in (58cm) **Eden Bébé**. *H & J Foulke, Inc.*

Marked Eden Bebe: Ca. 1890. Perfect bisque head, fully-jointed or five-piece composition jointed body; beautiful wig, large set paperweight eyes, closed or open/closed mouth, pierced ears; lovely clothes; all in nice condition.

Closed mouth,
   15 - 16in (38 - 41cm)   **$2400 - 2500**
   19 - 22in (48 - 56cm)   **2800 - 3100**
   5-piece body, 12in (31cm)   **1200 - 1500**
Open mouth, 21 - 24in (53 - 61cm)
                        2300 - 2600

FACTS

EFFanBEE Doll Co., New York, N.Y., U.S.A. 1912 - on.
Marks: Various, but nearly always marked "EFFanBEE" on torso or head. Sometimes with doll's name. Wore a metal heart-shaped bracelet; later a gold paper heart label.
Metal Heart Bracelet: $45 - 50

Early Characters: Composition character face, molded painted hair, closed mouth, painted eyes; cloth stuffed body with metal disk joints at shoulders and hips, composition lower arms, sewn-on shoes; appropriate clothes; in fair condition.

12 - 16in (30 - 41cm)

Baby Grumpy, 1912. Molds 172, 174 or 176. $250 - 300
Coquette, 1912. 250 - 300**
Pouting Bess, 1915. Some mold 162 or 166. (For photograph see *9th Blue Book*, page 152.) 250 - 300**
Billy Boy, 1915. (For photograph see page 12.) 250 - 300**
Whistling Jim, 1916. 250 - 300**
Harmonica Joe, 1924. (For photograph see page 156.) 250 - 300**

Katie Kroose, 1918. (For photograph see *9th Blue Book*, page 152.) 250 - 300**
Buds, 1915 - 1918. 175 - 185

**Not enough price samples to compute a realiable range

18in (46cm) *Lovums*, all original. *H & J Foulke, Inc.* (For further information see page 158.)

EFFanBEE continued

Above left: 14in (36cm) *Harmonica Joe*, all original. *H & J Foulke, Inc.* (For further information see page 155.)

Above right: 12in (31cm) black *Baby Grumpy*, all original. *Kiefer Collection.* (For further information see page 158.)

Left: 28in (71cm) Mama doll, script mark. *H & J Foulke, Inc.* (For further information see page 158.)

11in (28cm) *Patsy Jr.*, all original. *H & J Foulke, Inc.* (For further information see page 159.)

16in (41cm) brown *Patsy Joan. Kiefer Collection.* (For further information see page 159.)

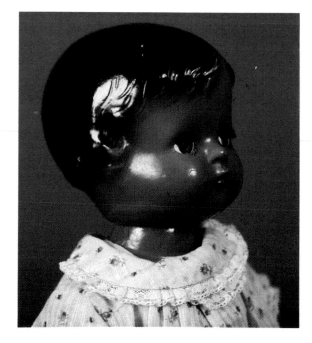

158

EFFanBEE continued

Shoulder Head Dolls: Composition shoulder head, painted molded hair or human hair wig, open or closed mouth, painted tin sleep eyes; cloth torso, composition arms and legs; original or appropriate old clothes; all in good condition. Came with metal heart bracelet.

Baby Grumpy, 1925 - 1939.
  12in (31cm) white   **$200 - 225**
  Black (For photograph see page 156.)
                           275 - 300
Pennsylvania Dutch Dolls: 1936-1940, all
  original and excellent. **190 - 210**
Baby Dainty, 1912 - 1922.
  15in (38cm)   **225**
Rosemary, 1925. **Marilee,** 1924.
  14in (36cm)   **225 - 250**
  17in (43cm)   **265 -295**
  25in (64cm)   **425 - 475**
  30in (76cm)   **500 - 550**
Mary Ann, 1928.
  16in (41cm)   **265 - 295**
Mary Lee, 1928.
  19in (48cm)   **300 - 350**
Early Mama Dolls, 1920s. (For photograph
  see page 156.)
  26 - 28in (66 - 71cm)   **500 - 600**

Mary Jane: 1917 - 1920. Composition "dolly face" head with metal sleeping eyes, painted eyebrows and eyelashes, open mouth with teeth, original human hair or mohair wig; jointed composition body with wood arms; dressed; all in very good condition. (For photograph see *7th Blue Book*, page 144.)
Mark: *Effanbee*

back of head and torso in raised letters
  20 - 24in (51 - 61cm)   **$250 - 300**

Babies: Composition head with painted hair or wigged, sleep eyes, open smiling mouth with teeth or closed mouth; cloth body, curved composition arms and legs; original or appropriate old clothes; all in good condition. Came with metal heart bracelet, later with gold heart hang tag.

Bubbles, 1924. (For photograph see *9th Blue Book*, page 153.)
Mark:

19 © 24   EFFANBEE
EFFanBEE   BUBBLES
DOLLS   COPYR 1924
WALK-TALK-SLEEP
MADE IN U.S.A   MADE IN U.S.A.

  16 - 18in (41 - 46cm)   **$325 - 375**
  22 - 24in (56 - 61cm)   **450 - 500**

Lovums, 1928. (For photograph see page 155.)
Mark: EFF AN BEE
              LOVUMS
                 ©
        PAT. N º. 1,283,558

  16 - 18in (41 - 46cm)   **250 - 300**
  22 - 24in (56 - 61cm)   **350 - 400**
Mickey, Baby Bright Eyes, Tommy Tucker, 1939-1949.
  16 - 18in (41 - 46cm)   **275 - 300**
  22 - 24in (56-61cm)   **350 - 400**
Sweetie Pie, 1942.
  16 - 18in (41 - 46cm)   **250 - 275**
  22 - 24in (56 - 61cm)   **325 - 375**
Baby Effanbee, 1925.
  12in (31cm)   **135 - 160**
Lambkin, 1930s.
  16in (41cm)   **375 - 425****
Sugar Baby, 1936. Caracul wig,
  16 - 18in (41 - 46cm)   **275 - 300**
Babyette, eyes closed,
  13in (33cm) boxed with pillow
                           550

**Not enough price samples to compute a reliable range.

Patsy Family: 1928 - on. All-composition jointed at neck, shoulders and hips; molded hair (sometimes covered with wig), bent right arm on some members, painted or sleep eyes; original or appropriate old clothes; may have some crazing. Came with metal heart bracelet. (See previous *Blue Books* for **Patsy** dolls not pictured here.)

Mark:

Bracelet

EFFANBEE
PATSY JR.
DOLL

EFFANBEE
PATSY
DOLL

EFFANBEE
PATSY
BABY KIN

6in (15cm) **Wee Patsy,**	**$325 - 350**
boxed with extra outfits	**525 - 625**
7in (18cm) **Baby Tinyette** (For photograph see page 161.)	**225 - 250**
9in (23cm) **Patsy Babyette**	**250 - 275**
Patsyette (For photograph see page 161.)	**325 - 350**
Brown	**425 - 450**
Hawaiian	**425 - 450**
11in (28cm) **Patsy Baby**	**250 - 275**
Brown	**425 - 450**
Patsy Jr. (For photograph see page 157.)	**300 - 325**
Patricia Kin	**300 - 325**
14in (36cm) **Patsy** (For photograph see page 160.)	**375 - 400**
15in (38cm) **Patricia** (For photograph see page 160.)	**425 - 450**
16in (41cm) **Patsy Joan**	**400 - 450**
Brown (For photograph see page 157.)	**550 - 600**
19in (48cm) **Patsy Ann**	**450 - 500**
22in (56cm) **Patsy Lou**	**475 - 525**
26in (66cm) **Patsy Ruth**	**750 - 850**
30in (76cm) **Patsy Rae**	**750 - 850**

Skippy: 1929. All-composition, jointed at neck, hips and shoulders, (later a cloth torso, still later a cloth torso and upper legs with composition molded boots for lower legs); molded hair, painted eyes to the side; original or appropriate clothes; all in good condition. Came with metal heart bracelet.

Mark:

EFFANBEE
SKIPPY
©
P.L. Crosby

14in (36cm)   **$450 - 500**

Below: 14in (36cm) *Skippy*, all original. *H & J Foulke, Inc.*

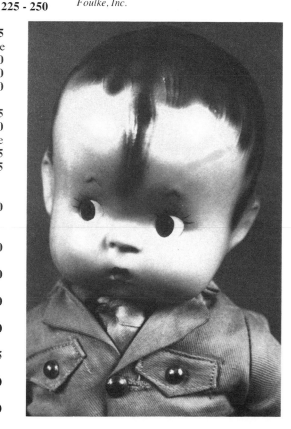

14in (36cm) *Patsy* with sleep eyes, all original. *H & J Foulke, Inc.*

14in (36cm) *Patricia*, all original. *H & J Foulke, Inc.*

(See page 159 for information on the dolls pictured on pages 160 and 161.)

9in (23cm) *Patsyette* and 7in (18cm) *Baby Tinyette*, all original. *H & J Foulke, Inc.*

EFFanBEE continued

All-Composition Children: 1933-on. All-composition jointed at neck, shoulders and hips; human hair or mohair wigs, sleep eyes, closed mouths; original clothes; all in very good condition. Came with metal heart bracelet or cardboard gold heart tag.

Anne Shirley, 1935 - 1940. Marked on back.

14 - 15in (36 - 38cm)	**$225 - 250**
17 - 18in (43 - 46cm)	**275 - 300**
21in (53cm)	**350 - 400**
27in (69cm)	**450 - 500**

Dy-Dee Baby: 1933 - on. First dolls had hard rubber head with soft rubber body, caracul wig or molded hair, open mouth for drinking, soft ears (after 1940). Later dolls had hard plastic heads with rubber bodies. Still later dolls had hard plastic heads with vinyl bodies. Came with paper heart label. Various sizes from 9 - 20in (23-51cm). Very good condition.
Mark:
"EFF-AN-BEE
DY-DEE BABY
US PAT.-1-857-485
ENGLAND-880-060
FRANCE-723-980
GERMANY-585-647
OTHER PAT PENDING"
Rubber body:

14 - 16in (36 - 41cm)	**$160 - 190**
24in (61cm)	**275 - 325**

Above:
Dy-Dee Baby with original trunk. *H & J Foulke, Inc.*

Right:
18in (46cm) ***Anne Shirley***, all original. *H & J Foulke, Inc.*

American Children, 1936 - 1939. Open mouth, unmarked. (For photograph see *10th Blue Book*, page 189.)

15in (38cm) **Barbara Joan**	**$ 550 -**	**650**
17in (43cm) **Barbara Ann**	**650 -**	**750**
21in (53cm) **Barbara Lou**	**750 -**	**850**

Closed mouth. (For photograph see *9th Blue Book*, page 157.)
19 - 21in (48 - 53cm) marked head on **Anne Shirley** body, sleep or painted eyes
$1300 - 1500

17in (43cm) boy, unmarked, painted eyes. (For photograph see *6th Blue Book*, page 131.) **$1300 - 1500**

Suzette, 1939. Painted eyes. (For photograph see *9th Blue Book*, page 159.)
11½in (29cm) **$ 225 - 250**

Suzanne, 1940. (For photograph see *8th Blue Book*, page 165.)
14in (36cm) **$275 - 300**
Little Lady, 1940 - 1949. Same prices as **Anne Shirley.**

Portrait Dolls, 1940. Ballerina, **Bo-Peep, Gibson Girl,** bride, groom, dancing couple, colonial. (For photograph see *7th Blue Book*, page 152.)
11in (28cm) **$250 - 275**

Candy Kid, 1946. Toddler, molded hair. (For photograph see *10th Blue Book*, page 190.)
12in (31cm) **$275 - 325**
Betty Brite, 1933. Caracul wig. (For photograph see *6th Blue Book*, page 130.)
16½in (42cm) **275 - 300**
Button Nose, 1939.
9in (23cm) **225 - 250**

9in (23cm) *Button Nose*, all original. *H & J Foulke, Inc.*

EFFanBEE continued

Charlie McCarthy: 1937. Composition head, hands and feet, cloth body; painted hair and eyes; strings at back of head to operate mouth; original clothes; all in very good condition.
Mark:
"EDGAR BERGEN'S CHARLIE McCARTHY,
AN EFFanBEE PRODUCT"

17 - 20in (43 - 51cm)	**$ 650 - 750**
Mint-in-box with button	**850 - 950**

Historical Dolls: 1939. All-composition, jointed at neck, shoulders and hips. Three each of 30 dolls portraying the history of American fashion, 1492 - 1939. "American Children" heads used with elaborate human hair wigs and painted eyes; elaborate original costumes using velvets, satins, silks, brocades, and so forth; all in excellent condition. Came with metal heart bracelet.
Marks: On head:
"EFFanBEE AMERICAN CHILDREN"
On body:
"EFFanBEE ANNE SHIRLEY"

21in (53cm)	**$1300 - 1500**

20in (51cm) *Charlie McCarthy*, all original. *H & J Foulke, Inc.*

Left:
21in (53cm) Historical doll, 1658 Carolina, all original. *H & J Foulke, Inc.*

Below:
14in (36cm) Historical doll, 1685 later Carolina, all original. *H & J Foulke, Inc.*

Historical Doll Replicas: 1939. All-composition, jointed at neck, shoulders and hips. Series of 30 dolls, popular copies of the original historical models (see above). Human hair wigs, painted eyes; original costumes all in cotton, copies of those on the original models. Came with metal heart bracelet. All in excellent condition.
Mark: On torso:
"EFFanBEE
ANNE SHIRLEY"
14in (36cm)   **$450 - 550**

Howdy Doody: 1949-1950. Hard plastic head and hands, molded hair, sleep eyes; cloth body; original clothes; all in excellent condition.
19 - 23in (48 - 58cm)   **$250 - 350**
Mint in Box   **525**

EFFanBEE continued

Honey: 1949 - 1955. All-hard plastic, jointed at neck, shoulders and hips; synthetic, mohair or human hair, sleep eyes; original clothes; all in excellent condition.
Mark: EFFANBEE

14in (36cm)	$225 - 250
18in (46cm)	300 - 325
24in (61cm)	400 - 425
Prince Charming	375
Cinderella	375
Alice	325 - 350

Vinyl Dolls: All original and excellent condition.
Mickey, 1956.

10 - 11in (25 - 28cm)	$100

Champagne Lady, 1959.

19in (48cm)	250**

Fluffy Girl Scout, 1957 on.

11in (28cm)	50 - 65

Patsy Ann Girl Scout, 1960 - 1961. (For photograph see *7th Blue Book*, page 154.)

	150 - 165

Mary Jane Nurse, 1959.

32in (81cm)	250 - 275

Effanbee Club Limited Edition Dolls: 1975 - on. All-vinyl jointed dolls; original clothes; excellent condition.

1975 Precious Baby	$200 - 300
1976 Patsy	225 - 275
1977 Dewees Cochran	125
1978 Crowning Glory	75 - 100
1979 Skippy	225 - 275
1980 Susan B. Anthony	75 - 100
1981 Girl with Watering Can	75 - 100
1982 Princess Diana	65 - 95
1983 Sherlock Holmes	65 - 95
1984 Bubbles	65 - 95
1985 Red Boy	60 - 70
1986 China Head	50

**Not enough price samples to compute a reliable range.

Cinderella and Prince Charming, all original. *H & J Foulke, Inc.*

French Bébé (Unknown Manufacturers)

H.
Marked H Bébé: Ca. late 1870s. Possibly by A. Halopeau. Perfect pressed bisque socket head of fine quality, paperweight eyes, pierced ears, closed mouth, cork pate, good wig; French-style wood and composition jointed body with straight wrists; appropriate clothes; all in excellent condition. (For photograph see *10th Blue Book*, page 195.)
Mark:

$$2 \cdot H$$

Size 0 = 16½in (42cm)
    2 = 19in (48cm)
    3 = 21in (56cm)
    4 = 24in (61cm)

21 - 23in (53 - 61cm)   **$75,000 - 85,000**

J.M.
Marked J.M. Bébé: Ca. 1880s. Perfect pressed bisque socket head, paperweight eyes, closed mouth, pierced ears, good wig; French-style composition body; appropriate clothes; all in good condition. (For photograph see following page.)
Mark:

$$5$$
$$J \quad M$$

19 - 21in (48 - 53cm)   **$24,000 - 25,000****

B.L.
Marked B.L. Bébé: Ca. 1880. Possibly by Lefebvre or perhaps Jumeau for the Louvre department store. Perfect bisque socket head, closed mouth, paperweight eyes, pierced ears, good wig; French-style jointed composition body; appropriate clothes; all in good condition. (For photograph see *Doll Classics*, page 41 or *5th Blue Book*, page 54.)
Mark:

$$B.9L.$$

18 - 21in (46 - 53cm)   **$ 4200 -   4700**

R.R.
Marked R.R. Bébé: Ca. 1880s. Some possibly made by Jumeau. Perfect bisque head, closed mouth, paperweight eyes, pierced ears, good wig; French-style jointed composition body; appropriate clothes; all in good condition. (For photograph see *9th Blue Book*, page 180.)
Mark:

$$R \: 10 \: R$$

21 - 23in (53 - 58cm)   **$4900 - 5300****

**Not enough price samples to compute a reliable range.

23in (58cm) **DEP**. *Carole Jean Stoessel Zvonar Collection.* (For information see following page.)

French Bébé (Unknown Manufacturers)

DEP.
Marked DEP: Ca. 1890. Perfect bisque head, swivel neck, lovely wig, set paperweight eyes, closed mouth, pierced ears; jointed French body; pretty costume; all in good condition. (For photograph see page 167.)

18 - 20in (46 - 51cm)   **$3200 - 3500**

J.
Marked J. Bébé: Ca. 1890. Perfect bisque socket head, closed mouth, paperweight eyes, pierced ears, good wig; jointed French body; appropriate clothes; all in good condition.

17in (43cm)   **$3000 - 3500**

**Not enough price samples to compute a reliable range.

Left: 19in (48cm) *J.M. Bébé. Private Collection.* (For information see preceding page.)

M.
Marked M. Bébé: Mid 1890s. Perfect bisque socket head, closed mouth, paperweight eyes, pierced ears, good wig; French-style jointed composition body; appropriate clothes; all in good condition. Some dolls with this mark may be Bébé Mascottes. (For photograph see *10th Blue Book*, page 196.)

Mark:

M
4

14 - 16in (36 - 41cm) $3000 - 3300**
21 - 23in (53 - 58cm)   4000 - 4500**

Right: 17in (43cm) *J1 Bébé. Private Collection.*

French Fashion-Type (Poupée)

Various French firms. Ca. 1860 - 1930.
Bisque shoulder head, gusseted kid
body (poupée peau), some with bisque
lower limbs or wood arms; or fully-
jointed wood body (poupée bois)
sometimes covered with kid; or cloth
body with kid arms.
(See also *Bru, Jumeau, Gaultier,
Gesland, Huret, Rohmer* and *Barrois*.)

(See information on following page.)

Right: 12in (31cm) French fashion (poupée peau)
incised "O." *H & J Foulke Inc.*

Below: 17½in (44cm) French fashion. *Nancy A.
Smith Collection.*

Below right: 19in (48cm) L.D. fashion, wood
body. *Jensen's Antique Dolls.*

French Fashion-Type (continued)

French Fashion Lady: Perfect unmarked bisque shoulder head, swivel or stationary neck, kid body or cloth body with kid arms — some with wired fingers; original or old wig, lovely blown glass eyes, closed mouth, earrings; appropriate old clothes; all in good condition. Fine quality bisque.

12 - 13in (31 - 33cm)	**$2200 up***
15 - 16in (38 - 41cm)	**2500 up***
18 - 19in (46 - 48cm)	**3200 up***
21in (53cm)	**3500 up***

Fully-jointed wood body,

15 - 17in (38 - 43cm)	**5000 up+**

Dainty oval face,

12 - 14in (31 - 36cm)	**$2300 - 2500**

Round face, cobalt eyes (shoulder head),

13 - 15in (33 - 38cm)	**2300 - 2500**

Twill-over-wood body (Simon & Halbig-type),

15 - 17in (38 - 43cm)	**$3900 - 4500**

Rochard head only with Stanhope shoulder plate, 8in (20cm) at auction **31,000**
(For photograph see page 8.)

Period Clothes, Fashion Lady clothing:

Dress	$ **500 - 1000**
Boots	**250 - 300**
Elaborate wig	**300**
Nice wig	**150**

*Allow extra for original clothing. Value of doll varies greatly depending upon the appeal of the face. Also, allow at least $400 additional for kid-over-wood upper and bisque lower arms.
+Allow extra for joints at ankle and waist.

13½in (34cm) French fashion (poupée peau). *Private Collection.*

Freundlich

FACTS

Freundlich Novelty Corp., New York, N.Y., U.S.A. 1923 - on. All-composition.

General Douglas MacArthur: Ca. 1942. All-composition portrait doll, molded hat, painted features, one arm to salute if desired; jointed shoulders and hips; original khaki uniform; all in good condition.
Mark: Cardboard tag: "General MacArthur"
18in (46cm)   **$275 - 325**

Military Dolls: Ca. 1942. All-composition with molded hats, jointed shoulders and hips, character face, painted features; original clothes. **Soldier, Sailor, WAAC**, and **WAVE**, all in good condition. (See photograph on following page.)
Mark: Cardboard tag.
15in (38cm)   **$150 - 200**

General MacArthur, all original.
H & J Foulke, Inc.

Freundlich continued

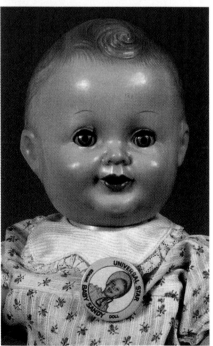

Baby Sandy: 1939 - 1942. All-composition with swivel head, jointed shoulders and hips, chubby toddler body; molded hair, smiling face, larger sizes have sleep eyes, smaller ones painted eyes; appropriate clothes; all in good condition. **Mark:** On head; "Baby Sandy"

8in (20cm)	**$135 - 165**
12in (31cm)	**190 - 210**
14 - 15in (36 - 38cm)	**300 - 350**

Other Composition Dolls:

Orphan Annie & Sandy, 12in (30cm)	**$250 - 300**
Red Ridinghood, Wolf & Grandmother Set 9in (23cm)	**400 - 500****
Dionne Quints and Nurse Set	**300 - 400**
Dummy Dan, 15in (38cm)	**100 - 125**
Goo Goo Eva, 20in (51cm)	**90 - 110**
Goo Goo Topsy (black), 20in (51cm)	**110 - 135**

**Not enough price samples to compute a reliable range.

Top:
15in (38cm) *WAVE*, all original. *H & J Foulke, Inc.* (For further information see page 171.)

Bottom:
15in (38cm) *Baby Sandy*, all original. *H & J Foulke, Inc.*

Frozen Charlotte
(Bathing Doll)

FACTS

Various German firms. Ca. 1850s - early 1900s. Glazed china; sometimes bisque. 1 - 18in (3 - 46cm).
Mark: None, except for "Germany," or numbers or both.

Frozen Charlotte: All-china doll, black or blonde molded hair parted down the middle, painted features; hands extended, legs separated but not jointed; no clothes; perfect condition. Good quality.

2 - 3in (5 - 8cm)	$ 45 - 55*
4 - 5in (10 - 13cm)	100 - 125*
6 - 7in (15 - 18cm)	150 - 175*
9 - 10in (23 - 25cm)	250 - 275*
14 - 15in (36 - 38cm)	450 - 500*
Pink tint, early hairdo,	
2½ - 3½in (6 - 9cm)	175 - 200
5in (13cm)	250 - 300
Pink tint with bonnet,	
3½ (9cm)	325 - 350
5in (13cm)	425 - 450
Black china, 5in (13cm)	150 - 175
Black boy, molded turban and pants,	
3in (8cm)	275 - 300
Black boy, molded shift,	
5in (13cm)	300 - 350
Blonde hair, molded bow,	
5½ (14cm)	165 - 185
Wig, lovely boots, 5in (13cm)	175 -185
Baby sitting in tub	225 - 250
Bisque, 5in (13cm)	135 - 160
Parian-type (1860s style),	
5in (13cm)	160 - 185
Alice style with pink boots,	
5in (13cm)	300 - 350
Fancy hairdo and boots,	
4½in (11cm)	250 - 300

*Allow extra for pink tint, fine decoration and modeling, unusual hairdo.

Top: 5in (13cm) china Frozen Charlotte with pink tint and molded bonnet. *H & J Foulke, Inc.*
Middle: 4½in (11cm) parian Frozen Charlotte. *H & J Foulke, Inc.*
Bottom: 3¾in (9cm) china Frozen Charlotte with molded ruffled bonnet. *H & J Foulke, Inc.*

Fulper

FACTS

Heads by Fulper Pottery Co., of
Flemington, N.J., U.S.A., for other
companies, often Amberg or Horsman.
1918 - 1921. Bisque heads; composition ball-jointed or jointed kid bodies.
Mark: "Fulper - Made in U.S.A."

Fulper Child Doll: Perfect bisque head,
good wig; kid jointed or composition ball-
jointed body; set or sleep eyes, open mouth;
suitably dressed; all in good condition. Good
quality bisque.

Kid body,
16 - 19in (41 - 48cm)	**$ 350 - 400***

Composition body,
18 - 22in (46 - 56cm)	**500 - 600***

Fulper Baby:
14 - 16in (36 - 41cm)	**450 - 550***
20 - 22in (51 - 56cm)	**650 - 750***

Toddler:

15 - 17in (38 - 43cm) very cute
	750 - 850*

Character Child: molded hair, intaglio
eyes, "O" mouth.
20in (51cm) at auction	**3750**

24in (61cm) Fulper character baby. *Richard
Wright Antiques.*

*Allow more for an especially pretty or cute doll.

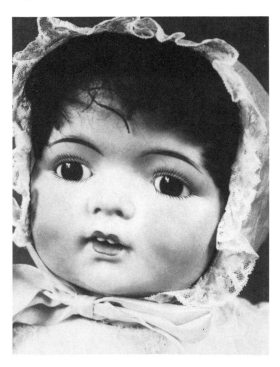

G. I. JOE®

FACTS

Hasbro (Hassenfeld Brothers, Inc.)
Pawtucket, RI, U.S.A. 1964 - 1979.
Hard plastic and vinyl. 12in (31cm)
fully-jointed.
Mark: G.I. Joe   After 1967 added:
Copyright 1964   Pat. No. 3,277,602
By Hasbro
Patent Pending
Made in U.S.A.

Marked G.I. Joe: Molded and painted hair and features, scar on right cheek; fully-jointed body; complete original outfit; all in good condition. Note: All **G.I. Joe** dolls have a scar on the right cheek except **Foreign Officers** and the **Nurse**. (See following page for photographs.)

Action Soldier, all original, boxed
$ 285

Action Sailor (painted hair), boxed
450

Action Marine, boxed   350
Action Pilot, boxed   600
Action Soldier Black
(painted hair), boxed   1300
Naked Dolls:
  Action Soldier (painted hair)   50
  Action Soldier (flocked hair*)   50
  Action Soldier (flocked hair and beard*)
50

  Black Action Soldier (painted hair)
300 - 350

*Hair must be in excellent condition.

Action Soldiers of the World (painted hair, no scars):
  German Soldier, boxed, large box
1200
  boxed, small box   600
  dressed doll only, no accessories
200
  Russian Infantry Man, boxed, large
box   1200
  boxed, small box   600
  dressed doll only, no accessories
200

British Commando, boxed, large box
$1250
  boxed, small box   225
  dressed doll only, no accessories   200
French Resistance Fighter, boxed, large
box   900
  boxed, small box   500
  dressed doll only, no accessories   200
Australian Jungle Fighter, boxed, large
box   700
  boxed, small box   400
  dressed doll only, no accessories   150
Japanese Imperial Soldier (unique model
used only for this type)
  boxed, large box   1300
  boxed, small box   800
  dressed doll only, no accessories   275
Talking Action Soldier, boxed   400
Talking Action Sailor, boxed   575
Talking Action Marine, boxed   475
Talking Action Pilot, boxed   800

Nurse Action Girl, boxed   1800
  dressed doll only   800
  naked doll   150

Man of Action (lifelike hair) Black, boxed
300
Man of Action (lifelike hair), boxed
200
Man of Action with Kung-Fu Grip
(lifelike hair), boxed   200
Talking Man of Action (lifelike hair)
boxed   225
Land Adventurer (lifelike hair and
beard), boxed   185
Talking Astronaut (lifelike hair), boxed
400 - 425
  dressed doll   275

G. I. JOE® continued

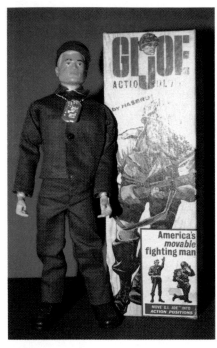

Outfits in unopened packages:

#7532 Green Beret Special Forces	$ 500
#7521 Military Police (brown)	400
#7521 Military Police (aqua)	1250
#7531 Ski Patrol	250
#7620 Deep Sea Diver	300
#7710 Dress Parade Set	225
#7824 Astronaut Suit	250
#7537 West Point Cadet	1200
#7624 Annapolis Cadet	1200
#7822 Air Cadet	1200
#7612 Shore Patrol	300
#7807 Scramble Set	275

(See preceding page for information about dolls pictured here.)

Left: *G.I. Joe Action Soldier*, all original, boxed. *Doodlebug Dolls.*

Bottom left: *G.I. Joe Action Marine Dress Parade*, (all original $125; outfit only $80). *Doodlebug Dolls.*

Bottom right: *G.I. Joe Talking Astronaut.* *Doodlebug Dolls.*

Gaultier

FACTS

Francois Gauthier (name changed to Gaultier in 1875); St. Maurice, Charenton, Seine, Paris, France. (This company made only porcelain parts, not bodies.) 1860 to 1899 (then joined S.F.B.J.) Bisque head for kid or composition body; all-bisque.

Marked F.G. Fashion Lady (Poupée): 1860 to 1930. Bisque swivel head on bisque shoulder plate, original kid body, kid arms with wired fingers or bisque lower arms and hands; original or good French wig, lovely large stationary eyes, closed mouth, ears pierced; dressed; all in good condition.
Mark: "F.G." on side of shoulder.

10½ - 11½in (27 - 29cm)	**$1600 - 1800***
13 - 14in (33 - 36cm)	**2100 - 2500***
16 - 18in (41 - 46cm)	**2600 - 2800***
21 - 23in (53 - 58cm)	**3000 - 3300***

Wood body,	
16 - 18in (41 - 46cm)	**$3800 - 4200***
Late doll in ethnic costume:	
8 - 9in (20 - 23cm)	**650 - 750**
Painted eyes:	
16in (41cm)	**1400 - 1600**

Approximate size chart:
Size 3/0 = 10½in (27cm)
2/0 = 11½in (29cm)
1 = 13½in (34cm)
2 = 15in (38cm)
3 = 17in (43cm)
5 = 20in (51cm)

*Allow extra for original clothes.

Bottom left:
16in (41cm) *F.G. Fashion* (poupée peau) with painted eyes. *H & J Foulke, Inc.*

Bottom right:
20in (51cm) *F.G. "5" Fashion* (poupée peau). *H & J Foulke, Inc.*

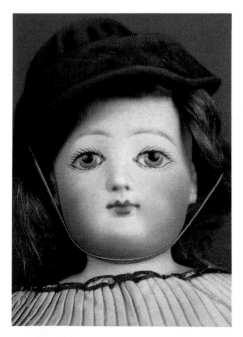

Gaultier continued

Marked F.G. Bébé: Ca. 1879 - 1887. Bisque swivel head on shoulder plate and gusseted kid body with bisque lower arms or chunky jointed composition body; good wig, large bulgy paperweight eyes, closed mouth, pierced ears; dressed; all in good condition. So-called "Block letters" mark.

Mark:

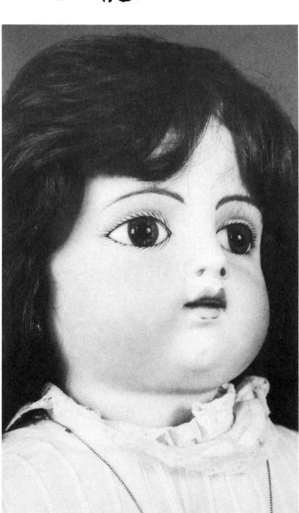

F . 7.G

14 - 16in (36 - 41cm)	**$4400 - 4700**
19 - 21in (48 - 53cm)	**4800 - 5100**
25 - 26in (64 - 66cm)	**5500 - 6000**
33 - 35in (84 - 89cm)	**7000**
Early style, kid body, 15in (38cm)	**5000 - 6000**
Wood body, 16in (41cm) at auction	**8500**

27in (69cm) "Block letters" F.G. *Ruth Noden Collection.*

22in (56cm) F.G. "Scroll" mark. *H & J Foulke, Inc.*

Marked F.G. Bébé: Ca. 1887 - 1900 and probably later. Bisque head, composition jointed body; good French wig, beautiful large set eyes, closed mouth, pierced ears; well dressed; all in good condition. So-called "Scroll" mark.

Mark:

5 - 6in (13 - 15cm)	**$ 675 - 775**
15 - 17in (38 - 43cm)	**2600 - 2900**
22 - 24in (56 - 61cm)	**3400 - 3700***
27 - 28in (69 - 71cm)	**4100 - 4400***
Open mouth:	
15 - 17in (38 - 43cm)	**1750 - 1950**
20 - 22in (51 - 56cm)	**2100 - 2400**

*Allow more for an especially pretty doll.

Gesland

FACTS

Heads: Francois Gaultier, Paris, France. **Bodies:** E. Gesland, Paris, France. 1860-1928. Bisque head, stockinette stuffed body on metal frame, bisque or composition lower arms and legs. (For photograph see *7th Blue Book*, page 175.)
Mark: Head: **F. G**

Body: Sometimes stamped E. Gesland

Fashion lady: Perfect bisque swivel head, good wig, paperweight eyes, closed mouth, pierced ears; stockinette body with bisque hands and legs; dressed; all in good condition.

Early face:
16 - 20in (41 - 51cm)	**$5500 - 6200**

F.G. face:
14 - 16in (36 - 41cm)	**3500 - 3800**
19 - 21in (48 - 53cm)	**4000 - 4300**

Bébé: Perfect bisque swivel head; composition shoulder plate, good wig, paperweight eyes, closed mouth, pierced ears; stockinette body with composition lower arms and legs; dressed; all in good condition. (For photograph see *8th Blue Book*, page 183.)

Beautiful early face:
14 - 16in (36 - 41cm)	**$4800 - 5000**
22 - 24in (56 - 61cm)	**5700 - 6200**

Scroll mark face:
22 - 24in (56 - 61cm)	**4000 - 4500**

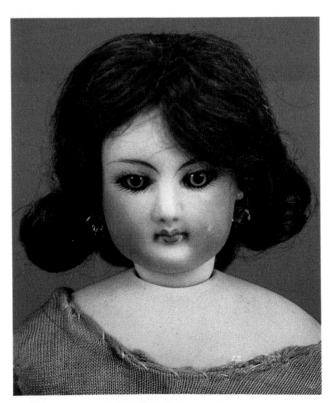

14in (36cm) F.G. fashion head on Gesland body. *H & J Foulke, Inc.*

FACTS

Heads made in Ohrdruf area, Germany, for George Borgfeldt, New York, N.Y., U.S.A. Bisque heads by ABG. 1929. Ceramic or bisque head, cloth torso, composition arms and legs.
Designer: Helen W. Jensen.
Mark:

[SIC]   *Gladdie*
Copyright By
Helen W. Jensen

Marked Gladdie: Biscaloid or ceramic head, molded and painted hair, glass eyes, open/closed mouth with molded teeth, laughing face; cloth torso, composition arms and legs; dressed; all in good condition.

16 - 19in (41 - 48cm) **$ 950 - 1150**
Bisque head **#1410** (For photograph see *8th Blue Book*, page 201.)
15 - 17in (38 - 43cm) **3700 - 4200**

17in (43cm) *Gladdie. H & J Foulke, Inc.*

Godey's Little Lady Dolls

FACTS

Ruth Gibbs, Flemington, N.J., U.S.A. 1946. China head and limbs, cloth body. Most 7in (18cm); a few 9, 10, 12 or 13in (23, 25, 31 or 33cm).
Designer: Herbert Johnson.
Mark: Paper label inside skirt "Godey's Little Lady Dolls;" "R.G." incised on back plate.

Ruth Gibbs Doll: China head with painted black, brown, blonde or auburn hair and features; pink cloth body with china limbs and painted slippers which often matched the hair color; original clothes, usually in an old-fashioned style.

7in (18cm)	$ 75 - 85
12 or 13in (31 or 33cm)	185 - 210
Boxed	215 - 235
Little Women, set of 5	600 - 675

12in (31cm) Ruth Gibbs lady doll.
H & J Foulke, Inc.

Goebel

Goebel Child Doll: 1895 - on. Perfect bisque socket head, good wig, sleep eyes, open mouth; composition jointed body; dressed; all in good condition. Some mold #120 or B.

Mark:

120 5/0
Germany

4½ - 5in (12 - 13cm)	**$175 - 190***
16 - 18in (41 - 46cm)	**375 - 450***
23 - 25in (58 - 64cm)	**550 - 600***

*Allow extra for very nice bisque.

21½in (55cm) Goebel 120 child. *Jensen's Antique Dolls.*

Pincushion Half Doll: Ca. 1915. Perfect china half figure usually of a lady with molded hair and painted features, sometimes with molded clothing, hats or accessories; lovely modeling and painting. Most desirable have fancy clothing or hair ornamentation and extended arms.

Mark:

2½in (6cm)	**$125 up***
4in (10cm)	**175 up***

Half-bisque child, (For photograph see *9th Blue Book*, page 197.)

3½in (9cm)	**110 - 135**

*Depending upon rarity.

Goebel Character Baby: Ca. 1910. Perfect bisque socket head, good wig, sleep eyes, open mouth with teeth; composition jointed baby body; dressed; all in good condition.

13 - 15in (33 - 38cm)	**$400 - 450**
19 - 21in (48 - 53cm)	**500 - 600**
Toddler, 17 - 19in (43 - 48cm)	**750 - 850**

Goebel Character Doll: Ca. 1910. Perfect bisque head with molded hair in various styles, some with hats, character face smiling or somber with painted features; papier-mâché five-piece body; all in excellent condition.

6½in (17cm)	**$325 - 375**

Top: 7in (18cm) Goebel 208 googly. *H & J Foulke, Inc.*

Bottom: 4½in (11cm) Goebel ***Jenny Lind*** pincushion doll. *H & J Foulke, Inc.*

Googly-Eyed Dolls

FACTS

J.D. Kestner, Armand Marseille, Hertel, Schwab & Co., Heubach, H. Steiner, Goebel and other German and French firms. Ca. 1911 - on. Bisque heads and composition or papier-mâché bodies or all-bisque.

All-Bisque Googly: Jointed at shoulders and hips, molded shoes and socks; mohair wig, glass eyes, impish mouth; undressed; in perfect condition.
#217, 501 and others:

4½ - 5in (11 - 13cm)	$ 475 - 525
5½ - 6in (14 - 15cm)	575 - 625

#189, 292 swivel necks:

4½ - 5in (11 - 13cm)	600 - 700
5½ - 6in (14 - 15cm)	700 - 800

Jointed elbows and knees (Kestner), swivel neck,

6 - 7in (15 - 18cm)	$2500 - 3000
Stiff neck, 5in (13cm)	1500 - 1650
Baby, 4½in (12cm)	400 - 425

Painted eyes, molded hair:

4½ (12cm)	350 - 375
6in (15cm)	500 - 525

K & R 131. 7in (18cm) $2600 - 3000**

**Not enough price samples to compute a reliable range.

Below left: 5in (13cm) all-bisque 401 googly with heart mark of Bähr & Pröschild. *H & J Foulke, Inc.*

Below right: 7in (18cm) E. Heubach 291 googly, rare model. *H & J Foulke, Inc.*

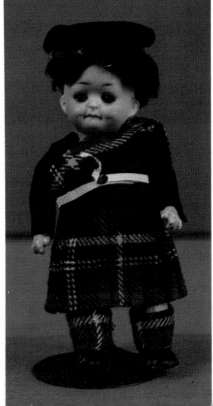

Googly-Eyed Dolls continued

Painted eyes, composition body: Perfect bisque swivel head with molded hair, painted eyes to the side, impish mouth; five-piece composition toddler or baby body jointed at shoulders and hips, some with molded and painted shoes and socks; cute clothes; all in good condition.

A.M., E. Heubach, Goebel, R.A.:

6 - 7in (15 - 18cm)	$ 425 - 500*
9 - 10in (23 - 25cm)	800 - 900*
#252 A.M. Kewpie-type baby,	
12in (31cm)	2000 - 2200

Gebrüder Heubach:

6 - 7in (15 - 18cm)	$ 525 - 600*
7in (18cm) Winker	750 - 850
9in (23cm) with top knot	1250
9in (23cm) #8995	2650

(For photograph see page 4.)

*Allow extra for unusual models.

Glass eyes, composition body: Perfect bisque head, mohair wig or molded hair, sleep or set large googly eyes, impish mouth closed; original composition body jointed at neck, shoulders and hips, sometimes with molded and painted shoes and socks; cute clothes; all in nice condition.

JDK 221: (For photograph see page 188.)
  12 - 15in (30 - 38cm) toddler

  $4500 - 5500

A.M. #323 and other similar models by H. Steiner, E. Heubach, Goebel and Recknagel:

6 - 7in (15 - 18cm)	$ 700 - 800
9 - 10in (23 - 25cm)	1100 - 1300
Baby body,	
10 -11in (25 - 28cm)	900 - 1100

A.M. #253 (watermelon mouth):

6 - 7in (15 - 18cm)	800 - 900
9in (23cm)	1300 - 1500

A.M. #200, 241:

8in (20cm)	1050 - 1150
11 - 12in (28 - 31cm)	2000 - 2200

A.M. #240: (For photograph see page 188.) 10in (25cm) toddler   **3000****

B.P. 686: 12in (31cm) at auction
  $3600

Demalcol (Dennis, Malley, & Co. London, England):
  9 - 10in (23 - 25cm)   **$ 650 - 750**

**Not enough price samples to compute a reliable range.

Above left: 10½in (26cm) H.S. & Co. 172 googly. *H & J Foulke, Inc.*

Below: 7in (18cm) A.M. 253 googly. *H & J Foulke, Inc.*

Hertel, Schwab & Co.:

#163, toddler, 15 - 16in (38 - 41cm)
                                   $5000 - 5600

#165, baby:

12 - 13in (31 - 33cm)	**3300 - 3800**
16in (41cm)	**4800 - 5000**
19in (48cm)	**5500**
Toddler 15in (38cm)	**3800 - 4200**

#172, 173:

Baby, 16in (41cm)	**5000****
Toddler,	
10 - 12in (25 - 31cm)	**4000 - 5000****
16in (41cm)	**6000 - 7000****

#222, Our Fairy:

5in (13cm)	**600 - 700**
10in (25cm)	**1200 - 1500**

G. Heubach:

Einco, 14 - 15in (36 - 38cm)
                                  $4000 - 5000

Elizabeth, 7 - 9in (18 - 23cm)
                                  1650 - 1850

Above right: 15½in (39cm) K * R 131 googly.
Richard Wright Antiques.

Below: 7in (18cm) E. Heubach 262 googly.
H & J Foulke, Inc.

#8678, 9573:

6 - 7in (15 - 18cm)	**800 - 850**
9in (23cm)	**1250 - 1500**

K * R 131:

8in (20cm), five-piece body
                                  $2400 - 2500**
15 - 16in (38 - 41cm)   **7500 - 8500****

Kley & Hahn 180:
  16½in (43cm)   **$3500****
P.M. 950:
  11in (28cm)   **$1600****

SFBJ #245:

8in (20cm), five-piece body
                                  $1500 - 1700**
11in (28cm) jointed body, with wardrobe
  at auction   **3750**
15in (38cm)   **4200 - 4600****

Schieler: 12in (31cm)   **$3200****

Disc Eyes: (See photograph on page 188.)
DRGM 954642 black or white
  11 - 12in (28 - 31cm)   **$1250 - 1500****

**Not enough price samples to compute a reliable range.

Googly-Eyed Dolls continued

16½in (42cm) JDK 221 googly. *Jackie Kaner.*

For further information about the dolls pictured on this page, see preceding pages.

10in (25cm) A.M. 240 googly. *H & J Foulke, Inc.*

Composition face: 1911 - 1914. Made by various companies in 9½ - 14in (24 - 36cm) sizes; marked with paper label on clothing. Called **Hug Me Kids, Little Bright Eyes**, as well as other trade names. Round all-composition or composition mask face, wig, round glass eyes looking to the side, watermelon mouth; felt body; original clothes; all in very good condition. (For photograph see *10th Blue Book*, page 151.)

10in (25cm)	**$ 650**
12 - 14in (31 - 36cm)	**750 - 850**

Googly with molded hat: 1915. Perfect bisque head with glass side-glancing eyes, watermelon mouth, molded hat; jointed composition body. Made for Max Handwerck, possibly by Hertel, Schwab & Co. All were soldiers: "U.S." (Uncle Sam hat); "E," (English Bellhop-type hat); "D," (German); "T," (Austrian/Turk-two faces) and Japanese.

Mark: "Dep
Elite"

10 - 13in (25 - 33cm)	**$2000 - 2200**
Double-Faced	**2200 - 2500**

10½in (26cm) disc-eyed black googly, all original. *H & J Foulke, Inc.*

Ludwig Greiner of Philadelphia, Pa.,
U.S.A. 1858-1883, but probably as early
as 1840s. Heads of papier-mâché, cloth
bodies, homemade in most cases, but
later some Lacmann bodies were used.
Various sizes, 13 - 38in (33-97cm) and
perhaps larger sizes "0" to "13."
Mark: Paper label on back shoulder:

GREINER'S
IMPROVED
PATENTHEADS
Pat.March 30th'58

or   **GREINER'S**
PATENT DOLL HEADS
No7
Pat. Mar. 30'58. Ext.'72

Greiner: Blonde or black molded hair,
painted features; homemade cloth body,
leather arms; nice old clothes; entire doll in
good condition.
'58 label:

15 - 17in (38 - 43cm)	$ 800 - 950
20 - 23in (51 - 58cm)	1150 - 1350
28 - 30in (71 - 76cm)	1500 - 1800
38in (97cm)	2500
Much worn:	
20 - 23in (51 - 58cm)	650 - 750
28 - 30in (71 - 76cm)	850 - 950
Glass eyes,	
20 - 23in (51 - 58cm)	2200**

'72 label:

19 - 22in (48 - 56cm)	475 - 525
29 - 31in (71 - 79cm)	750 - 850
35in (89cm)	1000 - 1100

**Not enough price samples to compute a reliable average.

15½in (39cm) 1858 Greiner. *Joan & Larry Kindler Antiques.*

22½in (57cm) 1858 Greiner. *Joan & Larry Kindler Antiques.*

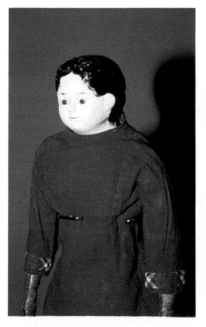

Heinrich Handwerck

FACTS

Heinrich Handwerck, doll factory, Waltershausen, Thüringia, Germany. Heads by Simon & Halbig. 1855 - on. Bisque head, composition ball-jointed body or kid body. **Trademarks:** Bébé Cosmopolite, Bébé de Réclame, Bébé Superior. **Mark:**

Germany   XANDWERCK

HEINRICH HANDWERCK   109-11
SIMON B HALBIG
                         Germany

Marked Handwerck Child Doll: Ca. 1885 - on. Perfect bisque socket head, original or good wig, sleep or set eyes, open mouth, pierced ears; ball-jointed body; dressed; entire doll in good condition.

No mold number:
14 - 16in (36 - 41cm)	$ 425 - 475*
19 - 21in (43 - 53cm)	525 - 575*
23 - 25in (58 - 64cm)	650 - 750*
28 - 30in (71 - 76cm)	1000 - 1200*
33 - 35in (84 - 89cm)	1450 - 1650*
42in (107cm)	2600 - 2800

Original lavish clothes and long mohair wig, 33in (84cm) **1900 - 2000**

#69, 79, 89, 99, 109, 119:
10 - 12in (25 - 31cm)	500 - 600*
14 - 16in (36 - 41cm)	550 - 600*
19 - 21in (43 - 53cm)	650 - 750*
23 - 25in (58 - 64cm)	800 - 900*
28 - 30in (71 - 76cm)	1200 - 1400*
33 - 35in (84 - 89cm)	1800 - 2100*
42in (107cm)	3500

#79, 89 closed mouth:
18 - 20in (46 - 51cm)	2300 - 2500
24in (61cm)	2800 - 3200

#189, open mouth,
18 - 20in (46 - 51cm) 850 - 950

#420 character five-piece toddler body, 22in (56cm) 900 - 1000**

*Allow extra for mint condition with original clothes.

**Not enough price samples to compute a reliable range.

18in (46cm) 189 Handwerck. *H & J Foulke, Inc.*

Max Handwerck

Max Handwerck, doll factory, Waltershausen, Thüringia, Germany. Some heads by Goebel. 1900 - on. Bisque head, ball-jointed composition or kid body.
Trademarks: Bébé Elite, Triumph-Bébé.
Mark:

Marked Bébé Elite Character: Perfect socket head with sleep eyes, open mouth with upper teeth, smiling character face; bent-limb composition baby body; appropriate clothes; all in good condition. (For photograph see *6th Blue Book*, page 171.)

14 - 16in (36 - 41cm)	**$ 425 - 475**
19 - 21in (48 - 53cm)	**550 - 650**
25in (64cm)	**800 - 900**

Marked Max Handwerck Child Doll: Perfect bisque socket head, original or good wig, set or sleep eyes, open mouth, pierced ears; original ball-jointed body; well dressed; all in good condition. Some mold #**283** or **297**.

16 - 18in (41 - 46cm)	**$ 375 - 400**
22 - 24in (56 - 61cm)	**525 - 575**
31 - 32in (79 - 81cm)	**1000 - 1100**
38 - 39in (97 - 99cm)	**2000 - 2200**

22in (56cm) 421 Max Handwerck.
H & J Foulke, Inc.

Hard Plastic, American (Unmarked)

FACTS

Various United States companies. 1948 into 1950s. All hard plastic.
Mark: None, or various letters and numbers, or "Made in U.S.A."

Unmarked Hard Plastic Doll: All hard plastic, jointed at neck, shoulders and hips; sleeping eyes with real eyelashes, synthetic wig in original set, open or closed mouth; original clothes; all in excellent condition.

14in (36cm)	$ 200 - 225
18in (46cm)	250 - 275
24in (61cm)	250 - 300

14in (36cm) hard plastic girl marked "Made in U.S.A.," all original. *June & Norman Verro.*

14in (36cm) hard plastic bride marked "Made in U.S.A.," all original. *June & Norman Verro.*

Hard Plastic, Italian

FACTS

Bonomi, Ottolini, Ratti, Furga and other Italian firms. Later 1940s and 1950s. Heavy hard plastic, sometimes painted, or plastic coated papier-mâché. **Mark:** Usually a wrist tag; company name on head;

       Ottolini - Lion head trademark.

Italian Hard Plastic: Heavy, fine quality material jointed at shoulders and hips; human hair wig, sleep eyes, sometimes flirty, often a character face; original clothes; all in excellent condition.

12in (31cm)	**$ 100 - 110**
15 - 17in (38 - 43cm)	**135 - 165**
19 - 21in (48 - 53cm)	**185 - 225**

19½in (49cm) Bonomi *Jenny*, all original. *H & J Foulke, Inc.*

Karl Hartmann

FACTS

Karl Hartmann, doll factory, Stockheim/
Upper Franconia, Germany. 1911 -
1926. Bisque head, jointed composition
body.

Mark:

Marked Karl Hartmann Doll: Perfect
bisque head, good wig, glass eyes, open
mouth; jointed composition body; suitable
clothing; all in good condition.

18 - 20in (46 - 51cm)	**$ 450 - 500**
22 - 24in (56 - 61cm)	**550 - 650**
28 - 30in (71 - 76cm)	**900 - 1000**

18in (46cm) Karl Hartmann girl.
H & J Foulke, Inc.

Hertel, Schwab & Co.

FACTS

Stutzhauser Porzellanfabrik, Hertel Schwab & Co., Stutzhaus, near Ohrdruf, Thüringia, Germany. 1910 - on. Bisque heads to be used on composition, cloth or leather bodies, all-bisque dolls, pincushion dolls.

Mark:

Made in Germany 151/2   152 4   Made in Germany 136/10   152 LW8C. 3

Marked Character Baby: Perfect bisque head, molded and painted hair or good wig, sleep or painted eyes, open or open/closed mouth with molded tongue; bent limb baby body; dressed; all in good condition.

#130, 142, 150, 151, 152:
10 - 12in (25 - 31cm)	**$ 425 - 475**
16 - 18in (41 - 46cm)	**625 - 675**
23 - 25in (58 - 64cm)	**900 - 1100**

#142 All-Bisque, 11in (28cm) painted eyes
750 - 850

#125 (so-called "Patsy Baby"):
11 - 12in (28 -31cm)   **800 - 900****

#126 (so called "Skippy"):
10 - 12in (25 - 31cm)   **800 - 1000****
19in (48cm) mulatto toddler
1650**

#169 Open mouth,
23in (58cm)   **1500****

**Not enough price samples to compute a reliable range.

25in (64cm) 152 character baby.
H & J Foulke, Inc.

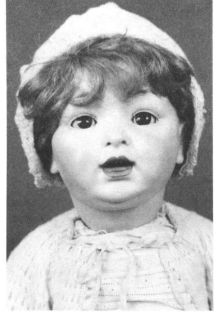

11in (28cm) 142 all-bisque baby.
H & J Foulke, Inc.

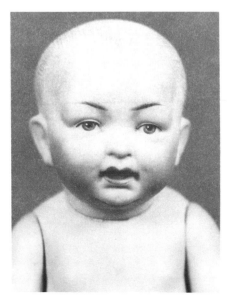

Hertel, Schwab & Co. continued

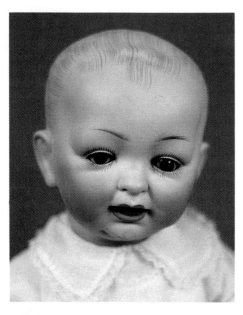

Child Doll: Ca. 1910. Perfect bisque head, mohair or human hair wig, sleep eyes, open mouth with upper teeth; good quality jointed composition body (some marked K & W); dressed; all in good condition. Mold **#136**.

16 - 18in (41 - 46cm)   **$ 500 - 550**
22 - 24in (56 - 61cm)   **600 - 700**
26in (66cm) mint condition, all
  orginal, lovely costume, at auction
                  1150

Top left: 15in (38cm) 142 character baby. *H & J Foulke, Inc.*

Bottom left: 24½in (62cm) 150 character baby. *H & J Foulke, Inc.*

Hertel, Schwab & Co. continued

Marked Character Child: Perfect bisque head, painted or sleeping eyes, closed mouth; jointed composition body; dressed; all in good condition.

#134, 149, 141:

16 - 18in (41 - 46cm)	**$5000 - 6000***
23in (58cm)	**8500***

#154 (closed mouth):

14 - 16in (36 - 41cm)	**2300 - 2500**

#154 (open mouth):

16 - 18in (41 - 46cm)	**1200 - 1400**

#169 (closed mouth):

19 - 21in (48 - 53cm) toddler

3500 - 4000

#127 (so-called "Patsy"):

16in (41cm)	**1100 - 1250***

*Glass eyes are more popular.

**Not enough price samples to compute a reliable range.

All-Bisque Doll: Jointed shoulders and hips; good wig, glass eyes, closed or open mouth; molded and painted shoes and stockings; undressed; all in good condition. Mold **#208**, often with **Prize Baby** label.

4 - 5in (10 - 13cm)	$ **225 - 275***
6in (15cm)	**350 - 375**
8in (20cm)	**500 - 550**
Swivel neck,	
7in (18cm)	**550 - 600**

*Do not pay as much for poor quality bisque.

24½in (62cm) 136 child. *H & J Foulke, Inc.*

Ernst Heubach

FACTS

Ernst Heubach, porcelain factory, Köppelsdorf, Thüringia, Germany. 1887 - on. Bisque head; kid, cloth or composition bodies.

Mark:

D.E.P. 1902   Heubach · Kopplesdorf.
                    300·14/0
2/0   Germany

Heubach Child Doll: Ca. 1888 - on. Perfect bisque head, good wig, sleep eyes, open mouth; kid, cloth or jointed composition body; dressed; all in good condition.

#275 or horseshoe, kid or cloth body:

13 - 15in (33 - 38cm)	$ 200 - 225
19 - 21in (48 - 53cm)	275 - 325
24in (61cm)	425 - 450

#250, composition body:

8 - 9in (20 - 23cm)	210 - 235
16 - 18in (41 - 46cm)	350 - 400
23 - 24in (58 - 61cm)	500 - 575
29 - 30in (74 - 76cm)	750 - 850

Painted bisque, **#250, 407**,

7 - 8in (18 - 20cm)	100 - 125

#312 SUR:

14in (36cm)	375 - 400
28in (71cm)	750 - 775
45in (113cm) at auction	3500

Left: 9in (23cm) 251 child, all original. *H & J Foulke, Inc.*

Below: 15in (38cm) 275 child, all original. *H & J Foulke, Inc.*

Character Children: 1910 - on. Perfect bisque shoulder head with molded hair in various styles, some with hair bows, painted eyes, open/closed mouth; cloth body with composition lower arms. (For photograph see *10th Blue Book,* page 242.)

#261, 262, 271 and others,
   12in (31cm)   **$400 - 450****

**Not enough price samples to compute a reliable range.

20in (51cm) 300 toddler. *H & J Foulke, Inc.*

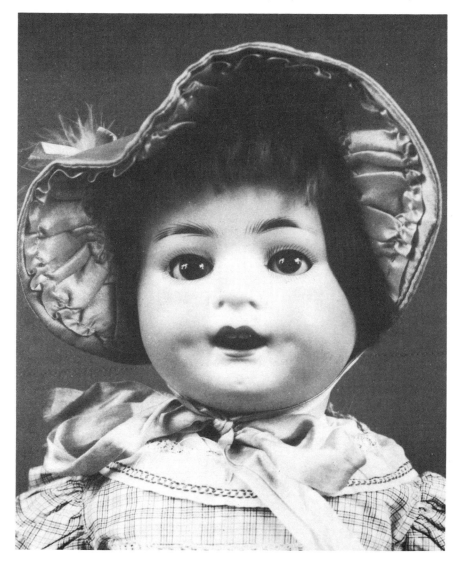

Ernst Heubach continued

Character Baby: 1910 - on. Perfect bisque head, good wig, sleep eyes, open mouth (sometimes also wobbly tongue and pierced nostrils); composition bent-limb baby or toddler body; dressed; all in good condition.

#300, 320, 342 and others:

6in (15cm)	$250 - 275
8 - 10in (20 - 25cm)	275 - 325
14 - 17in (36 - 43cm)	425 - 475
19 - 21in (48 - 53cm)	500 - 550
24 - 25in (61 - 64cm)	800 - 850

#300, 320, jointed composition body:

17in (43cm)	450
24in (61cm)	650

Toddler:

9in (23cm) five-piece body	350 - 400
15 - 17in (38 - 43cm)	500 - 550
23 - 25in (58 - 64cm)	850 - 950
Painted bisque, 28in (71cm) mint in box	950

Infant: Ca. 1925. Perfect bisque head, molded and painted hair, sleep eyes, closed mouth; cloth body, composition or celluloid hands, appropriate clothes; all in good condition.

#349, 339, 350:

13 - 16in (33 - 41cm)	$575 - 675**

#338, 340:

14 - 16in (36 - 41cm)	725 - 825**

**Not enough price samples to compute a reliable range.

Left: 28in (71cm) 342 toddler, painted bisque, all original and boxed. *H & J Foulke, Inc.*

Below: 16in (41cm) 349 baby. *H & J Foulke, Inc.*

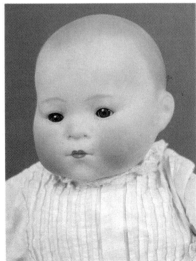

Gebrüder Heubach

FACTS

Gebrüder Heubach, porcelain factory, Licht and Sonneberg, Thüringia, Germany. 1820 - on; doll heads 1910 - on. Bisque head; kid, cloth or jointed composition body or composition bent-limb body, all-bisque.

Mark:

Heubach Character Child: Ca. 1910. Perfect bisque head, molded hair, glass or intaglio eyes, closed or open/closed mouth, character face; jointed composition or kid body; dressed; all in good condition. (For photographs of Heubach dolls see *Focusing On Dolls*, pages 30-68.)

#5636 laughing child, glass eyes:
12in (31cm)	**$1300 - 1500**
15 - 16in (38 - 41cm)	**2000 - 2200**

#5689 smiling child (For photograph see *6th Blue Book*, page 197.),
23 - 27in (58 - 69cm)	**2500 - 3000**

#5730 Santa, 19 - 21in (48 - 53cm)
2200 - 2500

#5777 Dolly Dimple:
19 - 22in (48 - 56cm)	**3000 - 3500**
Shoulder head, 15in (38cm)	**1000**

#6969, 6970, 7246, 7347, 7407, 8017, 8420 pouty child (must have glass eyes):
12 - 13in (31 - 33cm)	**2200 - 2600**
16 - 19in (41 - 48cm)	**3200 - 3700**
24in (61cm)	**4200 - 4500**

Below left: 20½in (52cm) 5730 *Santa. H & J Foulke, Inc.*

Below right: 16½in (42cm) 7246 pouty character girl. *Private Collection.*

#7604 and other smiling socket heads,
14 - 16in (36 - 41cm) **$ 800 - 1000**
#7602 and other socket head pouties (For photograph see page 5.),
14 - 16in (36 - 41cm) **750 - 950**
#7622 and other socket head pouties (wide lips),
14 - 17in (36 - 43cm) **1000 - 1250**
#7661 squinting eyes, crooked mouth,
19in (48cm) at auction **6750**
#7665 **Smiling**, 16in (41cm) **1800**
#7679 **Whistler** socket head:
10in (25cm) **800 - 900**
14in (36cm) **1100 - 1300**
#7684 **Screamer**, 16 - 19in (41 - 48cm)
  2500 - 3000
#7743 big ears, 17in (43cm) **5500**
#7764 singing girl, 16in (41cm)
  4000

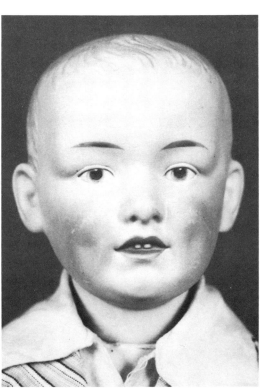

#7788 **Coquette**:
14in (36cm) **1150**
Shoulder head,
12in (31cm) **700 - 775**
#7865, 14in (36cm) **3000**
#7852 shoulder head, molded coiled braids, 16in (41cm) **2200**
#7853 shoulder head, downcast eyes,
14in (36cm) **1650 - 1850**
#7911, 8191 grinning:
11in (28cm) **900 - 1000**
15in (38cm) **1300 - 1400**
#7925, 7926 lady (For photograph see *9th Blue Book*, page 167.),
18 - 21in (46 - 53cm) **3000 - 3500**
#8050 smiling girl with hairbow (For photograph see *10th Blue Book*, page 157.),
18in (46cm) **8000**
#8381 **Princess Juliana**, 16in (41cm)
  8500 - 9500
#8550 molded tongue sticking out:
13in (33cm) intaglio eyes
  950 - 1050
13in (33cm) glass eyes
  1300 - 1400
#8556 (For photograph see *10th Blue Book*, page 157.)
  11,500
#9102 Cat, 6in (15cm)
  1150
#9141 Winker:
9in (23cm) glass eye
  1500
7in (18cm) painted eye
  850 - 950
#9467 Indian, 14in (36cm)
  2500 - 3000
#10532,
20 - 22in (51 - 53cm)
  1200 - 1300
#10586, 10633,
18 - 20in (46 - 51cm)
  750 - 850

19in (48cm) 7820 character boy.
H & J Foulke, Inc.

Gebrüder Heubach continued

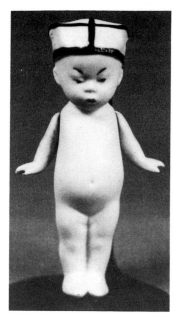

All-Bisque (For photographs see *Focusing on Dolls*, pages 71 - 77.):

Position Babies, 5in (13cm)	$ 500 - 700
Boy or Girl with bows or hair band:	
7 - 8in (18 - 20cm)	950 - 1150
9in (23cm)	1350 - 1650
Bunny Boy or **Girl**:	
5½in (14cm)	350 - 400
9in (23cm)	700 - 800
All-bisque boy or girl:	
4in (10cm)	300 - 400
5 - 6in (13 - 15cm)	650 - 750
Chin-Chin character,	
4in (10cm)	275 - 325
Action figures:	
6in (15cm)	500 - 700
4in (10cm)	275 - 375

Left: 4¼in (11cm) *Chin Chin*. *H & J Foulke, Inc.*

Below: 5in (13cm) 9743 position baby. *H & J Foulke, Inc.*

#11173 **Tiss Me** (For photograph see *8th Blue Book*, page 224.),
8in (20cm) **$1650 - 1850**
Shoulder heads, pouty or smiling (intaglio eyes):
14 - 16in (36 - 41cm)
750 - 950
20in (51cm) **1250 - 1350**
Walking, keywind mechanical
850 up*
Three-face Baby, 13in (33cm)
1800
Baby Bokaye, Bonnie Babe,
7 - 8in (18 - 20cm) **900 - 950**
#1907 **Jumeau** (For photograph see *10th Blue Book*, page 156.),
20 - 22in (51 - 56cm)
2400 - 2500

*Depending upon face.

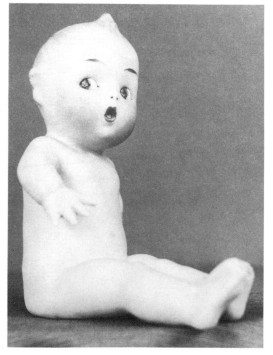

Gebrüder Heubach continued

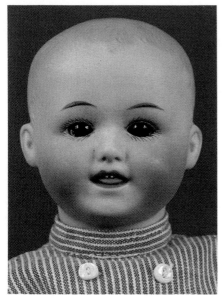

13in (33cm) 8550 character boy. *H & J Foulke, Inc.*

Heubach Babies: Ca. 1910. Perfect bisque head, molded hair, intaglio eyes, open or closed mouth, character face; composition bent-limb body; dressed; all in nice condition.

#6894, 7602, 6898, 7759 and other pouty babies:

4½in (12cm)	$ 225 - 275
6in (15cm)	275 - 300
10in (25cm)	425 - 475
14in (36cm)	650 - 750

#7604 laughing, 13 - 14in (33 - 36cm)
650 - 750

#7877, 7977 Baby Stuart:

10in (25cm)	1100 - 1200
16in (41cm)	1800
12in (31cm) glass eyes	2100

#7745 or 7746 laughing baby, at auction
4100

#8228 shoulder head **Baby Stuart**,
10½in (26cm)   750

#7959 molded pink cap, 10in (25cm)
1800 - 2000

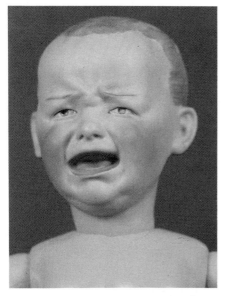

19in (48cm) 7684 *Screamer*. *Richard Wright Antiques.*

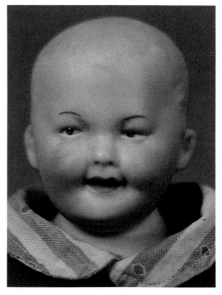

12½in (32cm) 7644 shoulder head smiling character boy. *H & J Foulke, Inc.*

FACTS

1986 - on. Hard vinyl and cloth.
Designer: Annette Himstedt
Distributor: Mattel, Inc., Hawthorne, CA., U.S.A. Dolls made in Spain.
Mark: Wrist tag with doll's name; cloth signature label on clothes; signature on lower back plate and on back of doll's head under wig.

Marked Himstedt Doll: Hard vinyl head swivels on long shoulder plate, cloth lower torso, vinyl arms and curved legs; inset eyes with real eyelashes, painted feathered eyebrows, molded upper eyelids, open nose, human hair wig; original cotton clothing, bare feet. All in excellent condition.

Bastian, all original. *H & J Foulke, Inc.*

26in (66cm) **Barefoot Children**, 1986:

Ellen	$ 650 - 750
Kathe	650 - 750
Paula	600 - 650
Fatou	900 - 1000
Bastian	600 - 650
Lisa	650 - 700

19 - 20in (48 - 51cm) **American Heartland Dolls**, 1987:

Timi	$ 350
Toni	350

31in (79cm) **The World Child Collection**, 1988:

Kasimir	$1100
Malin	800 - 1000
Machiko	700 - 800
Frederike	850 - 950
Makimura	600 - 700

26in (66cm) **Reflections of Youth**, 1989:

Adrienne	$ 600 - 650
Janka	500 - 600
Ayoka	800 - 900
Kai	450 - 550

Horsman

FACTS

E.I. Horsman Co., New York, N.Y., U.S.A. Also distributed dolls as a *verlager* for other manufacturers and imported French and German dolls. 1878 - on.

Billiken: 1909. Composition head with peak of hair at top of head, slanted slits for eyes, watermelon mouth; velvet or plush body; in very good condition. (For photograph see *9th Blue Book,* page 234.)
Mark: Cloth label on body; "Billiken" on right foot.

12in (31cm)	**$325 - 375**

Baby Bumps: 1910. Composition head with molded hair and painted features; stuffed cloth body. Good condition with some wear.
Mark: None.

12 - 14in (31 - 36cm)	**$200 - 250**
Black	**250 - 300**

Right: 13in (33cm) *Polly Pru*, original clothes, replaced shoes and socks. Courtesy of *Ursula Mertz.*

Below: Black *Baby Bumps* in tagged romper suit. *H & J Foulke, Inc.*

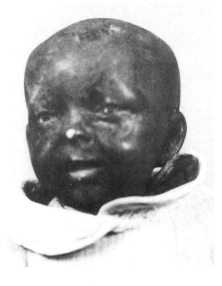

Can't Break 'Em Characters: Ca. 1910. Heads and hands of "Can't Break 'Em" composition, hard stuffed cloth bodies with swivel joints at shoulders and hips; molded hair, painted eyes, character faces; appropriate clothes; all in good condition.
Mark: "E.I.H.1911"

10 - 12in (25 - 31cm)	**$165 - 195***
Polly Pru, 13in (33cm)	**275 - 325**

*Allow extra for an unusual model.

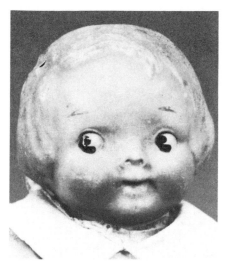

16in (41cm) *Campbell Kid*, all original. *H & J Foulke, Inc.*

Campbell Kid: 1910 - 1914. Designed by Grace Drayton. Marked composition head with flange neck, molded and painted bobbed hair, painted round eyes to the side, watermelon mouth; original cloth body, composition arms, cloth legs and feet; all in fair condition.
Mark: On head:

E.I.H. © 1910

Cloth label on sleeve:

The Campbell Kids Trademark by Joseph Campbell Mfg. by E. I. HORSMAN Co.

10 - 13in (25 - 33cm)	**$225 - 250**
16in (41cm)	**300 - 350**

Peterkin: 1914 - 1930. All-composition with character face, molded hair, painted eyes to side, watermelon mouth; various boy and girl clothing or simply a large bow; all in good condition. (For photograph see *9th Blue Book*, page 234.)
11in (28cm)   **$275 - 325****

** Not enough price samples to compute a reliable range.

Gene Carr Character: 1916. Composition head with molded and painted hair, eyes painted open or closed, wide smiling mouth with teeth; cloth body with composition hand; original or appropriate clothes; all in good condition. Names such as: **"Snowball"** (black boy); **"Mike"** and **"Jane"** (eyes open); **"Blink"** and **"Skinney"** (eyes closed). Designed by Bernard Lipfert from Gene Carr's cartoon characters. (For photograph see *10th Blue Book*, page 246.)
Mark: None.

13 - 14in (33 - 36cm)	**$300 - 325**
Black **Snowball**	**450 - 550**

Mama Dolls: Ca. 1920 - on. Composition head, cloth body, composition arms and lower legs; mohair wig or molded hair, sleep eyes; original clothes; all in very good condition.
Mark: "E. I. H. Co." or "HORSMAN"
Babies:

12 - 14in (31 - 36cm)	**$150 - 185**
18 - 20in (46 - 51cm)	**250 - 275**

Girls, including **Rosebud**:

14 - 16in (36 - 41cm)	**250 - 275**
22 - 24in (56 - 61cm)	**325 - 375**

Peggy Ann,

20in (51cm)	**300 - 350**

20in (51cm) *Peggy Ann*, all original. *H & J Foulke, Inc.*

Horsman continued

Ella Cinders: 1925. Composition head with molded hair, painted eyes; cloth body with composition arms and lower legs; original clothes; all in fair condition. From the comic strip by Bill Conselman and Charlie Plumb, for the Metropolitan Newspaper Service. (For photograph see *8th Blue Book*, page 229.)
Mark: "1925 © MNS"
    18in (46cm)   **$500 - 600**

Baby Dimples: 1928. Composition head with molded and painted hair, tin sleep eyes, open mouth, smiling face; soft cloth body with composition arms and legs; original or appropriate old clothes; all in good condition.
Mark: "©
      E. I. H. CO. INC."
    16 - 18in (41 - 46cm)   **$250 - 300**
    22 - 24in (56 - 61cm)   **350 - 400**

Left: 11in (28cm) *HEbee SHEbee*, all original. *H & J Foulke, Inc.*

Below: 18in (46cm) *Baby Dimples*, all original. *H & J Foulke, Inc.*

Jackie Coogan: 1921. Composition head with molded hair, painted eyes, closed mouth; cloth torso with composition hands; appropriate clothes; all in good condition. (For photograph see *8th Blue Book*, page 228.)
Mark: "E.I.H. Co. 19©21"
    14in (36cm)   **$450 - 550**

HEbee-SHEbee: 1925. All-composition, jointed at shoulders and hips, painted eyes, molded white chemise and real ribbon or wool ties in molded shoes; all in good condition. Blue shoes indicate a HEbee, pink ones a SHEbee.
    11in (28cm)   **$500 - 550**
    Fair condition (some peeling)
                      275 - 325
    Mint, all original   **700 - 750**

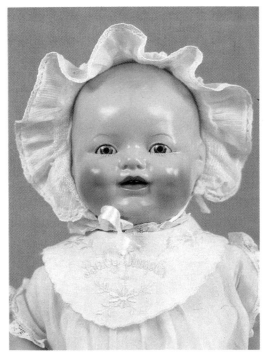

Child Dolls: Ca. 1930s and 1940s. All-composition with swivel neck, shoulders and hips; mohair wig, sleep eyes; original clothes; all in good condition.

Mark: "HORSMAN"

13 - 14in (33 - 36cm)	**$195 - 225**
16 - 18in (41 - 46cm)	**265 - 300**

Chubby toddler, 16 - 18in (41 - 46cm)

285 - 325

Jo-Jo, 1937. 12in (31cm) toddler

200 - 225

Jeanie, 1937. 14in (36cm)   **225 - 250**

Naughty Sue, 1937. 16in (41cm)

275 - 300

Whatsit Dolls, 1937. 14in (36cm)

275 - 300

Cindy: Ca. 1950. All-hard plastic, sleep eyes, open mouth with upper teeth and tongue, synthetic wig with braids.

Mark: "170 made in USA."

Walker, 16in (41cm)   **200 - 250**

16in (41cm) all original toddler. *H & J Foulke, Inc.*

Campbell Kid: 1948. Unmarked all-composition, molded painted hair, painted eyes to the side, watermelon mouth; painted white socks and black slippers; original clothes; all in good condition.

12in (31cm)   **$325 - 375**

15in (38cm) hard plastic *Cindy. H & J Foulke, Inc.*

Horsman continued

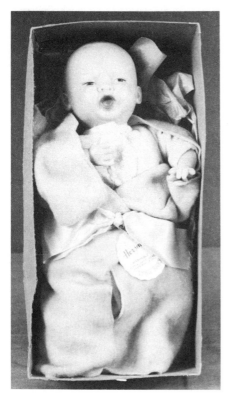

16in (41cm) *Tynie Baby*, all original. *H & J Foulke, Inc.*

15in (38cm) vinyl *Tynie Baby*, ca. 1950, all original. *H & J Foulke, Inc.*

Box for vinyl *Tynie Baby*. *H & J Foulke, Inc.*

Marked Tynie Baby: 1924. Bisque solid dome infant head with sleep eyes, closed mouth, slightly frowning face; cloth body with composition arms; appropriate clothes; all in good condition. Designed by Bernard Lipfert. (For photographs see *9th Blue Book*, page 237 and *10th Blue Book*, page 248.)

Mark: © 1924
E. I. Horsman Inc.
Made in
Germany

Bisque head, 12in (31cm) h.c.	**$750 - 800**	
All original with pin	**900**	
Composition head, 15in (38cm) long		
	275 - 300	
All-bisque with swivel neck, glass eyes,		
wigged or solid dome head,		
8 - 10in (20 - 25cm)	**1700 - 2000**	
Vinyl, Ca. 1950 crying face,		
15in (38cm) boxed	**90 - 110**	

Mary Hoyer

FACTS

The Mary Hoyer Doll Mfg. Co., Reading Pa., U.S.A. Ca. 1925 - on. First all-composition, later all-hard plastic. 14 and 18in (36 and 46cm).
Mark: Embossed on torso:
"The
Mary Hoyer
Doll"
or in a circle:
"ORIGINAL
Mary Hoyer
Doll"

Marked Mary Hoyer: Material as above; swivel neck; jointed shoulders and hips, original wig, sleep eyes with eyelashes, closed mouth; all in excellent condition. Original tagged factory clothes or garments made at home from Mary Hoyer patterns.

Composition, 14in (36cm)   **$350 - 400**
Hard plastic:
  14in (36cm)   **425 - 500**
  14in (36cm) boy with caracul wig
                              500 - 550
  18in (46cm), Gigi   **550 - 700**

18in (46cm) Mary Hoyer, all original. *H & J Foulke, Inc.*

Hülss

FACTS

Adolf Hülss, doll factory, Waltershausen, Thüringia, Germany; heads by Simon & Halbig. 1913 - on. Bisque socket heads, composition bodies (later heads of painted bisque)

Mark:

SIMON & HALBIG

Made in Germany 156/32

Marked Hülss Character Baby: 1925 - on. Mold number **156**. Perfect bisque head with good wig, sleep eyes, open mouth with teeth and tongue, smiling face; composition bent-limb body; nicely dressed; all in good condition.

15 - 17in (38 - 43cm)
                    $ 575 - 650
Toddler:
    11in (28cm)   **700 - 750**
    15 - 16in (38 - 41cm)
                     750 - 850*
    22 - 24in (56 - 61cm)
                   1350 - 1650*

Marked Hülss Child: 1920s. Mold number **176**. Perfect bisque head with good wig, flirty sleep eyes, open mouth with teeth and tongue. Jointed composition body with high knee joint; dressed; all in good condition.

    18in (46cm)   **$ 750 - 850****
    30in (76cm)   **1500 - 1650****

* Allow $50 - 100 extra for flirty eyes.
** Not enough price samples to compute a reliable range.

9¾in (25cm) 156 Toddler, all original. *H & J Foulke, Inc.*

Marked Huret Doll: China or bisque shoulder head, good wig, painted or glass eyes, closed mouth; kid body; beautifully dressed; all in good condition.

16 - 19in (41 - 48cm) **$ 5000 - 6000**

Wood body, 16 - 19in (41 - 48cm)
8000 - 9000 up
Gutta-percha body, 16 - 19in (41 -48cm)
**10,000 up **
Child, wood body, 16in (41cm)
**20,000 up **

** Not enough price samples to compute a reliable average.

17in (43cm) Signed Huret lady on wood body. *Private Collection.*

Ideal

FACTS

Ideal Novelty and Toy Co., Brooklyn, N.Y., U.S.A. 1907 - on.

Uneeda Kid: 1914 - 1919. Composition head with molded brown hair, blue painted eyes, closed mouth; cloth body with composition arms and legs with molded black boots; original bloomer suit, yellow slicker and rain hat; carrying a box of Uneeda Biscuits; all in good condition, showing some wear. (For photograph see page 216.)

16in (41cm)	**$450 - 475**
24in (61cm)	**650 - 700****

Snoozie: 1933. Composition head, character expression with yawning mouth, sleeping eyes, molded hair, composition arms and legs or rubber arms, cloth body; baby clothes; all in good condition. 13, 16 and 20 in (33, 41 and 51cm). (For photograph see *7th Blue Book*, page 216.)

Mark: ©

By B. LIPFERT

16 - 20in (41 - 51cm)   **$250 - 300**

** Not enough price samples to compute a reliable range.

Shirley Temple: 1935. For detailed information see pages 327-329.

Mama Doll: Ca. 1920 - on. Composition head, cloth body, composition arms and lower legs; mohair wig or molded hair, sleep eyes; appropriate old clothes; all in very good condition.

Mark:

14 - 16in (36 - 41cm)
                              $225 - 250
Characters, 14 - 16in (36 - 41cm)
                              225 - 250

Flossie Flirt: (For photograph see page 216.)
20in (51cm)   **$275 - 325**
Flirty-eyed Baby, 1938.
16 - 18in (41 - 46cm)
                              225 - 275

Betsy Wetsy: 1937 - on. Composition head with molded hair, sleep eyes; soft rubber body jointed at neck, shoulders and hips; drinks, wets; appropriate clothes; all in good condition. This doll went through many changes including hard plastic head on rubber body, later vinyl body, later completely vinyl. Various sizes.
Mark: "IDEAL"
14 - 16in (36 - 41cm)
    rubber body   **$110 - 135**

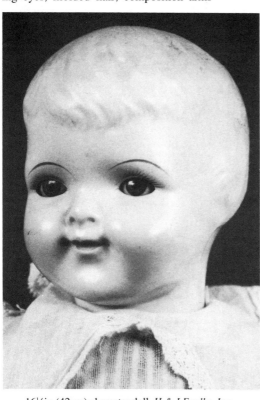

16½in (42cm) character doll. *H & J Foulke, Inc.*

Snow White: 1937. All-composition, jointed at neck, shoulders and hips; black mohair wig, lashed sleep eyes, open mouth; original dress with velvet bodice and cape, and rayon skirt, with figures of seven dwarfs; in good condition. 11in (28 cm), 13in (33cm) and 18in (46cm) sizes. (For photograph see *Doll Classics*, page 190.)
Mark: On body:
"SHIRLEY TEMPLE/18"
On dress: "An Ideal Doll"

11 - 13in (28 - 33cm)	**$450 - 475**
18in (46cm)	**550 - 650**

Molded black hair, painted blue bow, painted eyes,

13 - 14in (33 - 36cm)	**190 - 225**

Shirley Temple-Type Girl: 1930s - 1940s. All-composition with jointed neck, shoulders and hips; lashed sleeping eyes (sometimes flirty), open mouth with teeth; all original; very good condition.
Mark: IDEAL
            18
Betty Jane or **Little Princess:**

14in (36cm)	**$250 - 275**
18in (46cm)	**300 - 350**

Deanna Durbin: 1938. All-composition, jointed at neck, shoulders and hips; original human hair or mohair wig, sleep eyes, smiling mouth with teeth; original clothing; all in good condition. Various sizes. (For photograph see page 217.)
Mark: Metal button with picture:
"DEANNA DURBIN,
IDEAL DOLL, U.S.A."

14in (36cm)	**$450 - 500**
20 - 21in (51 - 53cm)	**625 - 675**
24in (61cm)	**850**

Top: 14in (36cm) *Little Princess*, all original. *H & J Foulke, Inc.*

Bottom: 22in (56cm) *Magic Skin* baby, all original. *H & J Foulke, Inc.* (For further information see page 218.)

Ideal continued

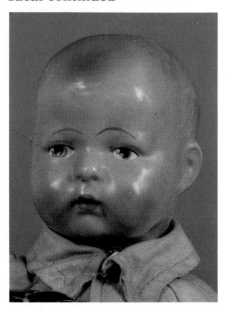

16in (41cm) *Uneeda Kid*. *H & J Foulke, Inc.* (For further information see page 214.)

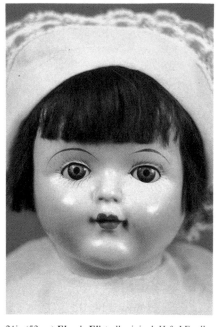

21in (53cm) *Flossie Flirt*, all original. *H & J Foulke, Inc.* (For further information see page 214.)

12in (31cm) *Fanny Brice* as *Baby Snooks*. *H & J Foulke, Inc.* (For further information see page 218.)

18in (46cm) *Saralee*, all original. *H & J Foulke, Inc.* (For further information see page 219.)

Opposite page: 14in (36cm) *Deanna Durbin*, all original. *H & J Foulke, Inc.* (For further information see page 215.)

Ideal continued

Judy Garland as Dorothy of the Wizard of Oz: 1939. All-composition, jointed at neck, shoulders and hips; dark human hair wig, dark sleep eyes, open mouth with teeth; original dress; all in good condition. (For photograph see *10th Blue Book*, page 159.)
Mark: On head: "IDEAL DOLL"
MADE IN U.S.A.
Body: U.S.A.
16

16in (41cm)	$1000 - 1200
Replaced dress	850

Flexy Dolls: 1938 - on. Head, hands and feet of composition; arms and legs of flexible metal cable, torso of wire mesh; in original clothes; all in good condition.
Mark: On head: "Ideal Doll"
12in (31cm)

Baby Snooks (Fanny Brice) (For photograph see page 216.)	$ 250 -	275
Mortimer Snerd	250 -	275
Soldier	200 -	225
Children	200 -	225

Composition and wood segmented characters: 1940. Molded composition heads with painted features, wood segmented bodies. Label on front torso gives name of character. (For photograph see *10th Blue Book*, page 160.)

Pinocchio, 10½in (27cm)	$ 265 -	285
King-Little, 14in (36cm)	225 -	250
Jiminy Cricket, 9in (23cm)	325 -	375

Magic Skin Baby and Plassie: 1940 - on. Composition or hard plastic head with molded hair, sleep eyes, closed or open mouth; stuffed latex rubber body; appropriate clothes; all in good condition. (For photograph see page 215.)
Mark: On head: "IDEAL"

14 - 15in (36 - 38cm)	$100 - 150
22in (56cm)	200 - 225
14in (36cm) Plassie, mint in box, at auction	235
Sparkle Plenty, 1947.	
15in (38cm) Baby	100 - 135
Toddler	125 - 175

Toni and P-90 and P-91 Family: 1948 - on. Series of girl dolls. Most were completely of hard plastic with jointed neck, shoulders and hips, nylon wig, sleep eyes, closed mouth; original clothes; all in excellent condition. Various sizes, but most are 14in (36cm).
Mark: On head: "IDEAL DOLL"
On body: "IDEAL DOLL
P-90
Made in USA"

Right: 21in
(53cm) P-93 *Toni*,
original dress.
H & J Foulke, Inc.

Far right: 14in
(36cm) *Miss
Curity. H & J
Foulke, Inc.*

Toni:

14 - 15in (36 - 38cm) P-90	**$250 - 300**
Mint in box	**400**
21in (53cm) P-93	**400 - 450**
22½in (57cm) P-94	**500****

Mary Hartline:

14in (36cm) P-90	**250 - 300**
22in (56cm) P-94	**550****

Betsy McCall, vinyl head,

14in (36cm)	**175 - 200**

Harriet Hubbard Ayer, vinyl head,

14in (36cm)	**175 - 200**
Miss Curity, 14in (36cm)	**250 - 300**
Sara Ann, 14in (36cm)	**250 - 300**

**Not enough price samples to compute a reliable range.

Saralee: 1950. Black vinyl head, painted hair, sleep eyes, open/closed mouth; cloth body, vinyl limbs; original clothes; all in excellent condition. Designed by Sarah Lee Creech; modeled by Sheila Burlingame. (For photograph see page 216.)

17 - 18in (43 - 46cm)	**$275 - 325**
Undressed	**125**

Bonnie Braids: 1951. Vinyl character head, molded hair, sleeping eyes; hard plastic body; original clothes; all in excellent condition.

13in (33cm)	**$150 - 200**
Mint in comic strip box	**325 - 350**

Saucy Walker: 1951. All-hard plastic, jointed at neck, shoulders and hips with walking mechanism; synthetic wig, flirty eyes, open mouth with tongue and teeth; original clothes; all in excellent condition. (For photograph see *8th Blue Book*, page 238.)

Mark: "IDEAL DOLL"

16 - 17in (41 - 43cm)	**$110 - 135**
20 - 22in (51 - 56cm)	**165 - 185**

Miss Revlon: 1955. Vinyl head with rooted hair, sleep eyes, closed mouth, earrings; hard plastic body with jointed waist and knees, high-heeled feet, vinyl arms with polished nails; original clothes; all in excellent condition. (For photograph see *6th Blue Book*, page 213.)

Mark: On head and body:
"IDEAL DOLL"

18in (46cm)	**$150 - 175**
20in (51cm)	**200 - 225**

Little Miss Revlon, 10½in (27cm)

	85 - 100

Peter and Patti Playpal: 1960. Vinyl heads with rooted hair, sleep eyes; hard vinyl body, jointed at shoulders and hips; appropriate clothes; all in excellent condition. (For photograph see *7th Blue Book*, page 221.)

Mark: Peter: "IDEAL TOY CORP.
BE-35-38"
Patty: "IDEAL DOLL
G-35"

35 - 36in (89 - 91cm):

Peter	**$325 - 375**
Patti, 18in (46cm)	**275 - 300**
Patti 42in (107cm)	**150 - 175**
Daddy's Girl, 29in (74cm)	**850**
Miss Ideal	**375 - 400**
Patti, ca. 1980 mint in box	**100**

13in (33cm) *Bonnie Braids*, all original. *H & J Foulke, Inc.*

Jullien

FACTS

Jullien, Jeune of Paris, France. 1875 -
1904 when joined with S.F.B.J. Bisque
head, composition and wood body.
Mark: "JULLIEN" with size number

JuLLiEN

1

Marked Jullien Bébé:
Bisque head, lovely wig, paperweight eyes,
closed mouth, pierced ears; jointed wood
and composition body; pretty old clothes;
all in good condition.

17 - 19in (43 - 48cm)	**$3500 - 3700**
24 - 26in (61 - 66cm)	**4200 - 4500**
Open mouth,	
19 - 21in (48 - 53cm)	**1600 - 1800**
29 - 30in (74 - 76cm)	**3000 - 3300**

29in (74cm) Jullien. *Jensen's Antique Dolls.*

Jumeau

FACTS

Maison Jumeau, Paris, France. 1842 - on. Bisque head, kid or composition body.
Trademark: Bébé Jumeau (1886)
Bébé Prodige (1886)
Bébé Francais (1896)

Poupée Peau Fashion Lady: Late 1860s - on. Usually marked with number only on head, blue stamp on body. Perfect bisque swivel head on shoulder plate, old wig, paperweight eyes, closed mouth, pierced ears; all-kid body or kid with bisque lower arms and legs; appropriate old clothes; all in good condition.
Mark:

JUMEAU
MEDAILLE D'OR
PARIS

Very Pretty Face:
15 - 17in (38 - 43cm) $ **3200 - 3500***
5½in (14cm) head and shoulder plate
only   **2900**
Standard face:
12 - 13in (31 - 33cm)   **2300 - 2600***
18 - 20in (46 - 51cm)   **3200 - 3500***

Wood body with bisque limbs,
18in (46cm)   **5000****
Later face with large eyes:
10 - 12in (25 - 31cm)   **1800 - 2000**
14 - 15in (36 - 38cm)   **2400 - 2500**
So-called "Portrait Face":
19 - 21in (48 - 53cm)   **5500 - 5800**
22in (56cm) boxed   **8500**
Wood body, 20in (51cm)   **11,000**

*Allow extra for all original clothes.
**Not enough price samples to compute a reliable range.

Period Clothes:
Bébé Clothing:
Jumeau shift $ **300 - 350**
Jumeau shoes   **400 - 500**
Jumeau dress   **650 up**

Left: Jumeau *poupee peau* standard face, all original. *H & J Foulke, Inc.*

Right: Jumeau *poupee peau* so-called "Portrait Face." *Private Collection.*

Jumeau continued

Long-Face Triste Bébé: Ca. 1870s. Usually marked with number only on head, blue
stamp on body. Perfect bisque socket head
with beautiful wig, blown glass eyes, closed
mouth, applied pierced ears; jointed composition body with straight wrists; lovely
clothes; all in good condition. (For photograph see page 12.)

20 - 21in (51 - 53cm)	**$16,000 - 20,000**
28 - 30in (71 - 76cm)	**25,000**

Size   9 = 21in (53cm)
       11 = 24in (61cm)
13, 14 = 29 - 30in (74 - 76cm)

Portrait Jumeau: Ca. 1870s. Usually
marked with size number only on head, blue
stamp on body; skin or other good wig;
unusually large paperweight eyes, closed
mouth, pierced ears; jointed composition
body with straight wrists; nicely dressed;
all in good condition.

Standard faces:

10 - 12in (25 - 30cm)	**$ 5000 - 5500***
14 - 15in (36 - 38cm)	**6000 - 7000***
18 - 19in (46 - 48cm)	**7000 - 8000***
23in (58cm	**11,500**

*Allow extra for original clothes.

Incised "Déposé": (For photograph see page
224.)

16 - 18in (41 - 46cm)	**7500 - 8500**

Almond-eyed:

10 - 12in (25 - 31cm)	**6500 - 7000**
17 - 19in (43 - 48cm)	**9500 - 10,500**
23in (58cm)	**16,000 - 17,000**

Extreme almond-eyed: (For photograph see
page 225.)

17in (43cm)	**20,000 up**
22in (56cm)	**35,000 up**

E.J.Bébé: Ca. 1880. Head incised as below, blue stamp on body. Perfect bisque
socket head with good wig, paperweight
eyes, closed mouth, pierced ears; jointed
composition body with straight wrists, early
models with separate ball joints; lovely
clothes; all in good condition.

Mark:

E. 8 J.

10in (25cm)	**$ 5000 - 5500**
14 - 16in (36 - 41cm)	**5700 - 6200**
19 - 21in (48 - 53cm)	**6500 - 7200**
25 - 26in (64 - 66cm)	**8500 - 10,000**

Later Tête-style face:

18 - 19in (46 - 48cm)	**5000 - 5500**
25 - 26in (64 - 66cm)	**6800 - 7500**

Early Mark:

$\overset{8}{E.J.}$

Soft eyebrows, applied ears, threaded eyes,

20 - 22in (51 - 56cm)	**$ 9000 - 11,000**
EJA, 26in (66cm) only	**25,000 - 30,000**

18½in (47cm) standard Portrait Jumeau face,
original fashion lady body. *Private Collection.*

Incised "Jumeau Déposé" Bébé Ca. 1880. Head incised as below, blue stamp on body. Perfect bisque socket head with good wig, paperweight eyes, closed mouth, pierced ears; jointed composition body with straight wrists; lovely clothes; all in good condition.

Mark: Incised on head:

DÉPOSÉ
JUMEAU
8

15 - 17in (38 - 43cm)	**$5500 - 6000**
20 - 21in (51 - 53cm)	**6700 - 7000**
24 - 26in (61 - 66cm)	**7500 - 8500**

Tête Jumeau Bébé: 1879 - 1899, then through S.F.B.J. Red stamp on head as indicated below, blue stamp or "Bebe Jumeau" oval sticker on body. Perfect bisque head, original or good French wig, beautiful stationary eyes, closed mouth, pierced ears; jointed composition body with jointed or straight wrists; original or lovely clothes; all in good condition. (For photograph see following page.)

Mark:

DÉPOSÉ
TETE JUMEAU
B^{TE} SGDG
6

10in (25cm) #1	**$3800 - 4200***
12 - 13in (31 - 33cm)	**2800 - 3100***
15 - 16in (38 - 41cm)	**3400 - 3800***
18 - 20in (46 - 51cm)	**3800 - 4000***
21 - 23in (53 - 58cm)	**4000 - 4200***
25 - 27in (64 - 69cm)	**4500 - 5000***
34 - 36in (86 - 91cm)	**7000 - 7500**
Lady body, 20in (51cm)	**5000 - 5500**

Open mouth: (For photograph see page 226.)

14 - 16in (36 - 41cm)	**2200 - 2500**
20 - 22in (51 - 56cm)	**2800 - 3000**
24 - 25in (61 - 64cm)	**3200 - 3300**
27 - 29in (69 - 74cm)	**3500**
32 - 34in (81 - 86cm)	**3800 - 4000**

* Allow extra for original clothes.

21in (53cm) incised "Déposé Jumeau." *Esther Schwartz Collection.*

19in (48cm) EJ size 8. *Private Collection.*

224

18½in (47cm) incised "Déposé" Portrait Jumeau. *H & J Foulke, Inc.* (For further information see page 222.)

19in (48cm) black incised "Déposé Jumeau," very rare. *Private Collection.* (For further information see preceding page.)

18in (46cm) Portrait Jumeau face with early EJ initials low on neck. *H & J Foulke, Inc.* (For further information see page 222.)

25in (64cm) Tête Jumeau. *H & J Foulke, Inc.* (For further information see preceding page.)

Extreme almond-eyed Portrait Jumeau. *Nancy A. Smith Collection.*
(For further information see page 222.)

Jumeau continued

Approximate sizes of E.J.s and Têtes:

1 = 10in (25cm)	8 = 19in (48cm)
2 = 11in (28cm)	9 = 20in (51cm)
3 = 12in (31cm)	10 = 21 - 22in (53 - 56cm)
4 = 13in (33cm)	11 = 24 - 25in (61 - 64cm)
5 = 14 -15in (36 - 38cm)	12 = 26 - 27in (66 - 69cm)
6 = 16in (41cm)	13 = 29 - 30in (74 - 76cm)
7 = 17in (43cm)	

22in (56cm) open-mouth Jumeau. *H & J Foulke, Inc.* (For further information see page 223.)

#230 Character Child: Ca. 1910. Perfect bisque socket head, open mouth, set or sleep eyes, good wig; jointed composition body; dressed; all in good condition. (For face see *10th Blue Book* page 369. Same mold as S.F.B.J. **230**.)

16in (41cm)	**$ 1450**
21 - 23in (53 - 58cm)	**1800 - 2000**

#1907 Jumeau Child: Ca. 1907 - on. Sometimes red-stamped "Tête Jumeau." Perfect bisque head, good quality wig, set or sleep eyes, open mouth, pierced ears; jointed composition body; nicely dressed; all in good condition.

16 - 18in (41 - 46cm)	**$ 2300 - 2500**
24 - 25in (61 - 64cm)	**3000 - 3200**
33 - 34in (84 - 87cm)	**3800 - 4000**

Jumeau Characters: Ca. 1900. Tête Jumeau mark. Perfect bisque head with glass eyes, character expression; jointed composition body; appropriately dressed; all in good condition.

#203, 208 and others: **$50,000 up**
Two-face   **12,000 - 15,000**
#221 Great Ladies, 10 - 11in (25 - 28cm)
     all original   **550 - 650**

Princess Elizabeth Jumeau: 1938 through S.F.B.J. Perfect bisque socket head highly colored, good wig, glass flirty eyes, closed mouth; jointed composition body; dressed; all in good condition. (For photograph see *9th Blue Book*, page 254.)

Mark: **Body Incised:**

18in (46cm) smiling side of two-face Jumeau. *Carole Jean Stoessel Zvonar Collection.*

71   UNIS FRANCE   149
306
JUMEAU
1938
PARIS

JUMEAU
PARIS
Princess

18 - 19in (46 - 48cm)	**$ 1400 - 1600**
32 - 33in (81 - 84cm)	**2400 - 2500**

K & K

FACTS

K & K Toy Co., New York, N.Y. U.S.A.
1915 - on. Bisque or composition head;
cloth and composition body.

Mark:

Germany
K & K
60
Thuringia

K. & K.
39
Made in Germany.

K & K Character Child: Perfect bisque shoulder head, mohair wig, sleep eyes, open mouth with teeth; cloth body with composition arms and legs or cloth or leather legs; appropriate clothes; all in good condition.

19 - 22in (48 - 56cm)	**$475 - 525**
Shoulder head only	**225 - 250**

Composition head, some marked "Fiberoid," original clothes.

20 - 24in (51 - 61cm)	**275 - 325**

Wear and light crazing, replaced clothes
150

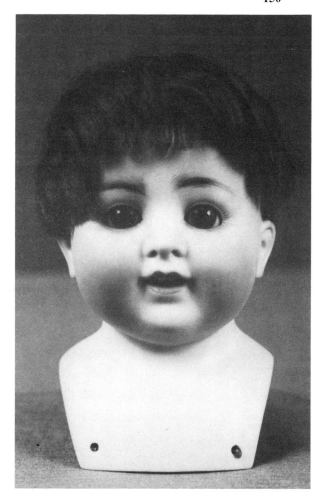

K & K bisque shoulder head character child. *H & J Foulke, Inc.*

Kamkins

FACTS

Louise R. Kampes Studios, Atlantic City, N.J. U.S.A. 1919 - 1928 and perhaps longer. Molded mask face, cloth stuffed torso and limbs. About 18 - 20in (46 - 51cm).

Mark: Red paper heart on left side of chest:

KAMKINS
A DOLLY MADE TO LOVE
PATENTED
FROM
L R KAMPES
ATLANTIC CITY
N. J.

Also sometimes stamped with black on foot or back of head:

KAMKINS
A DOLLY MADE TO LOVE
PATENTED BY L.R. KAMPES
ATLANTIC CITY,   N.J.

Marked Kamkins: Molded mask face with painted features, wig; cloth body and limbs; original clothing; all in excellent condition.

18 - 20in (46 - 51cm)	**$1200***
Fair to good condition	**750 - 850**

*Allow more for an especially nice example.

Kamkins, all original. *Private Collection.*

FACTS

Kämmer & Reinhardt of Waltershausen, Thüringia, Germany. Heads often by Simon & Halbig. 1886 - on. Bisque socket head, composition body, later papier-mâché, rubber or celluloid head, composition bodies. Size: 4½ - 42in (11 - 100cm).

Trademarks: Majestic Doll, Mein Liebling (My Darling), Der Schelm (The Flirt), Die Kokette (The Coquette).

Mark: In 1895 began using K(star)R, sometimes with "S & H." Mold number for bisque socket head begins with a 1; for papier-mâché, 9; for celluloid, 7. Size number is height in centimeters.

SIMON & HALBIG
116/A
50

Child Doll: 1886 - 1895. Perfect bisque head, original or good wig, sleep or set eyes, open or closed mouth, pierced ears; ball-jointed composition body; dressed; all in good condition.

#192:

Closed mouth:

6 - 7in (15 - 18cm)	$ 600 - 700*
10in (25cm)	900
16 - 18in (41 - 46cm)	2500 - 2800
22 - 24in (56 - 61cm)	3000 - 3500

Open mouth:

7 - 8in (18 - 20cm)	500 - 600*
12in (31cm)	700
14 - 16in (36 - 41cm)	775 - 875
20 - 22in (51 - 56cm)	1150 - 1300
26 - 28in (66 - 71cm)	1600 - 1900
8in (20cm) in original presentation trunk with wardrobe	2100 - 2300

*Allow more for a fully-jointed body.

8in (20cm) 192 child in original presentation trunk with wardrobe. *H & J Foulke, Inc.*

Kämmer & Reinhardt continued

Child Doll: 1895 - 1930s. Perfect bisque head, original or good wig, sleep eyes, open mouth, pierced ears; dressed; ball-jointed composition body; all in good condition. Numbers 15-100 low on neck are centimeter sizes, not mold numbers.

#191, 290, 403 or size number only:

12 - 14in (31 - 36cm)	$ 600 - 700*+
16 - 17in (41 - 43cm)	750 - 800*+
19 - 21in (48 - 53cm)	850 - 950*+
23 - 25in (58 - 64cm)	1050 - 1150*
29 - 31in (74 - 79cm)	1400 - 1600*
35 - 36in (89 - 91cm)	2000 - 2200*
39 - 42in (99 - 107cm)	3200 - 3600*

*Allow $50-100 additional for flirty eyes; allow $200 extra for flapper body.

+Allow 50% additional for fantastic totally original clothes, wig and shoes in pristine condition.

Tiny Child Doll: Perfect bisque head, mohair wig, sleep eyes, open mouth; five-piece composition body with molded and painted shoes and socks.

4½ - 5in (11 - 13cm)	$ 400 - 425
6 - 7in (15 - 18cm)	425 - 475
8 - 9in (20 - 23cm)	500 - 550
Walker, 6 - 7in (15 - 18cm)	500 - 550
Closed mouth, 6in (15cm)	500 - 600
Jointed body, 8 - 10in (20 - 25cm)	
	675 - 775

11in (28cm) in original presentation trunk with trousseau **$2800**

Below: 4½in (11cm) K & R tiny child. *H & J Foulke, Inc.*

Below: 25in (64cm) K & R 403 walker. *H & J Foulke, Inc.*

Character Babies or Toddlers: 1909 - on. Perfect bisque head, original or good wig, sleep eyes, open mouth; composition bent-limb or jointed toddler body; nicely dressed; may have voice box or spring tongue; all in good condition. (See *Simon & Halbig Dolls, The Artful Aspect* for photographs of mold numbers not pictured here.)

#100 Baby, painted eyes:

12in (31cm)	$ 550 - 600
14 - 15in (36 - 38cm)	700 - 750
18 - 20in (46 - 51cm)	950 - 1150
Glass eyes, 16in (41cm)	2000

#126, 22, 26 Baby Body:

10 - 12in (25 - 31cm)	500 - 525*
15 - 18in (38 - 46cm)	625 - 700*
22 - 24in (56 - 61cm)	950 - 1100*
30 - 33in (76 - 84cm)	1800 - 2200

#126 All-Bisque Baby:

6in (15cm)	750 - 800
8½in (21cm)	1000 - 1100

#126, 22 five-piece Toddler Body:

6 - 7in (15 - 18cm)	675 - 725*
9 - 10in (23 - 25cm)	750 - 850*
15 - 17in (38 - 43cm)	800 - 900*
23in (58cm)	1150 - 1250

#126 All-Bisque Toddler,

7in (18cm)	1400 - 1500

#126 Toddler fully jointed:

15 - 17in (38 - 41cm)	900 - 1000*
23 - 25in (58 - 64cm)	1600 - 1700*
28 - 30in (71 - 76cm)	2200 - 2500*

*Allow $50-75 extra for flirty eyes.

#121 Baby Body:

11 - 12in (28 - 31cm)	550 - 600
16 - 18in (41 - 46cm)	800 - 900
22in (56cm)	1250
24 - 25in (61 - 64cm)	1450 - 1650

#122, 128 Baby Body:

10 - 11in (25 - 28cm)	700 - 750
15 - 16in (38 - 41cm)	900 - 1000
23 - 24in (58 - 61cm)	1400 - 1600

#121, 122, 128 Toddler Body:

13 - 14in (33 - 36cm)	1150 - 1300
20 - 23in (51 - 58cm)	1600 - 1800
27 - 28in (69 - 71cm)	2300 - 2500

#118A Baby Body:

18in (46cm)	$2500 - 2600**

#119 Baby Body:

24in (61cm)	5000**

#135 Baby Body:

20in (51cm)	2200 - 2500**

Composition Head **#926**, five-piece toddler body: (For photograph see page 234.)

17in (43cm)	$ 500 - 600*
23in (58cm)	750 - 850
Baby, 18in (46cm)	550*

"Puz": (For photograph see page 234.)

8½in (21cm)	200 - 250*
17 - 19in (43 - 48cm)	400*
25in (64cm)	650 - 750*

*Allow $50 additional for flirty eyes.

**Not enough price samples to compute a reliable range.

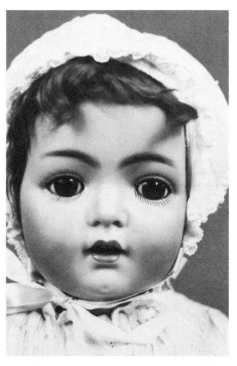

22in (56cm) 121 character baby. *H & J Foulke, Inc.*

Kämmer & Reinhardt continued

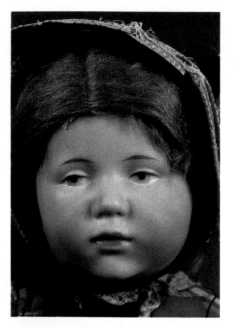

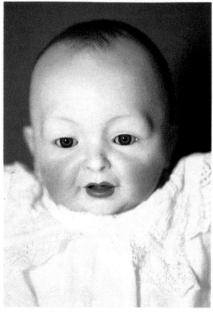

Top left: 15in (38cm) 114 character girl. *H & J Foulke, Inc.* (For further information see page 234.)

Top right: 171 infant. *H & J Foulke, Inc.* (For further information see page 235.)

Left: 17in (43cm) *Max and Moritz* characters. *Private Collection.* (For further information see page 235.)

Opposite page: 22in (55cm) 107 character boy. *Richard Wright Antiques.* (For further information see page 234.)

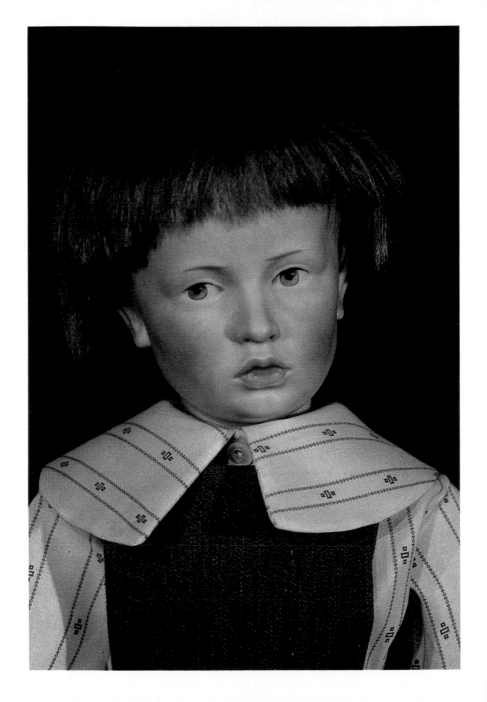

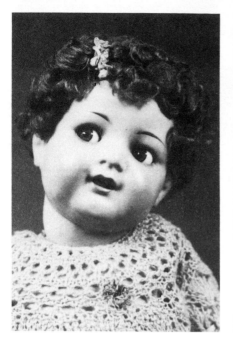

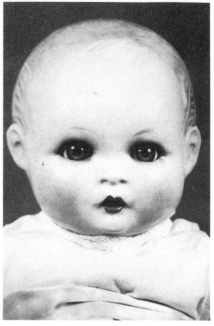

18in (46cm) 926 composition character baby. *H & J Foulke, Inc.*

17in (43cm) composition **"Puz."** *H & J Foulke, Inc.*

Character Children: 1909 - on. Perfect bisque-socket head, good wig, painted or glass eyes, closed mouth; composition ball-jointed body; nicely dressed; all in good condition. (See *Simon & Halbig, The Artful Aspect* for photographs of mold numbers not pictured here.)

#101 (Peter or Marie):

8 - 9in (20 - 23cm) five-piece body	
	$ 1800 - 2000
8 - 9in (20 - 23cm) jointed body	
	2200 - 2300
12in (31cm)	**2800 - 3000**
15 - 16in (38 - 41cm)	**3800 - 4200**
19 - 20in (48 - 51cm)	**6000 - 6500**

Glass eyes:

13in (33cm)	**7800****
20in (51cm)	**12,000****

#102:

12in (31cm)	**30,000 - 35,000****
22in (55cm)	**50,000 - 60,000****

#103, 104, 105, 106:

22in (56cm)	**75,000 up**
(seldom available)	

#107 (Carl): (For photograph see page 233.)

12in (30cm)	**$14,000 - 16,000**
22in (55cm)	**40,000 - 50,000**

#109 (Elise):

9 - 10in (23 - 25cm)	**3000 - 3500**
14in (36cm)	**8500**
19 - 21in (48 - 53cm)	**13,000 - 15,000**

#112, 112x:

16 - 18in (41 - 46cm)	**12,500**

#114 (Hans or Gretchen): (For photograph see page 232.)

8 - 9in (20 - 23cm) five-piece body	
	1800 - 2200
12in (31cm	**3500**
15 - 16in (38 - 41cm)	**4500 - 4800**
19 - 20in (48 - 51cm)	**5800 - 6800**
24in (61cm)	**8500 - 9000**

Glass eyes:

17in (43cm)	**12,000**
24in (61cm)	**17,000**

#115:

15 - 16in (38 - 41cm) toddler	
	6000**

**Not enough price samples to compute a reliable range

#115A:
Baby, 14 - 16in (36 - 41cm)
$ 4100 - 4500
Toddler, 15 - 16in (38 - 41cm)
5000 - 5500
19 - 20cm (48 - 51cm) 6500 - 7000
#116:
16in (41cm) toddler 5000**
#116A, open/closed mouth:
Baby 14 - 16in (36 - 41cm)
2300 - 2600
Toddler,
16in (41cm) 3000 - 3500
24in (61cm) 5000 - 5500
#116A, open mouth:
Baby, 14 - 16in (36 - 41cm)
2000 - 2500
Toddler, 16 - 18in (41 - 46cm)
2500 - 2750
#117, 117A, closed mouth:
9in (23cm) five-piece body
2750
12 - 14in (31 - 36cm) 3500 - 4000
18 - 20in (46 - 51cm) 5000 - 5500
23 - 25in (59 - 64cm) 6800 - 7800
28 - 31in (71 - 79cm) 8500 - 10,500
#117n, flirty eyes:
14 - 16in (36 - 41cm) 1300 - 1500*
20 - 22in (51 - 56cm) 2000 - 2200*
28 - 30in (71 - 76cm) 2600 - 3000*

#117n, sleep eyes:
14 - 16in (36 - 41cm) $ 1000 - 1200*
22 - 24in (56 - 61cm) 1600 - 1800*
30 - 32in (76 - 81cm) 2200 - 2500*
#117, open mouth:
27in (69cm) 4700 - 5000**
#123, 124 (Max & Moritz): (For photograph see page 232.)
17in (43cm) 20,000**
#127:
Baby, 10in (25cm) 800 - 850
14 - 15in (36 - 38cm) 1300 - 1400
20 - 22in (51 - 56cm) 1800 - 2000
Toddler or child, 15 - 16in (38 - 41cm)
1250 - 1500
Toddler, 25 - 27in (64 - 69cm)
2500 - 2750
#135 Child, 14 - 16in (36 - 41cm)
1700 - 2000
#201, 13in (33cm) 1500 - 1900**
Infant: 1924 - on. Perfect bisque head, molded and painted hair, glass eyes; cloth body, composition hands; nicely dressed; all in good condition. (For photograph see page 232.)
#171, 172:
14 - 15in (36 - 38cm) $ 3500
#175:
11in (28cm) h.c. 1100**

*Allow extra for flapper body.
**Not enough price samples to compute a reliable range.

30in (76cm) 117A character girl. *Private Collection.*

Kestner

FACTS

J.D. Kestner, Jr., doll factory, Waltershausen, Thüringia, Germany. Kestner & Co., porcelain factory, Ohrdruf. 1816 - on. Bisque heads, kids or composition bodies, bodies on tiny dolls are jointed at the knee, but not the elbow, all bisque. Up to 42in (107cm), size Q 20.

Child doll, early socket head: Ca. 1880. Perfect bisque head, plaster dome, good wig, paperweight or sleep eyes; composition ball-jointed body, some with straight wrists and elbows; well dressed; all in good condition. Many marked with size numbers only.

#169, 128, and unmarked pouty face, closed mouth:

6½in (17cm) five-piece body

	$ 900 - 1100
7½ - 8in (19 - 20cm)	**1350 - 1550**
11 - 12in (28 - 31cm)	**2200 - 2500**
14 - 16in (36 - 41cm)	**2600 - 2800**
19 - 21in (48 - 53cm)	**3000 - 3200**
24 - 25in (61 - 64cm)	**3400 - 3700**
27in (69cm)	**3800 - 4000**
24in (61cm) with original wardrobe	
	6000

#XI, 103 and very pouty face, closed mouth:

10 - 12in (25 - 31cm)	**$2800 - 3000***
14 - 16in (36 - 41cm)	**3200 - 3500***
19 - 21in (48 - 53cm)	**3800 - 4000***
24 - 25in (61 - 64cm)	**4200 - 4300***
27in (69cm)	**4500***
32in (81cm)	**5000***

*Allow less for a kid body.

29in (74cm) pouty Kestner, size M16. *H & J Foulke, Inc.*

Bru-type Kestner. *Maxine Salaman Collection.*

A.T.-type:
Closed mouth, any size   **$15,000 up***
Open mouth, 19in (48cm)   **2500***
Bru-type, molded teeth, jointed ankles:
20in (51cm)   **$ 5000**
Kid body, 24in (61cm)   **3200**

Open mouth, square cut teeth:
10 - 11in (25 - 28cm)   **$ 750 - 850**
14 - 16in (36 - 41cm)   **900 - 950**
24 - 25in (61 - 64cm)   **1300 - 1400**

*Allow less for a kid body.

26in (66cm) A.T.-type Kestner, kid body. *Jensen's Antique Dolls.*

Kestner continued

Child doll, early shoulder head: Ca. 1880s. Perfect bisque head, plaster dome, good wig, set or sleep eyes; sometimes head is slightly turned; kid body with bisuqe lower arms; marked with size letters or numbers. (No mold numbers.)

Closed mouth:

12in (31cm)	$ 850*
14 - 16in (36 - 41cm)	900 - 950*
20 - 22in (51 - 56cm)	1100 - 1250*
26in (66cm)	1500 - 1650*

Open/closed mouth:

16 - 18in (41 - 46 cm)	750 - 850

Open mouth:

14 - 16in (36 - 41cm)	500 - 600
20 - 22in (51 - 56cm)	700 - 775
25in (64cm)	800 - 900

*Allow $100 - 200 extra for a very pouty face or swivel neck.

Child doll, bisque shoulder head, open mouth: Ca. 1892. Kid body, some with rivet joints. Plaster dome, good wig, sleep eyes, open mouth; dressed, all in good condition. (See *Kestner, King of Dollmakers* for photographs of mold numbers not pictured here.)

HEAD MARK: *154. 8 dep.*
D made in Germany

BODY MARK:

#145, 154, 147, 148, 166, 195:

8in (20cm)	$ 275 - 300
12 - 13in (31 - 33cm)	350 - 400*
16 - 18in (41 - 46cm)	500 - 550*
20 - 22in (51 - 56cm)	600 - 650*
26 - 28in (66 - 71cm)	900 - 1000*

*Allow additional for a rivet jointed body.

Top: 19½in (49cm) "L" closed mouth Kestner. *H & J Foulke, Inc.*

Bottom: 16in (41cm) open/closed mouth shoulder head Kestner. *H & J Foulke, Inc.*

Child doll, open mouth: Bisque socket head on ball-jointed body; plaster dome, good wig, sleep eyes, open mouth; dressed; all in good condition. (See *Kestner, King of Dollmakers* for photographs of mold numbers not pictured here.)

HEAD MARK: *made in*
   D   *Germany.* 8.
      162.

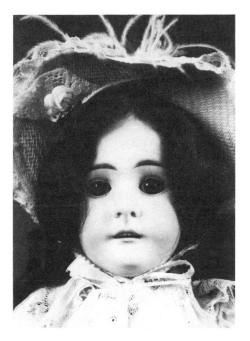

BODY MARK: Excelsior
      DRP N. 70686
      Germany

Mold numbers 142, 144, 146, 164, 167, 171: (See photograph on page 240.)

10 - 21in (25 - 31cm)	$ 700 - 800*
14 - 16in (36 - 41cm)	700 - 800*
18 - 21in (46 - 53cm)	850 - 950*
24 - 26in (61 - 66cm)	1000 - 1100*
30 - 32in (76 - 81cm)	1200 - 1500
36in (91cm)	2000 - 2300
42in (107cm)	3750 - 4000
32in (81cm) mint condition with elaborate original clothes	2200

*Allow 10 - 20% additional for molds #129, 149, 152, 160, 161, 173, 174.

#155: fully-jointed body,
7 - 8in (18 - 20cm)	$ 800 - 850

#171: Daisy, blonde mohair wig,
18in (46cm) only	900 - 1000

#168, 196, 214:
18 - 21in (46 - 53cm)	700 - 750
26 - 28in (66 - 71cm)	800 - 900
32in (81cm)	1000 - 1100

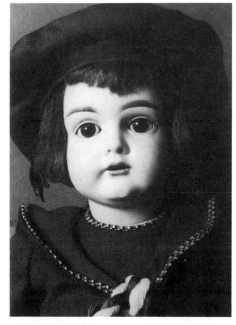

Top: 22in (56cm) "G" open-mouth Kestner. *H & J Foulke, Inc.*

Bottom: 24in (61cm) 161 Kestner boy. *H & J Foulke, Inc.*

Kestner continued

29in (74cm) 171 Kestner child. *H & J Foulke, Inc.* (For further information see page 239.)

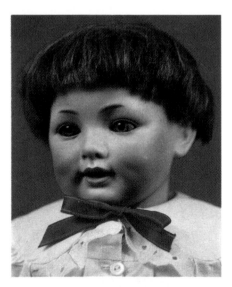

16in (41cm) JDK 220 toddler. *H & J Foulke, Inc.*

Character Child: 1909 - on. Perfect bisque head character face, plaster pate, wig, painted or glass eyes, closed, open or open/closed mouth; good jointed composition body; dressed; all in good condition. (See *Kestner, King of Dollmakers* for photographs of mold numbers not pictured here.)

#143 (Pre 1897):

7in (18cm)	$	**725 -**	**750**
9 - 10in (23 - 25cm)		**800 -**	**900**
12 - 14in (31 - 36cm)		**950 -**	**1100**
18 - 20in (46 - 51cm)		**1400 -**	**1500**
27in (69cm)		**1800**	

#178-190:

Painted Eyes:

12in (31cm)	**1800 -**	**2000**
15in (38cm)	**2800 -**	**3200**
18in (46cm)	**3800 -**	**4300**

Glass Eyes:

12in (31cm)	**2800 -**	**3200**
15in (38cm)	**3800 -**	**4300**
18in (46cm)	**4800 -**	**5300**
Boxed set, 15in (38cm)	**7500 up****	

#191, glass eyes, 19in (48cm) at auction
                                    6200

#206:

12in (31cm)	**4000 -**	**5000****
19in (48cm)	**12,000 -**	**15,000****

#208:

Painted Eyes:

12in (31cm)	**4000 -**	**5000****
23 - 24in (58 - 61cm)	**12,000 -**	**15,000****

#220 Toddler:

16in (41cm)	**5000 -**	**6000****
24in (61cm)	**7500 -**	**8000****

#239 Toddler:

15 - 17in (38 - 43cm)	**4000****

#241:

21 - 22in (53 - 56cm)	**6500 -**	**7000****

#249:

13 - 14in (33 - 36cm)	**1100 -**	**1200**
20 - 22in (51 - 56cm)	**1800**	

**Not enough price samples to compute a reliable range.

#260:

8in (20cm) Toddler	$ 700 -	750
10in (25cm) Toddler	850 -	950
12 - 14in (31 - 36cm)	800 -	850
18 - 20in (46 - 51cm)	900 -	1100
29in (75cm)	1500	

Character Baby: 1910 - on. Perfect bisque head, molded and/or painted hair or good wig, sleep or set eyes, open or open/closed mouth; bent-limb body; well dressed; nice condition. (See *Kestner, King of Dollmakers* for photographs of mold numbers not pictured here.)

Mark:

made in
F. Germany. 10
211
J. D. K.

#211, 226, 262, 263, JDK solid dome:

11 - 13in (28 - 33cm)	$ 575 -	675*
16 - 18in (41 - 46cm)	750 -	850*
20 - 22in (51 - 56cm)	1050 -	1200*
25in (64cm)	1500 -	1750*

*Allow $50 - 100 extra for an original skin wig.

Top: 15in (38cm) JDK 239 toddler. *H & J Foulke, Inc.*

Bottom: 16in (41cm) JDK 247 character baby. *H & J Foulke, Inc.* (For further information see page 242.)

Kestner continued

#234, 235, 238 shoulder heads:
  16in (41cm)   **$1000**
Hilda, **#237, 245,** Solid Dome Baby:
  11 - 13in (28 - 33cm)   **$2800 - 3200**
  16 - 17in (41 - 43cm)   **4200 - 4600**
  20 - 22in (51 - 56cm)   **5300 - 5600**
  24in (61cm)   **7000 - 7500**
Toddler:
  14in (36cm)   **4500 - 5000**
  17 - 19in (43 - 48cm)   **6000 - 6500**
  27in (69cm)   **8500 - 9000**
#247: (For photograph see page 241.)
  11in (28cm)   **1100**
  14 - 16in (36 - 41cm)   **1800 - 2100**
  26in (66cm) at auction   **4100**
#257:
  9 - 10in (23 - 25cm)   **600 - 700**
  14 - 16in (36 - 41cm)   **750 - 850**
  21in (53cm)   **1250 - 1350**
  25in (64cm)   **1650 - 1750**

Solid dome, fat-cheeked (So-called "Baby Jean"):
  12 - 13in (31 - 33cm)   **$1100 - 1250**
  17 - 18in (43 - 46cm)   **1500 - 1650**
  23 - 24in (58 - 61cm)   **2000 - 2100**
All-bisque:
Painted eyes, stiff neck,
  5 - 6in (13 - 15cm)   **225 - 275**
Swivel neck,
  7½in (19cm)   **425**
  9in (23cm)   **600**
Glass eyes, swivel neck,
  9 - 10in (23 - 25cm)   **900 - 950**

Below left: 22in (56cm) JDK 237 **Hilda.** *H & J Foulke, Inc.*

Below right: 12in (31cm) Kestner 130 girl. *H & J Foulke, Inc.*

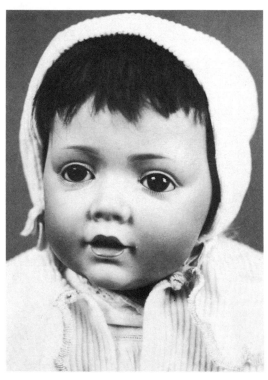

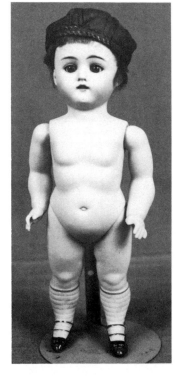

All-Bisque Child: Perfect all-bisque child jointed at shoulders and hips; mohair wig, sleeping eyes, open mouth with upper teeth; blue or pink painted stockings, black strap shoes. Naked or with appropriate clothes. Very good quality.

#130, 150, 160, 184 and 208:

4 - 5in (10 - 13cm)	$ 225 - 325*
6in (15cm)	350 - 375*
7in (18cm)	400 - 450*
8in (20cm)	500 - 550*
9in (23cm)	700 - 800
11in (28cm)	1100 - 1200
12in (31cm)	1300 - 1400

*Allow 30 - 40% extra for swivel neck; allow $25 - 50 extra for yellow boots.

Gibson Girl: Ca. 1910. Perfect bisque shoulder head with good wig, glass eyes, closed mouth, up-lifted chin; kid body with bisque lower arms (cloth body with bisque lower limbs on small dolls); beautifully dressed; all in good condition; sometimes marked "Gibson Girl" on body.

#172:

10in (25cm)	$1100 - 1300
15in (38cm)	2000 - 2400
20 - 21in (51 - 53cm)	3600 - 4100

Lady Doll: Perfect bisque socket head, plaster dome, wig with lady hairdo, sleep eyes, open mouth with upper teeth; jointed composition body with molded breasts, nipped-in waist, slender arms and legs; appropriate lady clothes; all in good condition.

Mark: *made in D Germany. 8. 162.*

#162:

16 - 18in (41 - 46cm) **$1400 - 1600**
Naked, 16 - 18in (41 - 46cm)
1000 - 1200
All original clothes, 16 - 18in (41 - 46cm)
2300

O.I.C. Baby: Perfect bisque solid dome head with glass eyes, open mouth with molded tongue; cloth body, dressed; all in good condition.

MARK: "255
3
O.I.C."

10in (25cm) h.c.   **$1500**

Siegfried: Perfect bisque solid dome head with molded hair and flange neck, sleep eyes, closed mouth, side nose, pronounced philtrum; cloth body with composition hands; dressed; all in good condition. Mold #272.

MARK: *Siegfried made in Germany 9*

10in (25cm)	**$1500****
14in (36cm)	**2000****

**Not enough price samples to compute a reliable average.

10in (25cm) 172 Kestner *Gibson Girl. Private Collection.*

244

Kewpie

FACTS

Various makers. 1913 - on. 2in (5cm) up.
Designer: Rose O'Neill, U.S.A. U.S. Agent:
George Borgfeldt & Co., New York, N.Y., U.S.A.
Mark: Red and gold paper heart or shield on chest
and round label on back.

All-Bisque: Made by J. D.
Kestner and other German firms.
Often have imperfections in making. Sometimes signed on foot
"O'Nei ". Standing, legs together, arms jointed, blue wings,
painted features, eyes to side.

2½in (5 - 6cm)	$ 90 -	100
4in (10cm)	**125**	
5in (13cm)	**150**	
6in (15cm)	**200**	
7in (18cm)	**250**	
8in (20cm)	**400**	
9in (23cm)	**550 -**	**600**
10in (25cm)	**750 -**	**800**
12in (31cm)	**1300 -**	**1500**
Jointed hips:		
4in (10cm)	**500**	
6in (15cm)	**750**	
8in (20cm)	**900 -**	**950**
Shoulder head, 3in (8cm)		
	425	
Perfume bottle, 4½in (11cm)		
	550 -	**600**
Black Hottentot, 5in (13cm)		
	550	
Button hole, 2in (5cm)		
	165 -	**175**
Pincushion, 2 - 3in (5 - 8cm)		
	250 -	**300**
Painted shoes and socks:		
5in (13cm)	**500 -**	**550**
11in (28cm)	**1500 -**	**1800**

Left: 8in (20cm) all-bisque *Kewpie*
with unusual jointed hips. *H & J
Foulke, Inc.*

Opposite page: 11½in (29cm) black
composition *Kewpie*, all original with
label. *H & J Foulke, Inc.* (For further
information see page 248.)

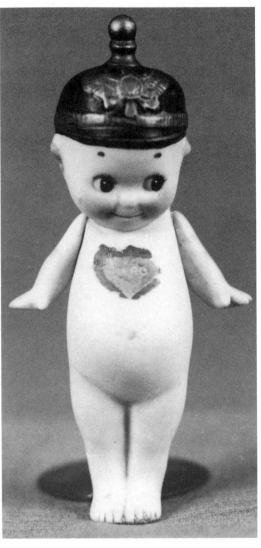

4¾in (12cm) *Kewpie* with helmet. *H & J Foulke, Inc.*

Action Kewpies (sometimes
  stamped: ©):
Thinker:
  4in (10cm) $ 275 - 325
  7in (18cm)   500 - 550
Kewpie with cat, 3½in (9cm)
                      450 - 500
Kewpie holding pen, 3in (8cm)
                      425 - 475
Reclining or sitting,
  3 - 4in (8 - 10cm) 425 - 475
Gardener, Sweeper, Farmer,
  4in (10cm)   475 - 525
Kewpie 2in (5cm) with rabbit,
  rose, turkey, pumpkin,
  shamrock, etc.   325 - 375
Doodledog:
  3in (9cm)   1500 - 1800
  1½in (4cm)   750 - 800
Huggers, 3½in (9cm)
                      200 - 225
Guitar player, 3½in (9cm)
                      350 - 400
Traveler, 3½in (9cm)
                      325 - 350
Governor, 3½in (9cm)
                      375 - 400
Kewpie and Doodledog
  bench, 3½in (9cm)
                      3000 up
Kewpie sitting on inkwell,
  3½in (9cm)   650 - 750
Kewpie Traveler with
Doodledog, 3½in (9cm)
                     1250 - 1350
Kewpie Soldiers,
  5 - 6in (13 - 15cm) 750 - 850
Kewpie reading book,
  3in (8cm) sitting   850
Two Kewpies reading book,
  3½in (9cm), standing
                        850
Kewpie at tea table 1800 up
Kewpie with basket,
  4in (10cm)   1000
Kewpie Mountain with
  17 figures   17,000 up

Bisque head on chubby jointed composition toddler body, glass eyes: Made by J.D. Kestner. (For photograph see *9th Blue Book,* page 276.)

Mark: "Ges.gesch.
O'Neill J.D.K."

10in (25cm) five-piece body
$4000
12 - 14in (31 - 36cm) **5000 - 6000**

Bisque head on cloth body: Mold **#1377** made by Alt, Beck & Gottschalck. (For photograph see *10th Blue Book*, page 282.)
12in (31cm) Glass eyes **$2600 - 2800****
Painted eyes **1600 - 2000****

Celluloid: Made by Karl Standfuss, Deuben near Dresden, Saxony, Germany. Straight standing, arms jointed, blue wings; very good condition.

2½in (6cm)	**$ 35 - 40**
5in (13cm)	**75 - 85**
8in (20cm)	**160 - 185**
12in (31cm)	**250**
22in (56cm)	**450**
Black, 2½in (6cm)	**75 - 85**
5in (13cm)	**125 - 135**

**Not enough price samples to compute a reliable range.

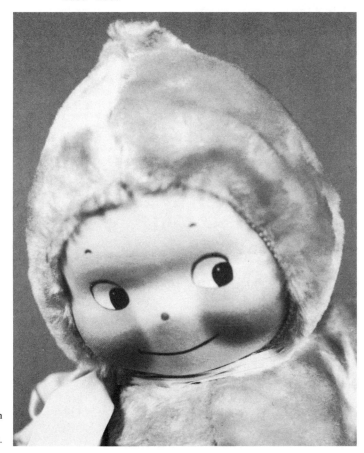

18in (46cm) cloth
Cuddle Kewpie.
H & J Foulke, Inc.

Kewpie continued

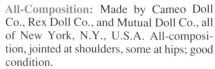

All-Composition: Made by Cameo Doll Co., Rex Doll Co., and Mutual Doll Co., all of New York, N.Y., U.S.A. All-composition, jointed at shoulders, some at hips; good condition.

8in (20cm)	**$150 - 175**
11 - 12in (28 - 31cm)	**225 - 275**

Black, 12 - 13in (31 - 33cm) (For photograph see page 245.) **350 - 400**
Talcum container, 7in (18cm) **175 - 225**
13in (33cm) mint and all original with
   wrist tag **400**
Composition head, cloth body,
   12in (31cm) **175 - 200**

All-Cloth: Made by Richard G. Krueger, Inc. or King Innovations, Inc., New York, N.Y., U.S.A. Patent number 1785800. Mask face with fat-shaped cloth body, including tiny wings and peak on head. Cloth label sewn in side seam.

10 - 12in (25 - 31cm)	**$175 - 200**
18 - 22in (46 - 56cm)	**325 - 375**

Hard Plastic: Ca. 1950s.
   Standing **Kewpie**, one-piece
   with jointed arms 8in (20cm)
      $110 - 125
   Boxed **165**
   Fully jointed with sleep eyes; all
   original clothes, 13in (33cm)
      400 - 450∗∗

∗∗Not enough price samples to compute a reliable range.

Vinyl: Ca. 1960s.
   Kewpie Baby with hinged
      body, 16in (41cm)
         $200 - 225
   16in (41cm) standing, white
         75 - 95
   16in (41cm) standing, black
         125 - 135

Top: 11½in (29cm) composition *Kewpie* with label. *H & J Foulke, Inc.*

Bottom: 12in (31cm) composition *Kewpie*, all original. *H & J Foulke, Inc.*

Kley & Hahn

FACTS

Kley & Hahn, doll factory, Ohrdruf, Thüringia, Germany. Heads by Hertel, Schwab & Co. (100 series), Bähr & Pröschild (500 series) and J.D. Kestner (250, 680 and Walküre). 1902 - on. Bisque head, composition body.
Trademarks: Walküre, Meine Einzige, Special, Dollar Princess.
Mark:

>K&H<
Germany

K H
Walküre

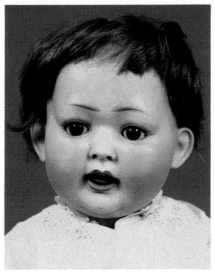

Character Baby: Perfect bisque head with molded hair or good wig, sleep or painted eyes, open or closed mouth; bent-limb baby body; nicely dressed; all in good condition.

#138, 158, 160, 167, 176, 458, 525, 531, 680 and others:

11 - 13in (28 - 33cm)	$ 475 - 525*
18 - 20in (46 - 51cm)	700 - 800*
24in (61cm)	1000 - 1100*
28in (71cm)	1500 - 1600*

20in (51cm) 167 character baby. *H & J Foulke, Inc.*

Toddler:

15in (38cm)	800 - 900*
22 - 23in (56 - 58cm)	1550 - 1650*
26 - 27in (66 - 69cm)	1950 - 2250*

Two-Face Baby, 13in (33cm)
1800 - 2000**

Character Child: Perfect bisque head, wig, glass or painted eyes, closed mouth; jointed composition child or toddler body; fully dressed; all in good condition.
#520, 526:

15 - 16in (36 - 38cm)	$3100 - 3500
19 - 21in (48 - 53cm)	4000 - 4500

#536, 546, 549:

15 - 16in (36 - 38cm)	3500 - 4000
19 - 21in (48 - 53cm)	4500 - 5000

*Allow extra for mold #568.
**Not enough price samples to compute a reliable range.

20in (51cm) 546 character girl. *Geri Gentile.*

Kley & Hahn continued

#547, 18½in (47cm) at auction
$6825
#154, 166, closed mouth:
  16 - 17in (41 - 43cm) jointed body
    2500 - 2650
  15in (38cm) baby   1300 - 1500
#154, 166, open mouth:
  17 - 18in (43 - 46cm) jointed body
    1200 - 1400
  25in (64cm)   1850 - 1950
  20in (51cm) baby   1300 - 1400
#169, closed mouth:
  13 - 14in (33 - 36cm) toddler
    2200 - 2400
  17 - 19in (43 - 48cm) toddler
    3400 - 3500

#169, open mouth, 23in (58cm) baby
$1500 - 1650**

Child Doll: Perfect bisque head, wig, glass eyes, open mouth; jointed composition child body; fully dressed; all in good condition.
#250 or **Walküre:**
  7½in (19cm) $ 325 - 375
  16 - 18in (41 - 46cm)   500 - 550
  22 - 24in (56 - 61cm)   600 - 700
  28 - 30in (71 - 76cm)   900 - 1000
  35 - 36in (89 - 91cm)   1500 - 1600
  42in (100cm)   2800 - 3000
Special, Dollar Princess,
  23 - 25in (58 - 64cm)   525 - 575

25in (64cm) *Walküre* flapper. *H & J Foulke, Inc.*

FACTS

Kling & Co., porcelain factory, Ohrdruf, Thüringia, Germany. 1836 - on (1870 - on for dolls). Bisque or china shoulder head, cloth body, bisque lower limbs; bisque socket head, composition body, all-bisque.
Mark:

Bisque shoulder head: Ca. 1880. Molded hair or mohair wig, painted eyes, closed mouth; cloth body with bisque lower limbs; dressed; in all good condition. Mold numbers such as **140** and **186**.

12 - 14in (31 - 36cm)	$ **300 - 375***
18 - 20in (46 - 51cm)	**500 - 550***
23 - 25in (58 - 64cm)	**600 - 700***

Glass eyes and molded hair,
11in (28cm)	**425 - 475**

Boy styles, such as **131**:
11in (28cm)	**600 - 650**
16 - 18in (41 - 46cm)	**900 - 1000**

Girl styles, such as #**186, 176,**
15 - 17in (38 - 43cm)	**900 - 1000**

Lady styles with decorated bodice, such as
#**135, 170**	**1500 up**

*Allow extra for unusual or elaborate hairdo.

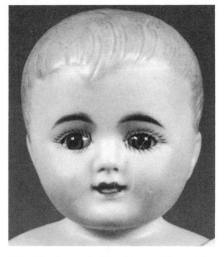

10in (25cm) unmarked shoulder head boy or baby probably Kling. *H & J Foulke, Inc.*

All-Bisque Child: Jointed shoulders and hips; wig, glass eyes, closed mouth; molded footwear (usually two-strap boots with heels, blue shirred hose with brown strap shoes or black hose with green shoes).
Mark: on back or in leg joint

#**36** or **69**:
4in (10cm)	$ **200 - 225**
5½in (14cm)	**300**

#**99** baby with bare feet, 4in (10cm)
	225**

**Not enough price samples to compute a reliable range.

Right: 4½in (11cm) 36 all-bisque girl. *H & J Foulke, Inc.*

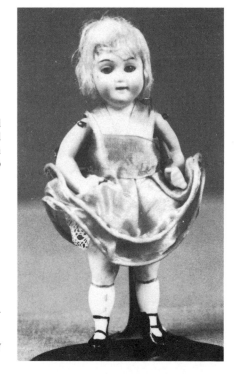

China shoulder head: Ca. 1880. Black- or blonde-haired china head with bangs, sometimes with a pink tint; cloth body with china limbs or kid body; dressed; all in good condition.

#188, 189, 200 and others:

13 - 15in (33 - 38cm)	**$275 - 325**
18 - 20in (46 - 51cm)	**400 - 450**
24 - 25in (61 - 64cm)	**525 - 575**

Bisque head: Ca. 1890. Perfect bisque head, mohair or human hair wig, glass sleep eyes, open or closed mouth; kid or cloth body with bisque lower arms or jointed composition body; dressed; all in good condition. (For photograph see *10th Blue Book*, page 287.)

#123, closed mouth shoulder head:

10 - 12in (25 - 31cm)	
Original costume	**$ 500 - 700**
Redressed	**250 - 300**

#166, closed mouth shoulder head,

15 - 16in (38 - 41cm)	**1000 - 1100**

#373 or **377** shoulder head, open mouth:

13 - 15in (33 - 38cm)	**375 - 425****
19 - 22in (48 - 56cm)	**475 - 525****

#370 or **372, 182** socket head, open mouth:

14 - 16in (36 - 41cm)	**450 - 500**
22 - 24in (56 - 61cm)	**600 - 700**
27in (69cm)	**900 - 1000**

**Not enough price samples to compute a reliable range.

Above: 16in (41cm) 189 china head. *H & J Foulke, Inc.*

FACTS

Knickerbocker Doll & Toy Co., New York, N.Y., U.S.A. 1937. All-composition.
Mark: (Embossed on dwarfs)
"WALT DISNEY
KNICKERBOCKER TOY CO."

Composition Snow White: All-composition jointed at neck, shoulders and hips; black mohair wig with hair ribbon, brown lashed sleep eyes, open mouth; original clothing; all in very good condition.

20in (51cm)   **$450 - 500**

With molded black hair and blue ribbon,
13 - 15in (33 - 38cm)   **300 - 400**

Snow White, all original with hang tag. *H & J Foulke, Inc.*

Knickerbocker continued

Composition Seven Dwarfs: All-composition jointed at shoulders, stiff hips, molded shoes, individual character faces, painted features; mohair wigs or beards; jointed shoulders, molded and painted shoes; original velvet costumes and caps with identifying names: "Sneezy," "Dopey," "Grumpy," "Doc," "Happy," "Sleepy" and "Bashful." Very good condition.

9in (23cm)   **$225 - 275 each**

Additional composition dolls:

Jiminy Cricket, 10in (25cm)	**$450 - 550**
Pinocchio, 13in (33cm)	**250 - 275**

Additional cloth dolls:

Seven Dwarfs, 14in (36cm)	**$250 each**
Snow White, 16in (41cm)	**300 - 350**
Donald Duck	**500 up**
Mickey Mouse	**500 up**
Minnie Mouse	**500 up**

9in (23cm) composition *Sleepy*, all original with hang tag. *H & J Foulke, Inc.*

König & Wernicke

FACTS

König & Wernicke, doll factory, Waltershausen, Thüringia, Germany. Heads by Hertel, Schwab & Co. and Bähr & Pröschild. 1912 - on. Bisque heads, composition bodies or all-composition. **Trademarks:** Meine Stolz, My Playmate

Mark: Body Mark:

K & W Character: Bisque head with good wig, sleep eyes, open mouth; composition baby or toddler body; appropriate clothes; all in good condition.

#98, 99, 100, 1070:

8½in (21cm)	**$ 350**
10 - 11in (25 - 28cm)	**425 - 450***
14 - 16in (36 - 41cm)	**550 - 650***
19 - 21in (48 - 53cm)	**750 - 850***
24 - 25in (61 - 64cm)	**1000 - 1100***

Character child, closed mouth, wig, glass eyes, 24in (61cm) toddler **$3600****

*Allow $50-75 extra for flirty eyes.
*Allow $100-200 extra for toddler body.
**Not enough price samples to compute a reliable range.

22in (56cm) K & W character baby. *H & J Foulke, Inc.*

Richard G. Krueger, Inc.

FACTS

Richard G. Krueger, Inc., New York, N.Y., U.S.A. 1917 - on. All-cloth, mask face.
Mark: Cloth tag or label.

Label: Krueger, N.Y.
Reg, U.S. Pat Off.
Made in U.S.A.

16in (41cm)	**$ 100 - 125**
20in (51cm)	**150 - 175**

All-Cloth Doll: Ca. 1930. Mask face with painted features, rosy cheeks, yarn hair or curly mohair wig on cloth cap; oil cloth body with hinged shoulders and hips; original clothes; in excellent condition.

Pinocchio: Ca. 1940. Mask character face with black yarn hair, attached ears, round nose, large oval eyes, curved mouth; cloth torso, wood jointed arms and legs; original clothes, all in good condition. (For photograph see *10th Blue Book*, page 230.)

15in (38cm)	**$ 250 - 300**

Kewpie: See page 248.

Tagged Krueger girl, all original.
H & J Foulke, Inc.

Käthe Kruse

FACTS

Käthe Kruse, Bad Kösen, Germany; after World War II, Donauworth. 1910 - on. Molded muslin head (hand-painted), jointed cloth body, later of hard plastic material.
Mark: On cloth: "Käthe Kruse" on sole of foot, sometimes also "Germany" and a number.
Hard plastic on back: Turtle mark and "Käthe Kruse."

Käthe Kruse *Made in*
81971 *Germany*

Cloth Käthe Kruse: Molded muslin head, hand-painted; jointed at shoulders and hips:

Doll I (1910 - 1929), 16in (41cm), Early model, wide hips:

Mint, all original	**$3800 - 4800**
Very good	2500 - 3000
Fair	1500 - 2000
Jointed knees	5500**

Doll I (1929 - on), 17in (43cm), Later model, slim hips:

Molded hair, mint	**$2800 - 3500**
Very good	1800 - 2300

Doll 1H (wigged): (For photograph see *Doll Classics*, page 174.)

Mint all original	**$2500 - 3200**
Very good	1500 - 2000

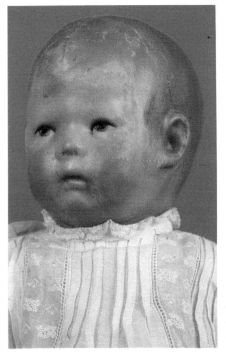

Early *Doll I. H & J Foulke, Inc.*

Doll VII with *Du Mein* head. *CC Collection.*

Käthe Kruse continued

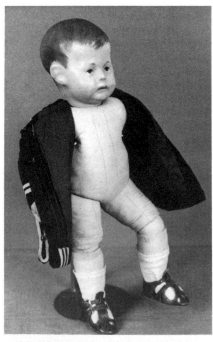

Doll II "Schlenkerchen" Smiling Baby (1922 - 1936). (For photograph see *10th Blue Book*, page 292.)

  13in (33cm)   **$3000****
Doll V & VI Babies "Traumerchen"(five-pound weighted "Sand Baby") and "Du Mein"(unweighted). Cloth head; later head of Magnesit. (For photograph see *9th Blue Book*, page 287.)

  19½ - 23½in (50 - 60cm)   **$3500 - 4000**
Doll VII (1927 - 1952) and Doll X (1935 - 1952), 14in (36cm):

  Redressed   **$1300**
  All original   **1800 - 2000**
  Mint in box, at auction   **4000**
  With Du Mein head (1928 - 1930), 14in (36cm):
    Showing wear   **1600**
    Mint   **2900**

**Not enough price samples to compute a reliable average.

Doll VIII "German Child" (1929 - on), 20½in (52cm) wigged, turning head: (For photograph see *9th Blue Book*, page 287.)
  Mint, all original   **$2500 - 3000**
  Good condition, suitably dressed
                                  1500 - 1800
Doll IX "Little German Child" (1929 - on), wigged, turning head, 14in (36cm):
  Redressed   **$1300**
  All original   **1800 - 2000**
U.S. Zone Germany: Dolls IX or X with cloth or Magnesit heads, very thick paint finish; all original, very good condition (1945 - 1951):
14in (36cm)
  Cloth head, mint   **$1200 - 1500**
  Magnesit, mint   **750 - 850**
  Hard plastic, mint   **600 - 700**
17 - 18in (43 - 46cm) Doll I, mint. (For photograph see page 260.)   **2500 - 3000**

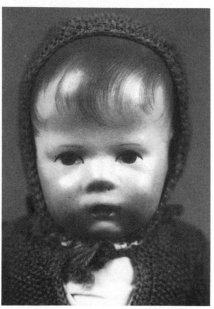

Top: Early model with jointed knees. *Nancy A. Smith Collection.*

Bottom: 1930 *Doll I*. *H & J Foulke, Inc.*

Hard Plastic Head: Ca. 1952 - on. Hard plastic head with human hair wig, painted eyes; pink muslin body; original clothes; all in excellent condition.

Ca. 1952 - 1975:

14in (36cm)	**$375 - 425**
19 - 21in (48 - 53cm)	**500 - 575**

1975 - on:

14in (36cm)	**300 - 350***
19 - 21in (48 - 53cm)	**400 - 450***
20in (51cm) **Du Mein**	**550 - 650***

*Retail store prices may be higher.

Hanna Kruse Dolls:
10in (25cm) **Däumlinchen** with foam rubber stuffing (1957 - on) **$200 - 225***

13in (33cm) **Rumpumpel Baby** or
Toddler (1959 - on) **350 - 400**
10in (25cm) **Doggi** (For photograph see
10th Blue Book, page 293.) (1964 - 1967)
200 - 225**

All-Hard Plastic (Celluloid) Käthe Kruse: Wig or molded hair and sleep or painted eyes; jointed neck, shoulders and hips; original clothes; all in excellent condition. Turtle mark. (1955 - 1951). (For photograph see *10th Blue Book*, page 293.)

16in (41cm)	**$425 - 475**

**Not enough price samples to compute a reliable range.

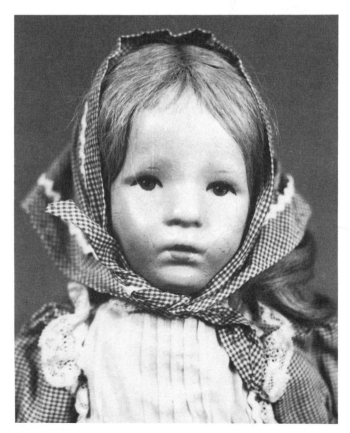

Doll IX Little German Child, redressed. *H & J Foulke, Inc.*

Käthe Kruse continued

Doll I, U.S. Zone Germany, all original. *H & J Foulke, Inc.* (For further information see page 258.)

FACTS

Gebrüder Kuhnlenz, porcelain factory, Kronach, Bavaria. 1884 - on. Bisque head, composition or kid body.

Mark: "G.K."

G^{br} 165 K
9
Germany   44-31

and/or numbers, such as:
41-28   56-18   44-15
The first two digits are mold numbers; second two are size number.

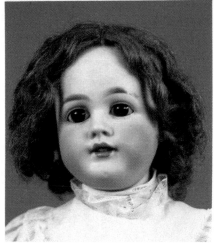

24in (61cm) 44 child. *H & J Foulke, Inc.*

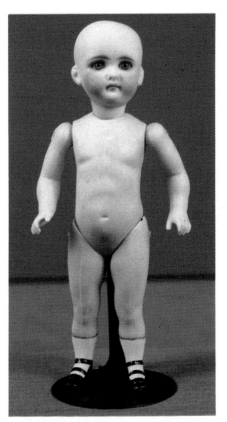

19in (38cm) 47 child. *H & J Foulke, Inc.*

Left: 8½in (21cm) all-bisque 31 child. *H & J Foulke, Inc.*

Gebrüder Kuhnlenz continued

G. K. doll with closed mouth: Ca. 1885 - on. Perfect bisque socket head (some with closed Belton-type crown), inset glass eyes, closed mouth, round cheeks; jointed composition body; dressed; all in good condition.
#32, 31:

8 - 10in (20 - 25cm)	**$ 850 - 1100***
16 - 18in (41 - 46cm)	**1600 - 1800***
22 - 24in (56 - 61cm)	**2200 - 2400***

#34, Bru-type, French Body:

18in (46cm)	**$3000 - 4000****

#38 shoulder head, kid body:

14 - 16in (36 - 41cm)	**725 - 825***
22 - 23in (56 - 58cm)	**1200 - 1300***

*Allow more for a very pretty doll.
**Not enough price samples to compute a reliable range.

7½in (19cm) 44 boy. *H & J Foulke, Inc.*

Gebrüder Kuhnlenz continued

G.K. child doll: Ca. 1890 - on. Perfect bisque socket head with distinctive face, almost a character look, long cheeks, sleep or paperweight-type eyes, open mouth, molded teeth; jointed composition body, sometimes French; dressed; all in good condition.

#41, 44, 56:

16 - 19in (41 - 48cm)	$ 800 - 900
24 - 26in (61 - 66cm)	1200 - 1400

#165:

18in (46cm)	425 - 450
22 - 24in (56 - 61cm)	500 - 550
34in (86cm)	1200 - 1300

#61, 47 shoulder head:

19 - 22in (48 - 56cm)	650 - 750

G.K. Tiny Dolls: Perfect bisque socket head, wig, stationary glass eyes, open mouth with molded teeth; five-piece composition body with molded shoes and socks; all in good condition. Usually mold #44.

7 - 8in (18 - 20cm):

Crude body	$ 185 - 210
Better body	225 - 275

All-Bisque Child: 1895 - on. Socket head with glass eyes, open mouth, nice mohair wig; pegged shoulders and hips, white painted stockings, light blue boots, black straps or two-strap shoes. Usually mold #44 or #31.

7½in (19cm)	$ 850 - 1000**
8½in (22cm)	1250 - 1400**

**Not enough price samples to compute a reliable range.

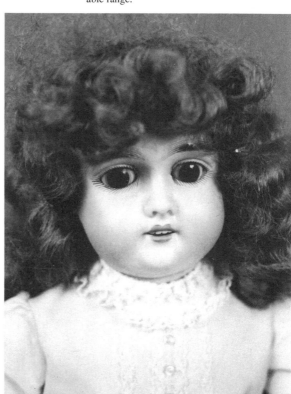

24in (61cm) 165 child. *H & J Foulke, Inc.*

Lanternier

FACTS

A Lanternier & Cie. Porcelain factory of Limoges, France. 1915 - 1924. Bisque head, papier-mâché body.
Mark:

Marked Lanternier Child: Ca. 1915. Perfect bisque head, good or original wig, large stationary eyes, open mouth, pierced ears; papier-mâché jointed body; pretty clothes; all in good condition.

Cherie, Favorite or **La Georgienne:**

16 - 18in (41 - 46cm)	$ 675 - 775*
22 - 24in (56 - 61cm)	900 - 1000*
28in (71cm)	1400 - 1600*

*Allow extra for lovely face and bisque.

Lanternier Lady: Ca. 1915. Perfect bisque head with adult look, good wig, stationary glass eyes, open/closed mouth with molded teeth; composition lady body; dressed; all in good condition. (For photograph see *7th Blue Book*, page 271.)
Lorraine, 16 - 18in (41 - 46cm)
$ 850 - 1250*

*Depending upon costume and quality.

Characters, "Toto" and others: Ca. 1915. Perfect bisque smiling character face, good wig, glass eyes, open/closed mouth with molded teeth, pierced ears; jointed French composition body; dressed; all in good condition. (For photograph see *10th Blue Book*, page 231.)
17 - 19in (43 - 48cm)
$ 900 - 1100

22in (56cm) child marked "Limoges." *H & J Foulke, Inc.*

Leather, French

Unknown French maker. Ca. 1920. All leather. 5 - 6in (13 - 15cm).
Mark: None on doll; may have "Made in France" label.

Leather Doll: Baby or child doll with molded and painted hair, painted features, jointed shoulders and hips; original clothes; excellent condition.

Baby, 5in (13cm)   **$2250**
Child, 6in (15cm)   **2500 - 3000****

5in (13cm) French leather baby, all original. *Jan Foulke Collection.*

**Not enough price samples to compute a reliable range.

Lenci

FACTS

Enrico & Elenadi Scavini, Turin, Italy. 1920 - on. Pressed felt head with painted features, jointed felt bodies. 5 - 45in (13 - 114cm).

Mark: "LENCI" on cloth and various paper tags; sometimes stamped on bottom of foot.

Lenci: All-felt (sometimes cloth torso) with swivel head, jointed shoulders and hips; painted features, eyes usually side-glancing; original clothes, often of felt or organdy; in excellent condition.

Miniatures and Mascottes:

8 - 9in (20 - 23cm) Regionals	**$ 275 - 325**
Children or unusual costumes	**375 - 425**

Children #300, 109, 149, 159, 111:

13in (33cm)	**$ 850 up**
16 - 18in (41 - 46cm)	**1200 up**
20 - 22in (51 - 56cm)	**1800 up**

#300 children, at auction, 17in (43cm):

Mozart	**$3700**
Russian Boy	**3000**
Russian Girl	**2400**
Albanian Boy	**3500**
Albanian Girl	**2500**

Madame Pomadour Lady Lenci, all original. *H & J Foulke, Inc.*

Left: 20in (51cm) ***Widow Allegra***, all original.
H & J Foulke, Inc.

Right: 7½in (19cm) ***Sailor***, all original.
H & J Foulke, Inc.

Lenci continued

"Laura" face, 16in (41cm)   **$1000 - 1500**
(For photograph see page 9.)
"Lucia" face, 14in (36cm):
  Child clothes   **800 - 1200**
  Regional outfits   **700 - 900**
Ladies and long-limbed novelty dolls,
  24 - 28in (61 - 71cm)   **1800 up**
  Glass eyes, 20in (51cm)   **2800 - 3000**
  Celluloid-type, 6in (15cm)   **50 - 65**
"Surprised Eye" (round painted eyes),
  fancy clothes, 20in (51cm) **2200 - 2600**
#1500, scowling face,
  17 - 19in (43 - 48cm)   **1800 - 2000**
Baby:
  14 - 18in (36 - 46cm)   **2000 - 2200**
  21in (53cm)   **2500**
Teenager, long legs, 17in (43cm)
                      1200 up
Orientals, 18in (46cm)   **3500 - 4000**
Sports Series, 17in (43cm)   **2200 up**
Golfer, 23in (58cm)   **3000**
Googly, watermelon mouth, 22in (56cm)
                    1600 - 2000
Winkers, 12in (31cm)   **750 - 950**
1935 Round face, 11in (28cm) **500 up**
1950 Characters   **300 up**
Benedetta, 18in (46cm)   **2000 up**
Catalogs   **900 - 1200**
Purse   **300**
Fascist Boy, 13in (33cm) **1200 - 1400**
Brown South Seas, 16in (41cm)
                    1800 - 2000
Mask face, disc eyes, 23in (58cm)
                    600 - 700

Collector's Note: Mint examples of rare dolls will bring higher prices. To bring the prices quoted, Lenci dolls must be clean and have good color. Faded and dirty dolls bring only about one-third to one-half these prices.

Top: 13in (33cm) Lenci child, all original. *H & J Foulke, Inc.*

Bottom: 14in (36cm) Lenci *"Lucia"* face child. *H & J Foulke, Inc.*

Lenci-Type

Top: 13in (33cm) Lenci-type girl. *H & J Foulke, Inc.*

Bottom: 12in (31cm) Lenci-type boy and girl, all original. *H & J Foulke, Inc.*

Lenci-type continued

Felt or Cloth Doll: Mohair wig, painted features; stuffed cloth body; original clothes or costume; excellent condition.
Child dolls, 16 - 18in (41 - 46cm) up to **$750** depending upon quality
Foreign costume, very good quality:

7½ - 8½in (19-22cm)	**$ 40 - 50**
12in (31cm)	**90 - 110**

Alma, Turin, Italy, 16in (41cm)
400 - 500
(For photograph see *9th Blue Book*, page 53.)

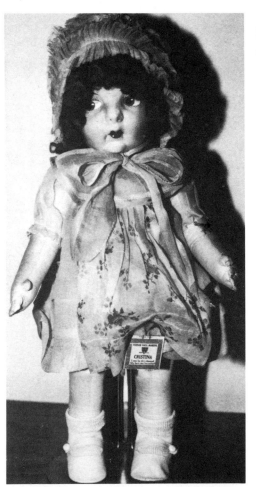

Dean's Rag Book Company, England:

14 - 16in (36 - 41cm)	**$500 - 600**
Printed Cloth, 10in (25cm)	**85 - 95**
16 - 18in (41 - 46cm)	**160 - 185**

Farnell's Alpha Toys, London, England:

14in (36cm)	**$400 - 500**

Coronation Doll of King George VI, 1937,
16in (41cm) **400 - 450**
(For photograph see page 13.)
Eugenie Poir, Gre-Poir French Doll Makers, Paris and New York, 17 - 21in (43 - 46cm):

Mint condition	**$500 - 600**
Good condition	**300 - 400**

Raynal, Paris France: (For photograph see *9th Blue Book*, page 339.)

17 - 18in (43 - 46cm)	**$400 - 500**

18in (46cm) *Cristina* by Eugenie Poir. *Courtesy of Carolyn Tracz.*

Liberty of London

FACTS

Liberty & Co. of London, England. 1906 - on. All-fabric. 5½ - 10in (14 - 25cm). **Mark:** Cloth label or paper tag "Liberty of London."

British Coronation Dolls: 1939. All-cloth with painted and needle-sculpted faces; original clothes; excellent condition. The **Royal Family** and **Coronation Participants.**

5½ - 9½in (14 - 24cm)   **$100 - 125***

Other English Historical and Ceremonial Characters: All-cloth with painted and needle-sculpted faces; original clothes; excellent condition.

9 - 10in (23 - 25cm)   **$100 - 125**

*Allow extra for Princesses Elizabeth and Margaret.

Queen Elizabeth II and *Prince Phillip*, all original. *H & J Foulke, Inc.*

Limbach

FACTS

Limbach Porzellanfabrik, Limbach, Thüringia, Germany (porcelain factory). Factory started in 1772. Bisque head, composition body; all-bisque.

Mark:

MADE IN GERMANY

All-Bisque Child: Ca. 1900. Child all of bisque (sometimes pink bisque) with wire jointed shoulders and hips; molded hair (often with a blue molded bow) or bald head with mohair wig, painted eyes, closed mouth, white stockings, blue garters, brown slippers or strap shoes.

Mark:

GERMANY

4 - 5in (10 - 13cm)	$ 75 -	95
6in (15cm)	125	
6½in (16cm) swivel neck	225	
Glass eyes:		
5in (13cm)	160 -	185
8in (20cm)	275 -	325
Character, jointed arms only,		
4 - 5in (10 - 13cm)	85 -	95

6½in (16cm) 573 child with swivel neck. *H & J Foulke, Inc.*

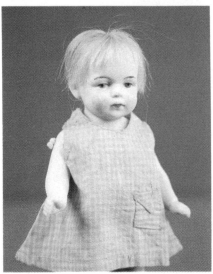

Above: 6in (15cm) 620 child. *H & J Foulke, Inc.*

Left: 6in (15cm) black 8675 baby with swivel neck. *H & J Foulke, Inc.*

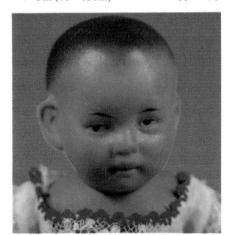

All-Bisque Baby: Ca. 1910. Baby with painted hair and facial features; wire jointed shoulders and hips, bent arms and legs; bare feet. (For photograph see *8th Blue Book*, page 299.)

Mark: Clover and number with "P."

4 - 5in (10 - 13cm)	**$ 85 - 100***
7in (18cm)	**135***
11 - 12in (28 - 31cm) fine quality	
	550 - 650
Black #8675, 6in (15cm)	**800 - 900****

*Allow more for fine quality.
**Not enough price samples to compute a reliable range.

Limbach Child Doll: 1893 - 1899; 1919 - on. Perfect bisque head, good wig, glass eyes, open mouth with teeth; composition jointed body; dressed; all in good condition. (For photograph see *9th Blue Book*, page 297.)

Wally, Rita, or **Norma** after 1919:

17 - 19in (43 - 48cm)	**$550 - 600***
23 - 24in (58 - 61cm)	**700 - 750***

Incised with clover (1893 - 1899):

14 - 17in (36 - 43cm) open mouth	
	900 - 1200**
27in (69cm) closed mouth	
	2100

#8682 Character Baby: open/closed mouth, 15in (38cm)   **900 - 1000****

*Allow 30 - 40% more for fine quality.
**Not enough price samples to compute a reliable range.

Armand Marseille (A.M.)

FACTS

Armand Marseille of Köppelsdorf, Thüringia, Germany (porcelain and doll factory). 1885 - on. Bisque socket and shoulder head, composition, cloth or kid body.

Marks:

A.M. - DE P
N°. 3600.
3.
Made in Germany.

A0½ M
Florodora
Armand Marseille
Made in Germany

1894
A M 5/0 DE P
Germany

18" Made in Germany
A (Baby 2½ Betty) M
D. R. G. M.

Child Doll: 1890 - on. Perfect bisque head, nice wig, set or sleep eyes, open mouth; composition ball-jointed body or jointed kid body with bisque lower arms; pretty clothes; all in good condition.

#390, (larger sizes marked only "A. [size] M."), **Florodora** (composition body):

9 - 10in (23 - 25cm)	**$ 235 - 265***

(Continued on next page.)

9in (23cm) 390 girl, fully jointed body, all original. *H & J Foulke, Inc.*

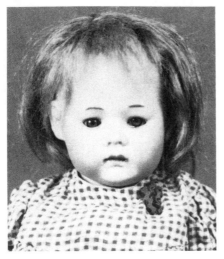

13in (33cm) 231 *Fany* character. *Private Collection.*

(Continued from preceding page.)

12 - 14in (31 - 36cm)	$ 250 - 300*
16 - 18in (41 - 46cm)	350 - 400*
20in (51cm)	425 - 450*
23 - 24in (58 - 61cm)	500 - 525*
28 - 29in (71 - 74cm)	700 - 750
30 - 32in (76 - 81cm)	850 - 950
35 - 36in (89 - 91cm)	1200 - 1500
38in (96cm)	1900 - 2100
40 - 42in (102 - 107cm)	2200 - 2400

Five-piece composition body,

6 - 7in (15 - 18cm)	175 - 200
9 - 10in (23 - 25cm)	235 - 265

Closed mouth, 5 - 5½in (12 - 14cm)
250 - 275

#1894 (composition body): (For photograph see page 276.)

10in (25cm)	350 - 375
14 - 16in (36 - 41cm)	450 - 500
21 - 23in (53 - 58cm)	750 - 850

#370, 3200, 1894, Florodora, Anchor 2015, Rosebud shoulder heads:

11 - 12in (28 - 31cm)	175 - 200
14 - 16in (36 - 41cm)	225 - 275
22 - 24in (56 - 61cm)	375 - 425

*Add $100 for factory original clothes; subtract $50-75 for cardboard and stick body.

#2000: 14in (36cm)   900**

Queen Louise, Rosebud (composition body):

12in (31cm)	**$325 - 350**
23 - 25in (58 - 64cm)	**500 - 550**
28 - 29in (71 - 74cm)	**650 - 750**

Baby Betty:

14 - 16in (36 - 41cm) composition body
525 - 575

19 - 21in (48 - 53cm) kid body
525 - 575

#1894, 1892, 1896, 1897 shoulder heads (excellent quality):

19 - 22in (48 - 56cm)   475 - 525

Name shoulder head child: 1898 to World War I. Perfect bisque shoulder head marked with doll's name, jointed kid or cloth body, bisque lower arms; good wig, glass eyes, open mouth; well dressed; all in good condition. Names include Rosebud, Lilly, Alma, Mabel, Darling, Beauty and Princess.

Marks: *Alma* *Lilly*
        5   10

12 - 14in (31 - 36cm)	**$185 - 215**
20 - 22in (51 - 56cm)	**325 - 375**
25in (64cm)	**425 - 475**

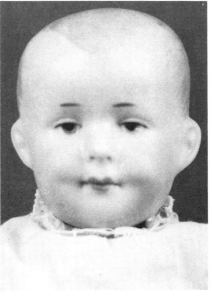

9½in (24cm) 600 character. *H & J Foulke, Inc.*

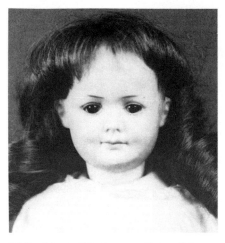

11½in (29cm) 550 character. *Esther Schwartz Collection.*

Character Children: 1910 - on. Perfect bisque head, molded hair or wig, glass or painted eyes, open or closed mouth; composition body; dressed; all in good condition.

#230 Fany (molded hair):
15 - 16in (38 - 41cm) **$5000 - 6000**
19in (48cm) **7500 - 8500**
20in (51cm) faint hairline **6000**

#231 Fany (wigged):
14 - 15in (36 - 38cm) **3500 - 4000**
#250, 11 - 13in (28 - 33cm) **750**
#340, 13in (33cm) **2600****
#372 Kiddiejoy shoulder head, "Mama" body, 19in (48cm) **850 - 900**
#400 (child body),
20in (51cm) **3500****
#500, 600, 13 - 15in (33 - 38cm)
650 - 750
#550 (glass eyes):
12in (31cm) **2200**
18 - 20in (46 - 51cm) **3450 - 3750****
#560, (For photograph see page 276.),
11 - 13in (28 - 33cm) **750**
#620 shoulder head, 16in (41cm)
1250**
#640 shoulder head (same face as **550** socket), 20in (51cm) **1500 - 1650****

**Not enough price samples to compute a reliable range.

#700:
13in (33cm) painted eyes **2000**
14in (36cm) glass eyes **3000 - 3500**
A.M. (intaglio eyes), 16 - 17in (41 - 43cm)
4500 up
Character Babies and Toddlers: 1910 - on. Perfect bisque head, good wig, sleep eyes, open mouth some with teeth; composition bent-limb body; suitably dressed; all in nice condition.
Marks: Armand Marseille Germany 990 A 9/0 M Germany 326 A 11 M

Mold #990, 985, 971, 996, 1330, 326, (solid dome), 980, 991, 327, 329 and others:
10 - 11in (25 - 28cm) **$ 325 - 350**
13 - 15in (33 - 38cm) **375 - 425**
18 - 20in (46 - 51cm) **500 - 550**
22in (56cm) **650**
24 - 25in (61 - 64cm) **750 - 850**
#233:
13 - 15in (33 - 38cm) **500 - 550**
20in (51cm) **700 - 800**
#251/248 (open/closed mouth),
18in (46cm) **1800 - 2100**
#251/248 (open mouth),
12 - 15in (31 - 38cm) **750 - 850**

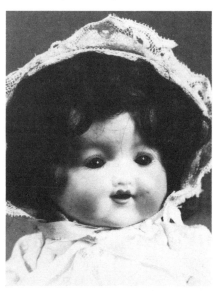

9in (23cm) 992 *Our Pet*. *H & J Foulke, Inc.* (For further information see page 277.)

Armand Marseille (A.M.) continued

23in (58cm) 1894 girl. *H & J Foulke, Inc.* (For further information see page 274.)

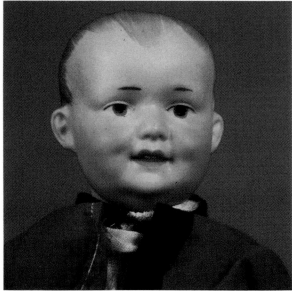

10in (25cm) 560 character. *Private Collection.* (For further information see page 275.)

Armand Marseille (A.M.) continued

#410 (2 rows of teeth),
  15 - 16in (38 - 41cm) **1200 - 1500** **
#518:
  16 - 18in (41 - 46cm) **600 - 700**
  25in (64cm) **1000 - 1200**
#560A:
  12in (31cm) **525 - 550**
  15 - 17in (38 - 43cm) **650 - 700**
#580, 590 (open/closed mouth):
  14 - 15in (31 - 38cm) **1200 - 1500**
  18in (46cm) **1600 - 1800**
#590 (open mouth):
  12in (31cm) **600**
  16 - 18in (41 - 46cm) **850 - 950**
#920 shoulder head, "mama" body,
  21in (53cm) **900** **
Melitta, 19in (48cm) **750 - 850**

Infant: 1924 - on. Solid-dome bisque head with molded and/or painted hair, sleep eyes; composition body or hard-stuffed jointed cloth body or soft-stuffed cloth body; dressed; all in good condition.

Mark: A. M.
         Germany.
         351.14K

#351, 341 Kiddiejoy and **Our Pet:** (See photograph on page 275.)
Head circumference:
  8 - 9in (20 - 23cm) **$225 - 250***
  10in (25cm) **275 - 300***
  12 - 13in (31 - 33cm) **350 - 425***
  15in (38cm) **600 - 650***
  6in (15cm) compo body **225 - 250**
  24in (61cm) wigged toddler
    950
#352, 17 - 20in (43 - 51cm) long
    575 - 625
#347:
Head circumference:
  12 - 13in (31 - 33cm) **475 - 525**
Baby Phyllis:
Head circumference:
  9in (23cm) black **500**
  12 - 13in (31 - 33cm) **425 - 475**
Baby Gloria, 15 - 16in (38 - 41cm)
    700 - 800

**Not enough price samples to compute a reliable range.
*Allow $25-75 extra for composition body.

17in (43cm) 590 character. *Richard Wright Antiques.*

9in (23cm) MH 300 lady, all original. *H & J Foulke, Inc.* (For further information see page 278.)

Armand Marseille (A.M.) continued

Marked "Just Me" Character: Ca. 1925. Perfect bisque socket head, curly wig, glass eyes to side, closed mouth; composition body; dressed; all in good condition. Some of these dolls, particularly the painted bisque ones, were used by Vogue Doll Company in the 1930s and will be found with original Vogue labeled clothes.

Mark:

Just ME
Registered
Germany
A 310/5/0 M

7½in (19cm)	**$1000**
9in (23cm)	**1250 - 1350**
11in (28cm)	**1500 - 1600**
13in (33cm)	**2000 - 2200**

Painted bisque:

7 - 8in (18 - 20cm) all original
                                              800 - 900
10in (25cm) all original   **1000 - 1100**

Lady: 1910 - 1930. Bisque head with mature face, mohair wig, sleep eyes, open or closed mouth; composition lady body with molded bust, long slender arms and legs; appropriate clothes; all in good condition. (For photograph see *9th Blue Book*, page 304.)

#401 and **400** (slim body):

12 - 13in (31 - 33cm):

Open mouth	**$1050 - 1250**
Closed mouth	**2000 - 2500**

#300 (naked M.H.): (For photograph see page 277.)

9in (23cm)	**1400 - 1500****
All original	**1650****

**Not enough price samples to compute a reliable range.

9½in (24cm) painted bisque 310 *"Just Me."*
H & J Foulke, Inc.

Mascotte

FACTS

May Freres Cie, 1890 - 1897; Jules Nicolas Steiner, 1898 - on. Paris, France. 1890 - 1902. Bisque head, composition and wood jointed body.

Mark:

"BÉBÉ MASCOTTE
PARIS"

Bébé Mascotte: Bisque socket head, good wig, closed mouth, paperweight eyes, pierced ears; jointed composition and wood body; appropriate clothes; all in good condition.

16 - 18in (41 - 46cm)	**$3500 - 4200**
23 - 24in (58 - 61cm)	**5200 - 5800**

20in (51cm) Mascotte. *Joanna Ott Collection.*

Metal Dolls

FACTS

Various U.S. companies, such as Atlas Doll & Toy Co. and Giebeler-Falk, N.Y., U.S.A. Ca. 1917 - on. All-metal, or metal head with cloth body (may have composition lower limbs).

Metal Child: All metal, body fully jointed at neck, shoulders, elbows, wrists, hips, knees and ankles; sleep eyes, open/closed mouth with painted teeth; dressed; all in good condition. (Body may be jointed composition with metal hands and feet.)
16 - 20in (41 - 51cm)   **$325 - 425**

Metal Baby: All metal (with bent limbs) jointed at shoulders and hips with metal springs; molded and painted hair and facial features, painted or sleep eyes, closed or open mouth; appropriate clothes; all in good condition.
11 - 13in (28 - 33cm)   **$100 - 125**
18 - 20in (46 - 51cm) metal head, cloth body with composition lower limbs
165 - 185

19in (48cm) Giebeler-Falk all metal girl. *H & J Foulke, Inc.*

Metal Heads

FACTS

Buschow & Beck, Germany (Minerva): Karl Standfuss, Germany (Juno); Alfred Heller, Germany (Diana). Ca. 1888 - on. Metal shoulder head, kid or cloth body.

Mark:

Mark may often be found on front of shoulder plate.

Marked Metal Head Child: Metal shoulder head on cloth or kid body, bisque or composition hands; dressed; very good condition, not repainted.

Molded hair, painted eyes,
12 - 14in (31 - 36cm)	**$110 - 135**

Molded hair, glass eyes,
12 - 14in (31 - 36cm)	**150 - 175**
20 - 22in (51 - 56cm)	**225 - 250**

Wig and glass eyes,
14 - 16in (36 - 41cm)	**225 - 250**
20 - 22in (51 - 56cm)	**275 - 325**

Below left: 14in (36cm) *Minerva* metal head. *H & J Foulke, Inc.*

Below right: 18in (46cm) *Minerva* metal head. *H & J Foulke, Inc.*

Missionary Ragbabies

FACTS

Julia Beecher, Elmira, N.Y., U.S.A.
1893 - 1910. All-cloth. 16 - 23in (41 -
58cm).
Designer: Julia Jones Beecher
Mark: None.

Beecher Baby: Handmade stuffed stockinette doll with looped wool hair, painted
eyes and mouth, needle-sculpted face; appropriately dressed; all in good condition.
  20 - 23in (51 - 59cm)   **$5000 up****
Fair condition, 18in (46cm)   **2500****

**Not enough price samples to compute a reli-
able average.

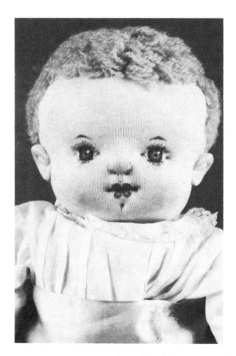 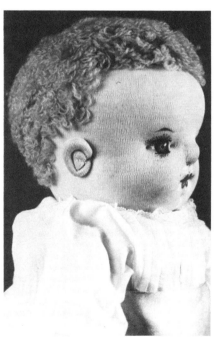

20in (51cm) *Missionary Ragbaby*. *Private Collection.*

Molly-'es

FACTS

International Doll Co., Philadelphia, Pa., U.S.A. Made clothing only. Purchased undressed dolls from various manufacturers. 1920s - on. All-cloth or all-composition, later hard plastic and vinyl.
Clothes Designer: Mollye Goldman.
Mark: Usually a cardboard tag, dolls unmarked except for vinyl.

Molly-'es Composition Dolls: All-composition, jointed at neck, shoulders and hips; molded hair or wig, sleep eyes; beautiful original outfits; all in good condition.

Babies, 15 - 18in (38 - 46cm)
$175 - 225

Toddlers, 14 - 16in (36 - 41cm)
225 - 275

Ladies, 18 - 21in (46-53cm)
450 - 550

Sabu, (For photograph see *10th Blue Book*, page 3.),
15in (38cm) **550 - 600**

Sultan, 19in (48cm)
650

Princess, 15in (38cm)
600 - 650

Internationals: All-cloth with mask faces, mohair wigs (sometimes yarn), painted features; variety of costumes, all original clothes; in excellent condition with wrist tag. (For photograph see *10th Blue Book*, page 330.)
13in (33cm) **75 - 95**
Mint in box **100 - 125**

15in (38cm) *Princess. H & J Foulke, Inc.*

Munich Art Dolls

FACTS

Marion Kaulitz. 1908 - 1912. All-composition, fully-jointed bodies.
Designer: Paul Vogelsanger and others.
Mark: Sometimes signed on doll's neck.

Munich Art Dolls: Molded composition character heads with hand-painted features; fully-jointed composition bodies; dressed; all in good condition.

13in (33cm)	**$2200 - 2500**
18 - 19in (46 - 48cm)	**3000 - 4000****
12in (31cm) fair condition	
	1100 - 1300

**Not enough price samples to compute a reliable range.

12in (31cm) Munich Art Doll. *Cookie Wershbale.*

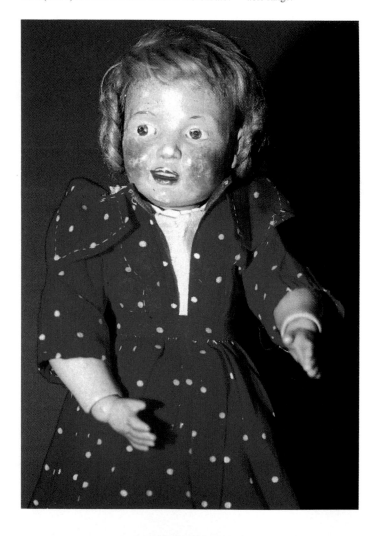

Nancy Ann Storybook Dolls Co.

FACTS

Nancy Ann Storybook Dolls Co., South San Francisco, CA., U.S.A. 1936 - on. Painted bisque in 1936 - 1947; 1948 on hard plastic.
Mark: Various as indicated.

Marked Storybook Doll: 1936 - 1942. Painted bisque, mohair wig, painted eyes; one-piece body, head and stiff legs, jointed arms; original clothes; excellent condition with sticker or wrist tag and box. 5½ - 7in (13-19cm).

1936 Babies only: Gold sticker on front of outfit; sunburst box. **Mark:** "88 Made in Japan" or "87 Made in Japan"
$400 up

1937 - 1938: Gold sticker on front of outfit; sunburst box, gold label. **Mark:** "Made in Japan 1146," "Made in Japan 1148," "Japan," "Made in Japan" or "AMERICA"
300 up

1938 - 1939: Gold sticker on front of skirt; sunburst transition to silver dot box. **Mark:** "JUDY ANN USA" (crude mark), "STORYBOOK USA" (crude mark). Molded sock/molded bang. **Mark:** "StoryBook Doll USA"
300 up

Judy Ann in storybook box with extra outfits
450 up

1940: Gold sticker on front of skirt; colored box with white polka dots. Molded Sock **Mark:** "StoryBook Doll USA"
200 up

1941 - 1942: Gold wrist tag; white box with colored polka dots; strung legs. **Mark:** "StoryBook Doll USA"
70 up

1943 - 1947: Gold wrist tag; white box with colored polka dots; stiff legs. **Mark:** "StoryBook Doll USA" (some later dolls with plastic arms)
50 up
Socket head
80 up

Marked Storybook Doll: Hard plastic, swivel head, mohair wig, painted eyes, jointed legs; original clothes, gold wrist tag; white box with colored polka dots, excellent condition.
40 up

Painted bisque *Alice in Wonderland* with molded socks, all original with sticker. *Courtesy of Jane Mann.*

Hard plastic *Storybook Baby. H & J Foulke, Inc.*

Nancy Ann Storybook Dolls Co. continued

Painted bisque *Pretty Maid*, all original with wrist tag. *H & J Foulke, Inc.*

Painted bisque *Pussy Cat*, all original. *Private Collection.*

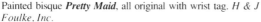

Bent-limb Baby:

Star hand baby	**$125 up**
Bisque with closed fist, open mouth	**135 up**
Painted bisque	**100 up**
Hard Plastic	**75 up**
Boxed furniture	**300 up**

Special Series Dolls:

Painted bisque with white painted socks	**$150 up**
Glow-in-Dark	**100 up**
Flower Girl Series	**200 up**
Masquerade, bisque strung leg	**250 up**
Around the World, bisque	**200 up**
Sports, bisque	**250 up**
Powder & Crinoline, bisque	**150 up**
Operetta, bisque	**100 up**
All Time Hit Parade, bisque	**100 up**
Topsy, bisque	**350 up**

Special Holiday inserts:

Bisque	**100 up**
Hard plastic	**75 up**
Nancy Ann Style Show, hard plastic, 17in (43cm)	**425 - 600**

Muffie, all hard plastic, wig, sleeping eyes, 8in (12cm) tall:

Mark: "StoryBook Dolls USA" some with "Muffie."

1953: straight leg nonwalker, painted lashes, no brows, dynel wig (side part with flip); 54 complete costumes. Original clothes, excellent condition **125 up**

1954: walker, molded eyeslashes, eyebrows after 1955, side part flip or braided wig; 30 additional costumes. Original clothes, excellent condition **125 up**

1956: hard plastic walker or bent-knee walker, rooted Saran wig (ponytail, braids or side part flip); vinyl head and hard plastic body; molded or painted upper lashes **125 up**

1968: reissued, unmarked, **Muffie Around the World,** straight leg walker, molded eyelashes, glued on wig. 12 dolls in polka dot cellophane see-through boxes **100 up**

FACTS

Gebrüder Ohlhaver, doll factory, Sonneberg, Thüringia, Germany. Heads made by Gebrüder Heubach, Ernst Heubach and Porzellanfabrik Mengersgereuth. 1912 - on. Bisque socket head, ball-jointed composition body.

Trademarks: Revalo.

Mark: Revalo Germany 3

Revalo Character Baby or **Toddler:** Perfect bisque socket head, good wig, sleep eyes, hair eyelashes, painted lower eyelashes, open mouth; ball-jointed toddler or baby bent-limb body; dressed; all in good condition.

#22:

14 - 16in (36 - 41cm)	**$500 - 550***
20 - 22in (51 - 56cm)	**750 - 850***

*Allow $200-250 extra for toddler body.

Revalo Child Doll: Bisque socket head, good wig, sleep eyes, hair eyelashes, painted lower eyelashes, open mouth; ball-jointed composition body; dressed; all in good condition. Mold #150 or #10727.

15 - 16in (38 - 41cm)	**$500 - 550**
22in (56cm)	**725 - 775**
25 - 27in (64 - 69cm)	**850 - 950**

Revalo Character Doll: Bisque head with molded hair, painted eyes, open/closed mouth; compositin body; dressed; all in good condition.

Coquette. (For photograph see *10th Blue Book*, page 333.)	
12in (31cm)	**$700 - 750**
Coquette with hairbows, 14in (36cm)	
	900 - 950

See following page for photographs.

Ohlhaver continued

See preceding page for further information.

13in (33cm) Revalo baby. *H & J Foulke, Inc.*

26in (66cm) Revalo child. *H & J Foulke, Inc.*

Old Cottage Dolls

FACTS

Old Cottage Toys, Allargate, Rustington, Littlehampton, Sussex, Great Britain. 1948. Composition or hard plastic heads, stuffed cloth bodies. Usually 8 - 9in (20 - 23cm).
Designers: Greta Fleischmann and her daughter Susi.
Mark: Paper label - "Old Cottage Toys" - handmade in Great Britain.

Old Cottage Doll: Hard plastic face with hand painted features, wig, stuffed cloth body; original clothing; excellent condition.

8 - 9in (20 - 23cm)	**$135 - 165**
12 - 13in (31 - 33cm), mint-in box	**300****

**Not enough price samples to compute a reliable average.

8in (20cm) Old Cottage Doll. *H & J Foulke, Inc.*

Oriental Dolls

Japanese Traditional Dolls:
Ichimatsu (play doll): 1850 - on. Papier-mâché swivel head on shoulder plate, hips, lower legs and feet (early ones have jointed wrists and ankles); cloth midsection, cloth (floating) upper arms and legs; hair wig, dark glass eyes, pierced ears and nostrils; original or appropriate clothes; all in good condition.

Ca. 1900:
12 - 14in (31 - 36cm)	**$ 350 - 400**
18 - 20in (46 - 51cm)	**500 - 600**
Boy, 18 - 20in (46 - 51cm)	**650 - 750**
Three-bend body, 11in (28cm) at auction	**2800**
Early exceptional quality, 24in (61cm)	**1600**

Ca. 1920s:
13 - 15in (33 - 38cm)	**150 - 175**
17 - 18in (43 - 46cm)	**210 - 250**
Ca. 1940s, 12 - 14in (31 - 36cm)	**85 - 95**

Traditional Lady:
Ca. 1900, 12in (31cm)	**$ 500 up**
1920s:	
10 - 12in (25 - 31cm)	**150 - 175**
16in (41cm)	**235 - 265**
1940s, 12 - 14in (31 - 36cm)	**85 - 95**

Traditional Warrior:
1880s, 16 - 18in (41 - 46cm)	**$ 800 up**
1920s, 11 - 12in (28 - 31cm)	**250 up**

Royal Personages:
Ca. 1890, 10in (25cm)	**$ 800 up**
1920s - 1930s:	
4 - 6in (10 - 15cm)	**100 - 125**
12in (31cm)	**350 up**

Baby with bent limbs:
Ca. 1910, 11in (28cm)	**$ 250 up**
Ca. 1930s, souvenir dolls,	
8 - 10in (20 - 25cm)	**65 - 85**

Oriental Bisque Dolls: Ca. 1900 - on. Made by German firms such as Simon & Halbig, Armand Marseille, J.D. Kestner and others. Bisque head tinted yellow; matching ball-jointed or baby body; original or appropriate clothes; all in excellent condition. (See previous *Blue Books* for photographs of dolls not pictured here.)

B.P. #220, 16 - 17in (41 - 43cm)
$3200 - 3500**

Belton-type, 10in (25cm)
1200 - 1500**

BSW #500, 14 - 15in (36 - 38cm)
$2000 - 2400**

Tête Jumeau, closed mouth,
19 - 20in (48 - 51cm)
$48,000 - 62,000

JDK 243:
13 - 14in (33 - 36cm)
$4500 - 5000
18 - 20in (46 - 51cm)   6250 - 6500
Molded hair, 14in (36cm)
6500 - 6800**

A.M. 353:
12 - 14in (31 - 36cm)
$1200 - 1350
10in (25cm) cloth body   900

A.M. Girl: 8 - 9in (20 - 23cm)
650 - 750

S&H 1329:
12 - 14in (31 - 36cm)
$1800 - 2200
18 - 19in (46 - 48cm)
2700 - 3000

Oriental Dolls continued

S&H 1099, 1129, & 1199:
15in (38cm)	**$2700 - 2800**
19 - 20in (48 - 51cm)	**3200 - 3500**

S PB H, 9in (23cm)   **$ 650 - 750**

#164, 16 - 17in (41 - 43cm)
                                         $2300 - 2500

Unmarked:
4½in (12cm) painted eyes	**175**
6in (15cm) glass eyes	**425 - 450**
11 - 12in (28 - 31cm) glass eyes	**850 - 950**

All-Bisque JDK Baby:
5½in (14cm)	**$1250 - 1350**
8in (20cm)	**1650**

All-Bisque S&H Child:
5½in (14cm)	**$ 650 - 750**
7in (18cm)	**850 - 950**

Unknown origin:
Lady with molded headband, wood jointed body, 13in (33cm)
                                 $ 650 - 750**
Character man with molded mustache, jointed body 11in (28cm)   **$1100****

Baby Butterfly: 1911 - 1913. Made by E.I. Horsman. Composition head and hands, cloth body; painted black hair, painted features. (For photograph see *6th Blue Book,* page 286.)
13in (33cm)	**$ 300****

Ming Ming Baby: Quan-Quan Co., Los Angeles and San Francisco, Calif., U.S.A. Ca. 1930. All-composition baby, jointed at shoulders and hips; painted facial features; sometimes with black yarn hair, original costume of colorful taffeta with braid trim; feet painted black or white for shoes.
10 - 12in (25 - 31cm)	**$ 175 - 200**

**Not enough price samples to compute a reliable average.

Oriental Dolls continued

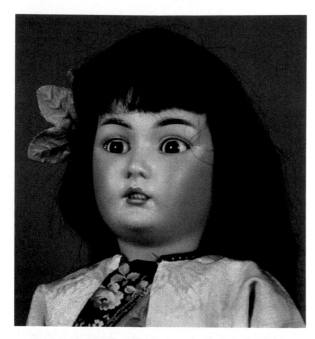

15½in (39cm) S&H 1329 girl.
Anna May Case Collection.

8in (20cm) JDK all-bisque
Oriental baby.
H & J Foulke, Inc.

11in (28cm) baby with painted hair. Ca. 1910. *Betty Lunz Collection.*

15½in (39cm) JDK 243 Oriental baby. *Betty Lunz Collection.*

12½in (32cm) portrait boy. Ca. 1900. *Betty Lunz Collection.*

13in (33cm) warrior, gold cardboard armor. 1900-1910. *Betty Lunz Collection.*

Papier-mâché (So-Called French-Type)

FACTS

Heads by German firms such as Johann Müller of Sonneberg and Andreas Voit of Hildburghausen, were sold to French and other doll makers. 1835 - 1850. Papier-mâché shoulder head, pink kid body.
Mark: None.

French-type Papier-mâché: Shoulder head with painted black pate, brush marks around face, nailed on human hair wig (often missing), set-in glass eyes, closed or open mouth with bamboo teeth, pierced nose; pink kid body with stiff arms and legs; appropriate old clothes; all in good condition, showing some wear.

18 - 20in (46 - 51cm)	**$1800 - 2000**
24 - 26in (61 - 66cm)	**2200 - 2500**
Painted eyes:	
14 - 16in (36 - 41cm)	**850 - 950**
6 - 8in (15 - 20cm)	**375 - 475**
Wood-jointed body, 6in (15cm)	
	750 - 800
Shell decoration:	
4½in (12cm)	**500 - 600**
8in (20cm) pair	**1000 - 1200**
Poupard, molded bonnet and clothes,	
18in (46cm)	**400 - 500**

Below left: 20in (51cm) French papier-mâché, missing original wig. *Private Collection.*

Below right: 13in (33cm) French papier-mâché with carton body. *Richard Wright Antiques.*

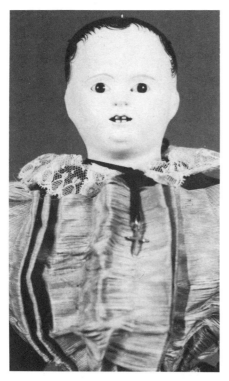

Papier-mâché (German)

FACTS

Various German firms of Sonneberg such as Johann Müller, Müller & Strasburger, F.M. Schilling, Heinrich Stier, A. Wislizenus, and Cuno & Otto Dressel. 1816 - on. Papier-mâché shoulder head, cloth body, sometimes leather arms or kid body with wood limbs.

22in (56cm) glass-eyed papier-mâché. *H & J Foulke, Inc.*

Papier-mâché Shoulder Head: Ca. 1840s to 1860s. Unretouched shoulder head, molded hair, painted eyes; some wear and crazing; cloth or kid body; original or appropriate old clothing; entire doll in fair condition.

16 - 18in (41 - 46cm)	**$ 900 - 1000**
22 - 24in (56 - 61cm)	**1100 - 1300**
32in (81cm)	**1900 - 2200**
Glass eyes, short hair:	
19in (48cm)	**1650 - 1850**
24in (61cm)	**2400**
Glass eyes, long hair,	
22in (56cm)	**1700 - 2000**
Flirty eyes, long hair,	
23in (58cm)	**2700 - 3000**

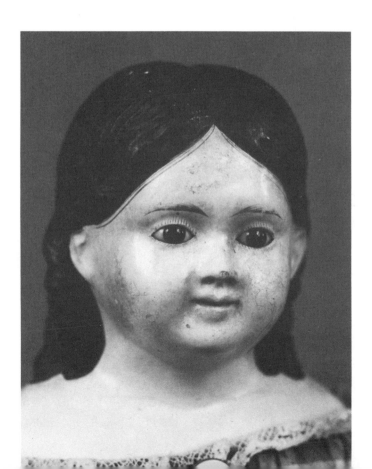

Papier-mâché (German) continued

Molded Hair Papier-mâché: (so-called "milliners' models") 1820s - 1860s. Unretouched shoulder head, various molded hairdos, eyes blue, black or brown, painted features; original kid body, wooden arms and legs; original or very old handmade clothing; entire doll in fair condition.

Long curls:

9in (23cm)	$ 550
13in (33cm)	675 - 725
23in (58cm)	1400 - 1500

Covered wagon hairdo:

7in (18cm)	275 - 325
11in (28cm)	450 - 500
15in (38cm)	675 - 775

Side curls with braided bun:

9 - 10in (23 - 25cm)	750 - 850
13 - 15in (31 - 38cm)	1300 - 1500

Left: 15in (38cm) papier-mâché with fancy hairdo. *Richard Wright Antiques.*

Below left: 23in (58cm) papier-mâché with long curls. *Richard Wright Antiques.*

Below right: 13in (33cm) papier-mâché with side curls and braided bun. *Richard Wright Antiques.*

Center part with molded bun:

7in (18cm)	$ 525
11in (28cm)	950 - 1000
Wood-jointed body	1200 - 1350

Side curls with high beehive, (Apollo knot):

11in (28cm)	950 - 1000
18in (46cm)	1900 - 2100

Coiled braids at ears, braided bun, 20in (51cm) **2000 - 2200**

Braided coronet, molded comb, painted side curls, all original, very good condition, 14½in (37cm) at auction

3850

Sonneberg-type Papier-mâché: Ca. 1880 - 1910. Shoulder head with molded and painted black or blonde hair, painted eyes, closed mouth; cloth body sometimes with leather arms; old or appropriate clothes; all in good condition, showing some wear.

Mark: Usually unmarked. Some marked:

13 - 15in (33 - 38cm)	$ 250 - 300*
18 - 19in (46 - 48cm)	350 - 400*
23 - 25in (58 - 64cm)	500 - 600*
Glass eyes, 13in (33cm)	475

*Allow extra for an unusual hairdo.

Patent Washable-type: 1880s to 1914.
See page 143.

26in (66cm) Sonneberg-type papier-mâché lady. *H & J Foulke, Inc.*

Pintel & Godchaux

FACTS

Pintel & Godchaux, Montreuil, France.
1880 - 1899. Bisque head, jointed composition body.
Trademark: Bébé Charmant.
Mark:　　B　　　　A
　　　　　　P 9 G　　P 7 G

Marked P.G. Doll: Perfect bisque head, paperweight eyes, closed mouth, good wig; jointed composition and wood body; appropriate clothing; all in good condition.

20 - 24in (51 - 61cm)　**$2500 - 3000**
Open mouth, 20in (51cm)　**1700 - 1900**

P.G. Bébé. *H & J Foulke, Inc.*

Parian-Type (Untinted Bisque)

FACTS

Various German firms. Ca. 1860s through 1870s. Untinted bisque shoulder head, cloth or kid body, leather, wood, china or combination extremities.
Mark: Usually none, sometimes numbers.

Unmarked Parian: Pale or untinted shoulder head, sometimes with molded blouse, beautifully molded hairdo (may have ribbons, beads, comb or other decoration), painted eyes, closed mouth; cloth body; lovely clothes; entire doll in fine condition.

Common, plain style:

8 - 10in (20 - 25cm)	**$135 - 185**
16in (41cm)	**300 - 350**
24in (61cm)	**475 - 525**

Very fancy hairdo and/or elaborately decorated blouse
800 - 2500

Very fancy with glass eyes
1500 - 3250

Pretty hairdo, simple ribbon or comb:

14in (36cm)	**425 - 475**
18 - 20in (46 - 51cm)	**650 - 750**

Simple hairdo with applied flowers,
20in (51cm)   **850**

Man, molded collar and tie, 16 - 17in (41 - 43cm)   **750**

Boy:
19in (48cm) short black hair
1800
23in (58cm) brown hair, glass eyes
3000

"Augusta Victoria," 17in (43cm)
1200

Molded plate, blonde curls, ribbon, glass eyes 14in (36cm)
1300 - 1500

Alice hairdo, 21in (53cm)   **$ 750 - 800**
"Countess Dagmar," 19in (48cm)
950
Molded blonde hair, blue ribbon, glass eyes, fashion face, swivel neck, 21in (53cm)
3500 - 4000
Blonde hair, blue glass eyes, 21in (53cm)
900 - 1000
"Irish Queen," Limbach 8552, 16in (41cm)
600 - 700
Brown hair, snood, 24in (61cm)
1200
Pink lustre hat or snood, 17in (43cm)
1700 - 1800
Molded gray bonnet, 5in (13cm)
1100 - 1200
Molded yellow bonnet, 4½in (12cm)
850

Parian lady with unusual hair decoration.
Richard Wright Antiques.

Parian-Type (Untinted Bisque)

All-Parian, pink lustre boots, 5½in (14cm)
$ 185 - 200

Blonde hair pulled back into individual
curls, glass eyes, swivel neck, pierced
ears, 23in (58cm) **2900**

"**Dolley Madison**," glass eyes, swivel
neck, 20in (51cm) **1600**

Pink lustre tiara, gold earrings, 12in
(31cm) **900**

Short blonde hair, wavy curls combed to
front, wide black hairband, 21in (53cm)
1350

Above: 14in (36cm) Parian lady with lovely
molding detail. *Richard Wright Antiques.*

Right: 18in (46cm) Parian lady with decorated
plate. *H & J Foulke, Inc.*

P.D.

FACTS

Probably Petit & Dumontier, Paris, France. Some heads made by Francois Gaultier. 1878 - 1890. Bisque head, composition body.

Mark:

P.2.D

P.D. Bébé: Perfect bisque head with paperweight eyes, closed mouth, pierced ears, good wig; jointed composition body (some have metal hands); appropriate clothes; all in good condition.

16 - 18in (41 - 46cm)	**$18,000 - 20,000**
26in (66cm)	**25,000 - 28,000**

23in (58cm) P.D. Bébé. *Private Collection.*

Philadelphia Baby

FACTS

J.B. Sheppard & Co., Philadelphia, Pa., U.S.A. Ca. 1900. All-cloth. 18 - 22in (46 - 56cm).
Mark: None.

Philadelphia Baby: All-cloth with treated shoulder-type head, lower arms and legs; painted hair, well-molded facial features, ears; stocking body; very good condition.

18 - 22in (46 - 56cm)	**$3500 - 4000**
Mint condition	**5000**
Fair, showing wear	**2500**
Very worn	**1600 - 1800**
Rare style face (see *6th Blue Book*, page 302 for exact doll) at auction	**9350**

21in (53cm) Philadelphia Baby, rare style face. *H & J Foulke, Inc.*

Pre-Greiner (So-called)

FACTS

Unknown and various. Ca. 1850. Papier-mâché shoulder head, stuffed cloth body, mostly homemade, wood, leather or cloth extremities.
Mark: None.

Unmarked Pre-Greiner: Papier-mâché shoulder head; molded and painted black hair, pupil-less black glass eyes; cloth (sometimes kid) stuffed body, leather extremities; dressed in good old or original clothes; all in good condition.

18 - 22in (46 - 56cm)	**$1000 - 1350**
28 - 32in (71 - 81cm)	**2000 - 2300**
Fair condition, much wear,	
20 - 24in (51 - 61cm)	**700 - 800**
Flirty eye, 30in (76cm)	**3000**

27½in (70cm) Pre-Greiner, all original. *Becky and Jay Lowe.*

Rabery & Delphieu

FACTS

Rabery & Delphieu of Paris, France.
1856 (founded) - 1899 - then with
S.F.B.J. Bisque head, composition body.
Mark: "R.D." (from 1890). R 5/0 D
Mark:
On back of head: BÉBÉ RABERY
Body mark: 5ᶜ
(Please note last two lines illegible)

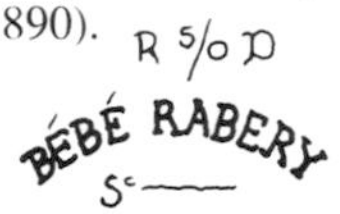

Very good quality bisque.

12 - 14in (31 - 36cm)	$ 2200 - 2700
18 - 19in (46 - 48cm)	3000 - 3500
24 - 25in (61 - 64cm)	3700 - 4200
28 (71cm)	4500 - 5000

28in (71cm) stunning face and clothes,
at auction **13,000**
Very beautiful, 14 - 15in (36 - 38cm)
3400
Lesser quality bisque (uneven coloring or
much speckling), 16 - 18in (41 - 46cm)
2250 - 2350
Open mouth, 19 - 22in (48 - 56cm)
2200 - 2500

Marked R.D. Bébé: Ca. 1880s. Bisque
head, lovely wig, paperweight eyes, closed
mouth; jointed composition body; beautifully dressed; entire doll in good condition.

17in (43cm) R.D. Bébé. *H & J Foulke, Inc.*

Raggedy Ann and Andy

Various makers. 1915 to present. All-cloth. 3 - 50in (8 - 125cm).
Creator Makers: Johnny B. Gruelle.

Early Raggedy Ann or **Andy:** Volland. All-cloth with movable arms and legs; brown yarn hair, button eyes, painted features; legs or striped fabric for hose and black for shoes; original clothes; all in good condition.
Mark: "PATENTED SEPT. 7, 1915"

16in (41cm)	**$1000 - 1200**
Much wear	**650 - 750**
Mint condition pair	**3000 - 3500**

Right: Volland *Raggedy Ann*. *Jan Foulke Collection.*

Below: Georgene *Raggedys*. *H & J Foulke, Inc.*

Raggedy Ann and Andy continued

Georgene *Beloved Belindy*. *Nancy A. Smith Collection.*

Georgene *Raggedy Andy*, original tag. *H & J Foulke, Inc.*

Volland **Percy**, **Uncle Clem** and two other Gruelle characters, 16in (41cm) at auction
$4200

Molly-'es Raggedy Ann or **Andy:** 1935 - 1938, manufactured by Molly-'es Doll Outfitters. Same as above, but with red hair and printed features; original clothes; all in good condition. (For photograph see *8th Blue Book*, page 195.)
Mark:
   "Raggedy Ann and Raggedy Andy Dolls, Manufactured by Molly'es Doll Outfitters" (printed writing in black on front torso)
   18 - 22in (46 - 56cm)   **$ 750 - 850**

Georgene Raggedy Ann or **Andy:** 1938 - 1963, manufactured by Georgene Novelties. Same as above, but with red hair and printed features; original clothes; all in good condition, some wear and fading acceptable.

Mark: Cloth label sewn in side seam of body.
   15 - 18in (38 - 46cm) **$ 225 - 275**
   Fair condition   **325 pair**
Asleep/Awake, 13in (33cm)
                         650 - 700 pair
Black Outlined nose, 19in (48cm)
                         450 - 500
   Pair, mint condition with individual name labels and tags   **2000**
Beloved Belindy   **1200 - 1500**

Knickerbocker Toy Co. Raggedy Ann or **Andy:** 1963 to 1982. Excellent condition.
   12 - 15in (28 - 38cm) **$ 25 - 35**
   24in (61cm)   **85 - 95**
   36in (91cm)   **125 - 150**
Beloved Belindy   **600 - 700**
Camel with Wrinkled Knees
                         150

Raleigh

FACTS

Jessie McCutcheon Raleigh, Chicago, Ill., U.S.A. 1916 - 1920. All-composition or composition heads and cloth bodies.
Designer: Jessie McCutcheon Raleigh.
Mark: None.

Raleigh Doll: Composition head, molded hair or wig, sleep or painted eyes; composition or cloth body; appropriate clothes; all in good condition. Child and baby styles.

11in (28cm) wigged	**$425 - 475**
13in (33cm) molded hair	**475 - 525**

Raleigh *Sonnie* redressed in copy of original outfit. *Joann Ott Collection.*

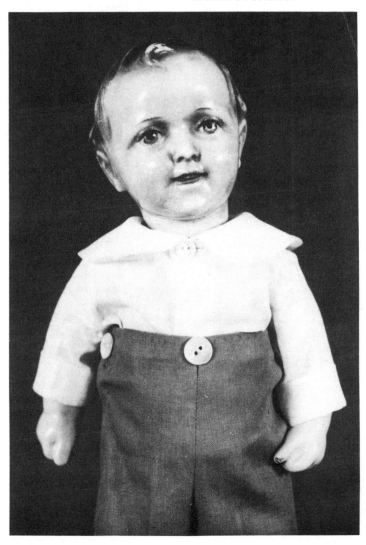

Ravca

FACTS _____
Bernard Ravca, Paris, France. After
1939, New York, N.Y., U.S.A. 1924 -
on. Cloth with stockinette faces.
Mark: Paper label: "Original Ravca
Fabrication Francaise."

Ravca Doll: Stockinette face individually
needle sculpted; cloth body and limbs; original clothes; all in excellent condition.
  10in (25cm)   **$ 90 - 110**
Ravca-type fine quality peasant man or
  lady 17in (43cm)   **$225 - 265 each**

Note: The dolls shown in the *9th Blue Book*,
page 338, and the *7th Blue Book*, page 256 should
have been captioned as Ravca-type dolls. These
dolls were not made by Mr. Ravca.

Above: 10in (25cm) Ravca stockinette lady with original label.
H & J Foulke, Inc.

Left: 17in (43cm) Ravca-type
stockinette fisherman. *H & J
Foulke, Inc.*

FACTS

Th. Recknagel, porcelain factory, Alexandrienthal, Thüringia, Germany. 1886 - on. Bisque head, composition or wood-jointed body. Usually small.

Mark: *1907*
        R/A DEP
            I 9/0

Above: R.A. 121 infant on composition body. *H & J Foulke, Inc.*

R.A. Child: Ca. 1890s - World War I. Perfect marked bisque head, jointed composition or wooden body; good wig, set or sleep eyes, open mouth; some dolls with molded painted shoes and socks; all in good condition.

1907, 1909, 1914:

8 - 9in (20 - 23cm)	**$160 - 185**
16 - 18in (41 - 46cm)	**325 - 375***
24in (61cm)	**500 - 550***

*Fine quality bisque only.

R.A. Character Baby: 1909 - World War I. Perfect bisque socket head; cloth baby body or composition bent-limb baby body; painted or glass eyes; nicely dressed; all in good condition.

#127, 1924 and other infants,
  8 - 9in (20 - 23cm) long
  $235 - 285
Character babies, **#23** and
  others, 7 - 8in (18 - 20cm)
  275 - 325
Bonnet babies, **#22** and **28,**
  8 - 10in (20 - 25cm) **475 - 525**
Character children,
  6 - 8in (15 - 20cm) **300 - 350**

R.A. Character #31 Max:
  molded hair, painted features,
  8in (20cm) **$600 - 650**

R.A. Googlies #45 and **46,**
  7in (18cm) **$400 - 500**

Below: 6in (15cm) 68 (girl) and 75 (boy) character children possibly by Recknagel. *H & J Foulke, Inc.*

Reliable

FACTS

Reliable Toy Co., Toronto, Canada.
1920 - on. All composition or cloth
and composition combination.
Mark: RELIABLE
              MADE IN
              CANADA

Marked Reliable Doll: All composition or composition shoulder head and lower arms, cloth torso and legs, sometimes composition legs; painted features, molded hair or wig; original clothes; all in good condition.

14in (36cm) Scots Girl $ 75 - 100
14in (36cm) Military Man
                        225 - 275
17in (43cm) Mountie   300 - 350
13in (33cm) Hiawatha or Indian
  Squaw   75 - 100
15in (38cm) Barbara Ann Scott
                        350 - 450

14in (36cm) Reliable *Aviator. Private Collection.*

Grace Corry Rockwell

Designer: Grace Corry Rockwell.
1920s. Bisque or composition head, cloth and composition body.
Mark:　　　Copr. by
　　　Grace C. Rockwell
　　　Germany

Grace Corry Child: 1927. **Little Brother** and **Little Sister.** Averill Mfg Co. Smiling face, molded hair (sometimes with a wig), painted eyes, closed mouth; cloth and composition body; appropriate clothes, some with Madame Hendren labels; all in good condition.

14in (36cm)　　　**$ 450 - 550**

Grace Corry Rockwell Child: Pefect bisque head with molded hair or wig, sleep eyes, closed mouth; cloth and composition body; appropriate clothes; all in good condition.

14in (36cm)　　　**$5000****

14in (36cm) Rockwell girl with molded hair.
H & J Foulke, Inc.

**Not enough price samples to compute a reliable average.

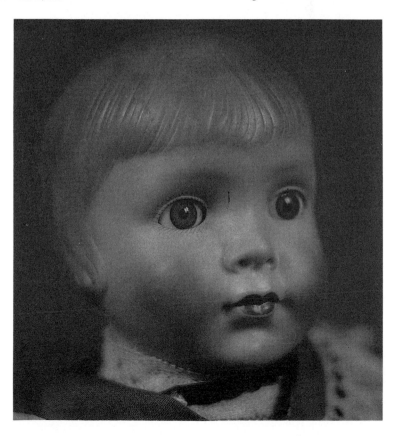

Rohmer Fashion

FACTS

Madame Marie Rohmer, Paris, France. 1857 - 1880. China or bisque shoulder head, jointed kid body.

Mark:

Rohmer Fashion: China or bisque swivel or shoulder head, jointed kid body, bisque or china arms, kid or china legs; lovely wig, set glass eyes, closed mouth, some ears pierced; fine costuming; entire doll in good condition.

 16 - 18in (41 - 46cm) $ **4500 - 5500***

All original doll with painted eyes, swivel neck, china limbs and four additional original gowns, 18in (46cm) at auction
$12,500

*Allow extra for original clothes.

15½in (39cm) Rohmer fashion with rare brown eyes. *Don Pinegar Collection.*

Rollinson Doll

FACTS

Utley Doll Co., Holyoke, Mass., U.S.A.
1916 - on. All-cloth. 14 - 28in (36 - 71cm).
Designer: Gertrude F. Rollinson.
Mark: Stamp in shape of a diamond with a doll in center, around border: "Rollinson Doll Holyoke, Mass."

Marked Rollinson Doll: All molded cloth with painted head and limbs; painted hair or human hair wig, painted features (sometimes teeth also); dressed; all in good condition.

Chase-type Baby with molded hair,
  18 - 22in (46 - 51cm) **$1250**
Child with wig. (For photograph see *8th Blue Book*, page 346.)
  26in (66cm) **1900 - 2200****
Toddler with wig. (For photograph see *10th Blue Book*, page 311.) 16in (41cm)
                          1500**

**Not enough price samples to compute a reliable range.

19in (48cm) Rollinson boy. *H & J Foulke, Inc.*

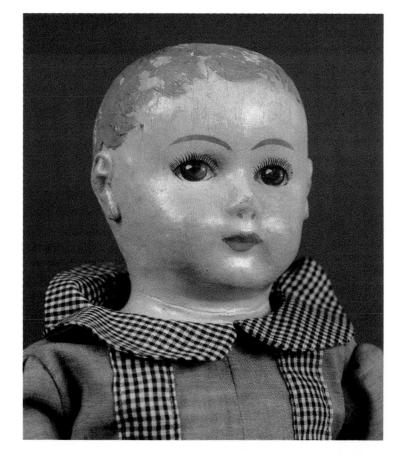

S.F.B.J.

FACTS

Société Française de Fabrication de Bébés & Jouets, Paris, France. 1899 - on. Bisque head, composition body.

Mark: *DÉPOSÉ* *S.F.B.J* S.F.B.J. *301 PARIS*

Child Doll: 1899 - on. Perfect bisque head, good French wig, set or sleep eyes, open mouth, pierced ears; jointed composition body; nicely dressed; all in good condition.
Jumeau-type, paperweight eyes (no mold number), 1899 - 1910:

14 - 16in (36 - 41cm)	$1100 - 1250
21 - 23in (53 - 58cm)	1700 - 1900
25 - 27in (64 - 69cm)	2200 - 2500

#301, end of World War I on:

12 - 14in (31 - 36cm)	$ 750 - 850
20 - 23in (51 - 58cm)	1100 - 1200
28 - 30in (71 - 76cm)	1700 - 1900
37in (94cm)	3000
Lady Body, 22in (56cm)	1200 - 1400

#60:

12 - 14in (31 - 36cm)	650 - 700
19 - 21in (48 - 53cm)	850 - 900
28in (71cm)	1300

Bleuette #301, (For photograph see *8th Blue Book*, page 347.),

10 - 11in (25 - 28cm) only	825 - 875

Walking, Kissing and Flirting,

22in (56cm)	1700 - 1800
All original,	2400

Papier-mâché head **#60**, fully-jointed body:

17in (43cm)	325 - 375

16in (41cm) S.F.B.J. 301 child.
H & J Foulke, Inc.

Character Dolls: 1910 - on. Perfect bisque head, wig, molded, sometimes flocked hair on mold numbers 237, 266, 227 and 235, sleep eyes, composition body; nicely dressed; all in good condition. (See previous *Blue Books* for illustrations of mold numbers not shown here.)

Mark:

S.F.B.J.
230
PARIS

S.F.B.J.
236
PARIS

#226, 235, 15 - 17in (38 - 43cm)
$1800 - 2100

#230, (sometimes Jumeau):
14 - 16in (36 - 41cm)
1400 - 1500
20 - 23in (51 - 58cm)
1800 - 2100
#233, Screamer, 20in (51cm)
3500**
#234, Baby, 15in (38cm)
2750 - 3000**
#236, Baby, 15 - 17in (38 - 43cm)
1100 - 1300
20 - 22in (51 - 56cm) **1700 - 1900**
Toddler:
14 - 15in (36 - 38cm) **1600 - 1800**
27 - 28in (69 - 71cm) **2600 - 2800**
#237, 238, 229, Child,
15 - 16in (38 - 41cm) **2200 - 2600**
#238, Lady, 23in (58cm) **3500 - 4000**
#239, Five-piece crude body, not original clothes, **Nenette** and **Rintintin**:
13in (33cm) **4000 - 4500**
With original wig, clothes and boxes, pristine condition, at auction
11,500 pair
#242, Nursing Baby 13in (33cm)
3250**
#245, Googly. See page 187.

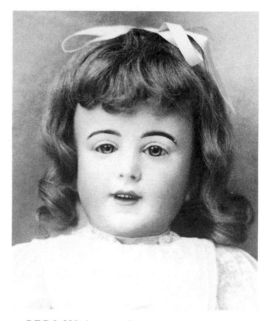

S.F.B.J. 238 character. *Courtesy of Lesley Hurford.*

#247, Toddler:
15 - 17in (38 - 43cm) $ **2300 - 2600**
25 - 27in (64 - 69cm) **3200 - 3700**
#251, Toddler:
14 - 15in (36 - 38cm) **1600 - 1700**
20in (51cm) **2000 - 2200**
27 - 28in (69 - 71cm) **2800 - 3000**
#252, Toddler:
13 - 15in (33 - 38cm) **5500 - 6000**
20in (51cm) **7500**
27 - 28in (69 - 71cm) **8500 - 9500****
Black papier-mâché **#247** head baby,
25in (64cm) **550**

**Not enough price samples to compute a reliable range.

See following page for additional photographs.

S.F.B.J. continued

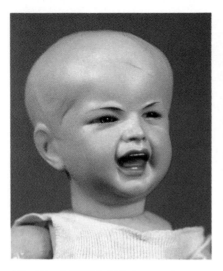

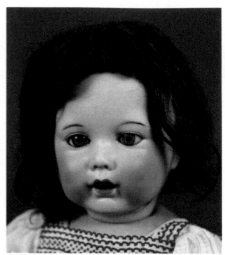

18in (46cm) S.F.B.J. 233 character boy. *Richard Wright Antiques.*

20in (51cm) S.F.B.J. 251 character. *Mary Barnes Kelley Collection.*

21in (53cm) S.F.B.J. 236 character. *H & J Foulke, Inc.*

For further information see preceding pages.

FACTS

Trendon Toys, Ltd., Reddish, Stockport, England. 1965 - 1986. All-vinyl.
Designer: Sasha Morgenthaler.

Sasha: All-vinyl of exceptionally high quality, long synthetic hair, painted features, wistful, appealing expression; original clothing, tiny circular wrist tag; excellent condition.

16in (41cm)	**$190 - 210**
Boxed	**250**
In cylinder package	**300 - 350**
Gregor (boy)	**190 - 210**
Boxed	**250**

Sasha Baby, white hair, all original. *H & J Foulke, Inc.*

Cora (black girl)	**$ 275 - 300**
Caleb (black boy)	**275 - 300**
Black Baby	**200 - 225**
White Baby	**165 - 185**
Sexed Baby, pre 1979	**250 - 275**
Limited Edition Dolls:	
1980 **Velvet Dress**	**$ 350 - 375**
1982 **Pintucks Dress**	**350 - 375**
1983 **Kiltie**	**350 - 375**
1985 **Prince Gregor**	**350 - 375**
Götz model, 1965 - 69	**800**
Boxed	**1000**
Early model 1950s	**5000 - 6000**
Fair condition and naked	**2500 - 2850**
Eskimo Pair, 20in (51cm) at auction	
	9000

Sasha #103 Brunette, all original. *H & J Foulke, Inc.*

F. M. Schilling

FACTS

Barbara, later her son Ferdinand Max Schilling, doll factory, Sonneberg, Thüringia, Germany. 1871 - on. Composition head and lower limbs, cloth body; Patent Washable-type. 8 - 39in (20 - 100cm).

Mark:

Schilling Täufling: Excellent quality composition head, good mohair or lamb's wool wig, paperweight eyes (sometimes sleeping eyes), closed mouth (sometimes open); cloth torso and upper limbs, composition lower limbs with molded boots or bare feet (the latter usually representing babies).

Excellent condition, all original:

13 - 15in (33 - 38cm)	$ 425 - 475
19 - 21in (48 - 53cm)	550 - 650
24in (61cm)	750 - 800
30 - 31in (76 - 79cm)	1000 - 1100

Fair condition, wear:

13 - 15in (33 - 38cm)	175 - 200
19 - 21in (48 - 53cm)	225 - 275
24in (61cm)	325 - 375
30 - 31in (76 - 79cm)	475 - 500

18in (46cm) unmarked composition shoulder head doll of the type made by Schilling. *H & J Foulke, Inc.*

Bruno Schmidt

FACTS

Bruno Schmidt, doll factory, Waltershausen, Thüringia, Germany. Heads by Bähr & Pröschild, Ohrdruf, Thüringia, Germany. 1898 - on. Bisque head, composition body.

Mark:

2096-4

Marked B. S. W. Child Doll: Ca. 1898 - on. Bisque head, good wig, sleep eyes, open mouth; jointed composition child body; dressed; all in good condition.

20 - 23in (51 - 58cm) $ 600 - 700
28 - 30in (71 - 76cm)   1000 - 1200
22in (56cm) flirty eyes   750 - 850

Marked B. S. W. Character Dolls: Bisque socket head, glass eyes; jointed composition body; dressed; all in good condition.
#2048, 2094, 2096 (so-called "Tommy Tucker"), molded hair, open mouth. (For photograph see *10th Blue Book*, page 373.)

13 - 14in (33 - 36cm)
        $1100 - 1200
19 - 21in (48 - 53cm)
        1400 - 1500
25 - 26in (64 - 66cm)
        1900 - 2000

#2048 (closed mouth),
16 - 18in (41 - 46cm)
        2500 - 2800**
#2072:
23in (58cm) toddler
        4500 - 5000**
17in (43cm)   3000 - 3500**

(For photograph see *7th Blue Book*, page 335.)

#2033 (so-called "Wendy") **(537)**. (For photograph see *9th Blue Book*, page 347.)
11 - 12in (28 - 31cm) $ 8000 - 10,000
17 - 18in (43 - 46cm)   20,000 - 23,000

#2025 (529) closed mouth, wigged,
22in (56cm)   4500 - 5000**
#2026 (538), 22in (56cm)
            3850 - 4250**
#2097, character baby open mouth. (For photograph see *9th Blue Book*, page 347.)
13 - 14in (33 - 36cm)   500 - 550
18in (46cm)   750 - 850
#425 all-bisque baby, 5½ - 6in (13 - 15cm)
            225 - 275

**Not enough price samples to compute a reliable range.

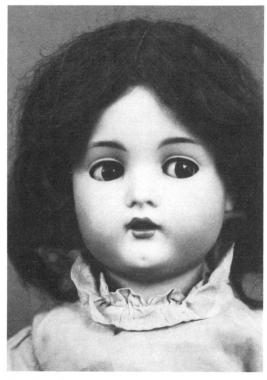

22in (56cm) B. S. W. child with flirty eyes. *H & J Foulke, Inc.*

Franz Schmidt

Franz Schmidt & Co., doll factory, Georgenthal near Waltershausen, Thüringia, Germany. Heads by Simon & Halbig, Gräfenhain, Thüringia, Germany. 1890 - on. Bisque socket head, jointed bent-limb or toddler body of composition.

Marked F.S. & Co. Character Baby: Ca. 1910. Perfect bisque character head, good wig, sleep eyes, open mouth, may have open nostrils; jointed bent-limb body; suitably dressed; all in good condition.

#1272, 1295, 1296, 1297, 1310:
Baby:

12 - 14in (31 - 36cm)	$ 500 - 600
20 - 21in (51 - 53cm)	800 - 850
26 - 27in (66 - 69cm)	1400 - 1600

Toddler:

7in (18cm), five-piece body	650 - 675
10in (25cm), five-piece body	700 - 800
13 - 15in (33 - 38cm)	750 - 850
19 - 21in (48 - 53cm)	1100 - 1200
27in (69cm)	1700 - 1800

#1286, molded hair with blue ribbon, glass eyes, open smiling mouth, 16in (41cm) toddler
$ 4000**
#1263 Character Child, closed pouty mouth, painted eyes, wig, 21in (53cm) at auction
$19,500

Mark:

1295
F. S. & Co.
Made in
Germany
30

Marked S & C Child Doll: Ca. 1890 - on. Perfect bisque socket head, good wig, sleep eyes, open mouth; jointed composition child body; dressed; all in good condition. Some are Mold #293.

6in (15cm)	$ 275 - 325
16 - 18in (41 - 46cm)	500 - 550
22 - 24in (56 - 61cm)	650 - 750
29 - 30in (74 - 76cm)	1050 - 1200
42in (107cm)	3000 - 3200

Mark:

S & C
SIMON & HALBIG
28

**Not enough price samples to compute a reliable average.

Below: 11in (28cm) 1272 character baby. *H & J Foulke, Inc.*

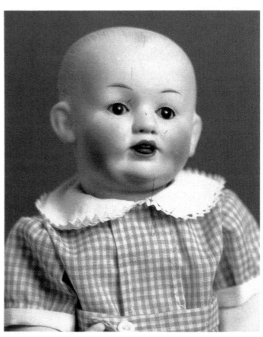

FACTS

Schmitt & Fils, Paris, France. 1854 -
1891. Bisque socket head, composition
jointed body.
Mark: On both head and body:

Marked Schmitt Bébé: Ca. 1879. Perfect
bisque socket head with skin or good wig,
large paperweight eyes, closed mouth,
pierced ears; Schmitt-jointed composition
body; appropriate clothes; all in good condition.

Long face:
  16 - 18in (41 - 46cm) **$12,000 - 14,000**
  23 - 25in (58 - 64cm)   **18,000 - 19,000**
Short face (For photograph see *10th Blue
Book*, page 375.)
  16 - 18in (41 - 46cm)   **15,500 - 16,500***
  22in (56cm)   **19,000 - 20,000***
Oval/round face:
  10 - 11in (25 - 28cm)   **8000 - 9000***
  15 - 17in (38 - 43cm) **12,000 - 14,000***
Cup and saucer neck:
  12 - 13in (31 - 33cm) **10,000 - 12,000**
  15in (38cm)   **15,000 - 18,000**

*Allow one-third less for dolls that do not have
strongly molded faces.

16in (41cm) Schmitt with round face. *Jackie
Kaner.*

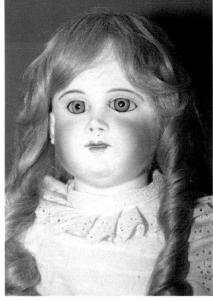

25in (64cm) Schmitt with long face. *Private Collection.*

Schoenau & Hoffmeister

FACTS

Schoenau & Hoffmeister, Porzellan-fabrik Burggrub, Burggrub, Bavaria, Germany. Arthur Schoenau also owned a doll factory. 1884 - on, dolls; 1901 - on, porcelain. Bisque head, composition body.
Trademarks: Hanna, Burggrub Baby, Bébé Carmencita, Viola, Kunstlerkopf, Das Lachende Baby.
Mark:

Child Doll: 1901 - on. Perfect bisque head; original or good wig, sleep eyes, open mouth; ball-jointed body; original or good clothes; all in nice condition. **#1906, 1909, 5700, 5800.**

14 - 16in (36 - 41cm)	$ 300 - 350
21 - 23in (53 - 58cm)	500 - 575
28 - 30in (71 - 76cm)	800 - 900
33in (84cm)	1100 - 1200
39in (99cm)	2000 - 2200

#1909, mint in box, very good quality, very nice clothes:

11in (28cm)	$ 700
20in (51cm)	950

26in (66cm) 1909 child.
H & J Foulke, Inc.

Schoenau & Hoffmeister continued

Character Baby: 1910 - on. Perfect bisque socket head, good wig, sleep eyes, open mouth; composition bent-limb baby body; all in good condition. **#169, 769**, "Burggrub Baby" or "Porzellanfabrik Burggrub." (For photograph see *8th Blue Book*, page 355.)

13 - 15in (33 - 38cm)	$ 375 - 425
18 - 20in (46 - 51cm)	500 - 550
23 - 24in (58 - 61cm)	700 - 800
28in (71cm)	1000 - 1100

Princess Elizabeth, 1932.
Chubby five-piece body,

17in (43cm)	$1900 - 2100
20 - 23in (51 - 58cm)	2400 - 2700

Pouty Baby: Ca. 1925. Perfect bisque solid dome head with painted hair, tiny sleep eyes, closed pouty mouth; cloth body with composition arms and legs; dressed; all in good condition. (For photograph see *8th Blue Book*, page 355.)

11 - 12in (28 - 31cm)	$ 750 - 800**

Hanna:
Baby:

14 - 16in (36 - 41cm)	$ 700 - 750
20 - 22in (51 - 56cm)	900 - 1100
26in (66cm)	1500
Toddler, 14 - 16in (36 - 41cm)	
	850 - 950
Brown, 7½in (19cm) toddler	
	275 - 325

Das Lachende Baby, 1930. (For photograph see *8th Blue Book*, page 355.)

23 - 24in (58 - 61cm)	$2200 - 2500**

**Not enough price samples to compute a reliable range.

21in (53cm) *Princess Elizabeth*. *Esther Schwartz Collection.*

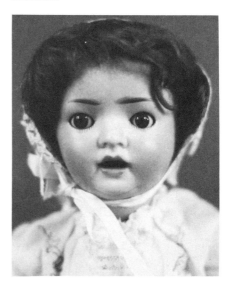

12½in (32cm) *Hanna*. *H & J Foulke, Inc.*

Schoenhut

FACTS

Albert Schoenhut & Co., Philadelphia, Pa., U.S.A. 1872 - on. Wood, spring-jointed, holes in bottom of feet to fit metal stand. 11 - 21in (28 - 53cm).
Designer: Early: Adolph Graziana and Mr. Leslie;
later: Harry E. Schoenhut.
Mark: Paper label:

Incised: SCHOENHUT DOLL
PAT. JAN. 17, '11, U.S.A.
& FOREIGN COUNTRIES

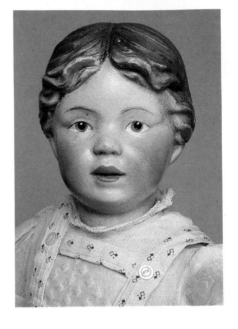

Right: 16/103 carved hair girl, transition period. *Private Collection. Photograph by Carol Corson.*

Below left: 16/202 G carved hair boy. *Private Collection. Photograph by Carol Corson.*

Below right: 16/203/605 carved hair boy, transition period, all original. *Private Collection. Photograph by Carol Corson.*

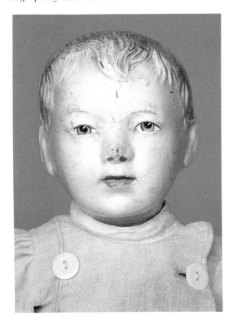

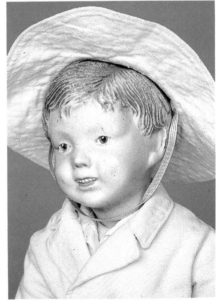

See following page for further information.

16/403 pouty boy. *H & J Foulke, Inc.*

17in (43cm) "Dolly Face" girl. *H & J Foulke, Inc.*

Schoenhut continued

Salesman's Cutaway Sample:
$ 800 - 1000

Character: 1911 - 1930. Wooden head and spring-jointed wooden body, marked head and/or body; original or appropriate wig, brown or blue intaglio eyes, open/closed mouth with painted teeth or closed mouth; original or suitable clothing; original paint may have light touch-up.
14 - 21in (36 - 53cm):

Excellent condition	**$1600 - 2100***
Good, some wear	**900 - 1400***

* Allow extra for rare faces.

Character with carved hair: Ca. 1911 - 1930. Wooden head with carved hair, comb marks, possibly a ribbon or bow, intaglio eyes, mouth usually closed; spring-jointed wooden body; original or suitable clothes; original paint may have light touch-up. (See photograph on page 12.)
14 - 21in (36 - 53cm)

Excellent condition	**$2500 - 3000**
Good, some wear	**1800 - 2200**
Early style	**3500 - 4000**
20in (51cm) man	**2200**

Tootsie Wootsie, 15in (38cm), very bad face, at auction **975**
Snickelfritz, 15in (38cm), wear **2500**

Baby Face: Ca. 1913 - 1930. Wooden head and fully-jointed toddler or bent-limb baby body, marked head and/or body; painted hair or mohair wig, painted eyes, open or closed mouth; suitably dressed; original paint; all in good condition, with some wear. (For photograph see *10th Blue Book*, page 379.)

Mark:

Baby:

12in (31cm)	$	**550 - 600**
15 - 16in (38 - 41cm)		**700 - 800**

Toddler:

11in (28cm)	**$ 800 - 900**
14in (36cm)	**800 - 850***
16 - 17in (41 - 43cm)	**850 - 950***

*Allow more for mint condition.

Dolly Face: Ca. 1915 - 1930. Wooden head and spring-jointed wooden body; original or appropriate mohair wig, decal eyes, open/closed mouth with painted teeth; original paint; original or suitable clothes.
14 - 21in (36 - 53cm):

Excellent condition	**$ 800 - 900**
Good condition, some wear	**600 - 700**

Walker: Ca. 1919 - 1930. All-wood with "baby face," mohair wig, painted eyes; curved arms, straight legs with "walker" joint at hip; original or appropriate clothes; all in good condition. Original paint. No holes in bottom of feet. (For photograph see *9th Blue Book*, page 355.)

13in (33cm)	**$ 800 - 900**
17in (43cm) excellent with original shoes	**1250**

Sleep Eyes: Ca. 1920 - 1930. Used with "baby face" or "dolly face" heads. Mouths on this type were open with teeth or barely open with carved teeth. Original paint. (For photograph see *9th Blue Book*, page 354.)
14 - 21in (36 - 53cm):

Excellent condition	**$1200 - 1400**
Good condition	**800 - 900**

All-Composition: Ca. 1924. Jointed at neck, shoulders and hips, right arm bent, molded blonde curly hair, painted eyes, tiny closed mouth; original or appropriate clothing; in good condition. (See photograph in *8th Blue Book*, page 359.)
Paper label on back:

13in (33cm)	**$ 500****

**Not enough price samples to compute a reliable average.

Shirley Temple

FACTS

Ideal Novelty Toy Corp., New York, N.Y., U.S.A. 1934 to present. 7½ - 36in (19 - 91cm).
Designer: Bernard Lipfert.

All-Composition Child: 1934 through late 1930s. Marked head and body, jointed composition body; all original including wig and clothes; entire doll in very good condition. Sizes 11 - 27in (28 - 69cm).
Mark: On body:

SHIRLEY TEMPLE
13

On head:
13
SHIRLEY TEMPLE

On cloth label:

```
Genuine
SHIRLEY TEMPLE
DOLL
REGISTERED U.S. PAT OFF
IDEAL NOVELTY & TOY CO     MADE IN USA
```

11in (28cm)	$ 850*
13in (33cm)	700 - 800*
15 - 16in (38 - 41cm)	800*
18in (46cm)	900*
20 - 22in (51 - 56cm)	1000*
25in (64cm)	1200*
27in (69cm)	1500 - 1600*
Button	135
Dress, tagged	150 up
Trunk	150 - 175
Carriage	500 - 600

*Allow 50 - 100% more for mint-in-box doll. Also allow extra for a doll with unusual outfit, such as *Texas Ranger* and *Little Colonel*.

Baby Shirley,
16 - 18in (41 - 46cm) **$1000 - 1200****
Made in Japan Composition Shirley, (For photograph see *8th Blue Book*, page 362.)
7½in (19cm) **250 - 300**
Hawaiian Shirley,
18in (46cm) **900 - 1000****

**Not enough price samples to compute a reliable range.

Vinyl and Plastic: 1957.
Mark: "Ideal Doll ST—12" (number denotes size)

Excellent condition, original clothes:

12in (31cm)	$ 175 - 200
15in (38cm)	275 - 300
17in (43cm)	350 - 375
19in (48cm)	400 - 425
36in (91cm)	1400 - 1500
Script name pin	25 - 30
Name purse	20 - 25

Vinyl and Plastic, 1973:

16in (41cm) size only	$ 100 - 110
Boxed	135 - 150
Boxed dress	35

See following page for photographs.

Shirley Temple continued

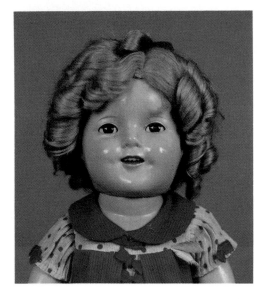

18in (46cm) composition *Shirley Temple*, all original. *H & J Foulke, Inc.*

22in (56cm) composition *Shirley Temple*, all original. *H & J Foulke, Inc.*

16in (41cm) composition *Baby Shirley*, all original. *H & J Foulke, Inc.*

12in (31cm) vinyl *Shirley Temple*, all original. *H & J Foulke, Inc.*

Simon & Halbig

Simon & Halbig, porcelain factory, Gräfenhain, Thüringia, Germany, purchased by Kämmer & Reinhardt in 1920. 1869 - on. Bisque head, kid (sometimes cloth) or composition body.

Mark:

$$S\ 13\ H$$
$$949$$

$$1079\text{-}2$$
$$DEP$$
$$S\ H$$
$$Germany$$

Child doll with closed mouth: Ca. 1879. Perfect bisque socket head on ball-jointed wood and composition body; good wig, glass set or sleep eyes, closed mouth, pierced ears, dressed; all in good condition. (See *Simon & Halbig Dolls, The Artful Aspect* for photographs of mold numbers not shown here.)

#719, 19 - 21in (48 - 53cm)
$3000 - 3500

#905, 908, 14 - 17in (36 - 43cm)
2500 - 3000

#929, 18 - 21in (46 - 53cm)
3500 - 4500**

#939:
14 - 15in (36 - 38cm)	**2500 - 2700**
19 - 22in (48 - 56cm)	**3100 - 3600**
27in (69cm)	**5000**

#949:
15 - 16in (38 - 41cm)	**1900 - 2300**
22 - 23in (56 - 58cm)	**2700 - 2900**
28in (71cm)	**3700 - 4000**

**Not enough price samples to compute a reliable range.

16in (41cm) 949 child. *Jensen's Antique Dolls.*

23in (53cm) 719 child with black Babyland Rag. *Jan Foulke Collection.*

Simon & Halbig continued

#979, 14 - 17in (36 - 43cm)   **2700 - 3200****

Kid or **Cloth Body:**
#720, 740, 940, 950:

9 - 10in (23 - 25cm)	**$ 550 - 650**
16 - 18in (41 - 46cm)	**1450 - 1650**
22in (56cm)	**1800 - 2000**
#949, 18 - 21in (46 - 53cm)	**1800 - 2000**

S.H. (no mold number):

13 - 15in (33 - 38cm)	**1300 - 1500**
15 - 16in (38 - 41cm) Fashion-type	**3000 - 3200**
9in (23cm) twill-covered body	**3000 - 3500**

Shoulder head:

9in (23cm)	**1000****
15in (38cm)	**1650 - 2000****

**Not enough price samples to compute a reliable range.

Above: 9in (23cm) shoulder head Simon & Halbig-type with painted eyes and molded lavender bow. *Richard Wright Antiques.*

Right: 6in (15cm) 886 blue stocking all-bisque, all original. *H & J Foulke, Inc.*

All-Bisque Child: 1880 - on. All-bisque child with swivel neck, pegged shoulders and hips; appropriate mohair wig, glass eyes, open or closed mouth; molded stockings and shoes.
#886 and **890**:

Over-the-knee black stockings:

5½ - 6in (14 - 15cm)	**$ 700 - 800***
7 - 7½ (18 - 19cm)	**900 - 1000***
8½in (22cm)	**1300 - 1500***

Early model with five-strap bootines,
  closed mouth, 7 - 8in (18 - 20cm)
                             1600 - 2000*

Open mouth with square cut teeth:

6in (15cm)	**1200**
8in (20cm)	**1600 - 1800***

*Allow extra for original clothes.

Child doll with open mouth and composition body: Ca. 1889 to 1930s. Perfect bisque head, good wig, sleep or paperweight eyes, open mouth, pierced ears; original ball-jointed composition body; very pretty clothes; all in nice condition. (See *Simon & Halbig Dolls, The Artful Aspect* for photographs of mold numbers not shown here.)

#719, 739, 749, 769, 939, 979:

12 - 14in (31 - 36cm)	$1350 - 1650
19 - 22in (48 - 56cm)	2200 - 2600
29 - 30in (74 - 76cm)	3000 - 3500

#759, 19in (48cm) 2500**

#905, 908, 12 - 14in (31 - 36cm) 1500 - 1800

#949:

15 - 16in (38 - 41cm)	1200 - 1400
19 - 21in (48 - 53cm)	1500 - 1900
25in (64cm)	2300

#969, 13in (33cm) 3600**

#1009:

15 - 16in (38 - 41cm)	900 - 1000
19 - 21in (48 - 53cm)	1200 - 1500
24in (61cm)	1800

**Not enough prices samples to compute a reliable average.

20½in (52cm) 1039 child. *H & J Foulke, Inc.*

#1039:

16 - 18in (41 - 46cm)	750 - 850
23 - 25in (58 - 64cm)	1050 - 1250

#1039, key-wind walking body,

16 - 17in (41 - 43cm)	1700 - 1800

#1039, walking, kissing,

20 - 22in (51 - 56cm)	1050 - 1250

#1078, 1079:

10 - 12in (25 - 31cm)	550 - 600
14 - 15in (36 - 38cm)	600 - 650
17 - 19in (43 - 48cm)	650 - 700
22 - 24in (56 - 61cm)	725 - 800
28 - 30in (71 - 76cm)	1100 - 1300
34 - 35in (86 - 89cm)	1800 - 2100
42in (107cm)	3500 - 3800

#1248, 1249, Santa:

13 - 15in (33 - 38cm)	850 - 900
21 - 24in (53 - 61cm)	1200 - 1400
26 - 28in (66 - 71cm)	1600 - 1800
32in (81cm)	2200
38in (96cm)	3100

#540, 550, 570, Baby Blanche,

22 - 24in (56 - 61cm)	625 - 675

#600, 14in (36cm) 850 - 1000

18in (46cm) 949 child. *H & J Foulke, Inc.*

Simon & Halbig continued

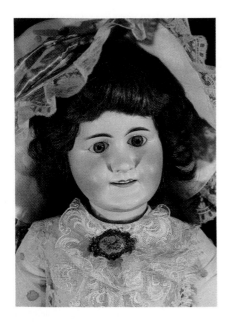

Child doll with open mouth and kid body:
Ca. 1889 to 1930s. Perfect bisque swivel head on shoulder plate or shoulder head with stationary neck, sleep eyes, open mouth, pierced ears; kid body, bisque arms, cloth lower legs; well costumed; all in good condition.

#1010, 1040, 1080, 1260:

9½in (24cm) cloth body	$ 325	
14 - 16in (36 - 41cm)	**500 -**	**600**
21 - 23in (53 - 58cm)	**700 -**	**800**
#1009, 17 - 19in (43 - 48cm)	**800 -**	**900**

#1250: (For photograph see title page.)

14 - 16in (36 - 41cm)	**550 -**	**650**
22 - 24in (56 - 61cm)	**800 -**	**900**
29in (74cm)	**1000 -**	**1100**
#949, 19 - 21in (48 - 53cm)	**1250 -**	**1350**

Tiny Child doll: Ca. 1889 to 1930s. Usually mold number **1079** or **1078.** Perfect bisque head, nice wig, sleep eyes, open mouth; composition body with molded shoes and socks; appropriate clothes; all in good condition.

7 - 8in (18 - 20cm)	**$ 425 -**	**475**
10in (25cm) walker, five-piece body		
	600 -	**625**

Fully-jointed, 8 - 10in (20 - 25cm)

550 - 600

So-called "Little Women" type: Ca. 1900. Mold number **1160.** Shoulder head with fancy mohair wig, glass set eyes, closed mouth; cloth body with bisque limbs, molded boots; dressed; all in good condition. (For photograph see *9th Blue Book,* page 365.)

5½ - 7in (14 - 18cm)	**$ 350 -**	**400**
10 - 11in (25 - 28cm)	**425 -**	**475**

Above: Rare smiling character child. *Richard Wright Collection.*

Left: 14½in (37cm) 1279. *Ruth West.*

Character Child: Ca. 1909. Perfect bisque socket head with wig or molded hair, painted or glass eyes, open or closed mouth, character face, jointed composition body; dressed; all in good condition. (See *Simon & Halbig Dolls, The Artful Aspect* for photographs of mold numbers not shown here.)

#120, 28 - 30in (71 - 76cm)

$ 3000 - 4000**

#150:
14in (36cm) — 12,000**
25in (51cm) — 28,000**

#151:
14 - 15in (36 - 38cm) — 4500 - 5000
18in (46cm) — 7000 - 8000
24in (61cm) — 11,000

#153, 13in (33cm) — $22,000**

#1279:
14 - 17in (36 - 43cm) — 2000 - 2400
19 - 21in (48 - 53cm) — 2700 - 3200
27in (69cm) — 5500 - 6000

#1299, 14 - 17in (36 - 43cm) — 1200 - 1600

#1339:
18in (46cm) — 1000 - 1100**
28 - 32in (71 - 81cm) — 1900 - 2100**

#1388, 23in (58cm) — 20,000**
#1398, 23in (58cm) — 20,000**
IV, #1448, 14 - 17in (36 - 43cm) — 22,000 - 24,000**

**Not enough price samples to compute a reliable range.

13½in (34cm) 1448 child. *Christine Lorman.*

Simon & Halbig continued

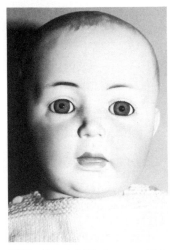

25½in (65cm) 1498 character. *Richard Wright Antiques.*

14in (36cm) 1469 lady. *H & J Foulke, Inc.*

Character Baby: Ca. 1909 to 1930s. Perfect bisque head, molded hair or wig, sleep or painted eyes, open or open/closed mouth; composition bent-limb baby or toddler body; nicely dressed; all in good condition. (See *Simon & Halbig Dolls, The Artful Aspect* for photographs of mold numbers not shown here.)

#1294:

Baby, 17 - 19in (43 - 48cm)	$ 725 -	800
23 - 25in (58 - 64cm)	1100 -	1300
Toddler, 20in (51cm)	1250 -	1450
28in (71cm) with clockwork eyes at auction		1900

#1428:

Baby, 13 - 14in (33 - 36cm)	1500 -	2000
Toddler, 15 - 18in (38 - 46cm)	2400 -	2600

#1488:

Baby, 20in (51cm)	4200 -	4600
Child, 16in (41cm)	3250	

#1489 Erika. (For photograph see *10th Blue Book,* page 352.) Baby, 21 - 22in (53 - 56cm)
3300 - 3700**

#1498:

Toddler, 17in (43cm)	3500 -	4000**
26in (65cm) at auction	10,000	

#172 Baby. (For photograph see *10th Blue Book,* page 353.)
3500

Lady doll: Ca. 1910. Perfect bisque socket head, good wig, sleep eyes, pierced ears; lady body, molded bust, slim arms and legs; dressed; all in good condition.

#1159:

12in (31cm)	$ 1100 -	1200
16 - 18in (41 - 46cm)	1800 -	2000
24in (61cm)	2500 -	2700
28in (71cm)	3000 -	3500

#1468, 1469:

13 - 15in (33 - 38cm) Naked	2000 -	2300
Original clothes	3000 -	4200

#1303 Lady, 15 - 16in (38 - 41cm)
10,000 - 12,000**

#152:

18in (46cm)	15,000 up**
25in (64cm)	25,000**
#1308 Man, 13in (33cm)	5500**
#1307, 21in (53cm)	20,000**
#1303 Indian, 21in (53cm)	7000**

**Not enough price samples to compute a reliable range.

Snow Babies

FACTS

Various German firms including
Hertwig & Co. and Bähr & Pröschild
after 1910. Ca. 1890 until World War II.
All-bisque. usually 1 - 3in (3 - 8cm).
Mark: Sometimes "Germany."

Snow Babies: All-bisque with snowsuits
and caps of pebbly-textured bisque; painted
features; various standing, lying or sitting
positions.

1½in (4cm)	$ 40 - 50
2½in (6cm)	100 - 125
3in (9cm) huskies pulling sled with snow baby	250
2½in (6cm) snowman	95 - 110
3in (8cm) baby riding snow bear	250
2½in (6cm) tumbling snow baby	150 - 165
2in (5cm) musical snow baby	85
2in (5cm) baby on sled	90 - 110
3in (8cm) baby on sled	175 - 200
2in (5cm) reindeer pulling snow baby	250
2in (5cm) early fine quality babies with high hoods	150 - 165
Three small babies on sled	150 - 175
Santa on snow bear	350 - 400

4½in (11cm) snow baby shoulder head with
ruffled bonnet. *H & J Foulke, Inc.*

Group of tiny snow babies and a snow bear. *H & J
Foulke, Inc.*

2½in (6cm) babies sliding on cellar door	250
2in (5cm) snow dog and snowman on sled	250
Santa going down chimney	300
Snow bears	40 - 75
Snow boy or girl on sled	150 - 165
Shoulder head, cloth body:	
4½in (11cm)	185
10in (25cm)	225 - 250
Train engine with coal car and Santa	400

"No Snows":
Boy and girl on sled, 2in (5cm)	$165
Skiing boy, 2½in (6cm)	95

Sonneberg Täufling (So-called Motschmann Baby)

FACTS

Various Sonneberg factories such as Heinrich Stier; many handled by exporter Louis Lindner & Söhn, Sonneberg, Thüringia, Germany. 1851 - 1880s. Papier-mâché, wood and cloth. 8in (20cm) to about 28 (71cm).
Mark: None.

Note: For many years it was thought that these dolls were made by Ch. Motschmann because some were found stamped with his name; hence, they were called **Motschmann Babies** by collectors. However, research has shown that they were made by various factories and that Motschmann was the holder of the patent for the voice boxes, not the manufacturer of the dolls.

Sonneberg Täufling: Papier-mâché or wax-over-composition head with painted hair or wig, dark pupil-less glass eyes; closed mouth or open mouth with bamboo teeth; composition lower torso; composition and wood arms and legs jointed at ankles and wrists, cloth covered midsection with voice box, upper arms and legs cloth covered, called floating joints; dressed in shift and bonnet.

Very good condition:

12 - 14in (31 - 36cm)	**$1000 - 1200**
18 - 20in (46 - 51cm)	**1600 - 2000**
24in (61cm)	**2200 - 2500**

Fair condition, with wear:

12 - 14in (31 - 36cm)	**500 - 600**
18 - 20in (46 - 51cm)	**800 - 900**

17in (43cm) Sonneberg Täufling. *H & J Foulke, Inc.*

6in (15cm) Sonneberg Täufling. *H & J Foulke, Inc.*

Steiff

FACTS

Fräulein Margarete Steiff, Würtemberg, Germany. 1894 - on. Felt, plush or velvet.

Mark: Metal button in ear.

Steiff Doll: Felt, plush or velvet, jointed; seam down middle of face, button eyes, painted features; original clothes; most are character dolls, many have large shoes to enable them to stand; all in excellent condition.

Children (Character Dolls):

11 - 12in (28 - 31cm)	**$1100**
16 - 17in (41 - 43cm)	**1500**

Caricature or Comic Dolls

	1400 - 4000*
Gnome, 12in (31cm)	**1500**
Soldiers, 18in (46cm)	**3000 - 4000**
Mickey Mouse, 9in (23cm)	
	1000
Minnie Mouse, 9in (23cm)	
	1750
Clown, 17in (43cm)	**2200**
Golliwog, 16in (41cm)	**4000**
Max and Moritz	**5000 - 6000 pair**
School room, 3 children, 1 teacher, desks and chairs	**9500**
Mama Katzenjammer Tea Cozy	**1500**

Collector's Note: To bring the prices quoted, Steiff dolls must be clean and have good color. Faded and dirty dolls bring only one-third to one-half these prices.

Above: Steiff **Golliwog**, all original. *Nancy A. Smith Collection.*

Below: Steiff characters and bears. *Private Collection.*

Herm Steiner

FACTS

Hermann Steiner of Sonneberg, Thüringia, Germany. 1921 - on. Bisque head, cloth or composition body. Various sizes, usually small.

Mark:

15
HS
Germany
240

Herm Steiner
HS
Germany

Herm Steiner Child: Perfect bisque head, wig, sleep eyes, open mouth; jointed composition body; dressed; in good condition.

  7 - 8in (18 - 20cm)   **$165 - 195**
  14 - 16in (36 - 41cm)   **300 - 350**
#128 with special eye movement,
  14in (36cm)   **375 - 425****

Herm Steiner Character Child: Perfect bisque head, molded hair and features; five-piece composition body; dressed; all in good condition.

  7in (18cm)   **$250 - 300**
#401 shoulder head, 15in (38cm)
    450 - 500**

Herm Steiner Infant: Perfect bisque head, molded hair, sleep eyes, closed mouth; cloth or composition bent-limb body; dressed; in good condition.

Head circumference:
  7 - 8in (18 - 20cm)   **$225**
  10 - 11in (25 - 28cm)
    275 - 300
#246, hand holding pacifier moves to the open mouth when doll is bounced,
  15in (38cm)   **$600**

Herm Steiner Character Baby: Perfect bisque socket head, good wig, sleep eyes, open mouth with teeth; composition jointed baby body; dressed; all in good condition.

  9 - 11in (23 - 28cm)
    $275 - 325

**Not enough price samples to compute a reliable range.

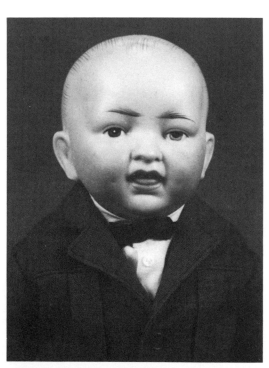

15in (38cm) 401 shoulder head boy.
H & J Foulke, Inc.

FACTS

Jules Nicolas Steiner and Successors, Paris, France. 1855 - 1908. Bisque head, jointed papier-mâché body.

Marked C or A Series Steiner Bébé: 1880s. Perfect socket head, cardboard pate, appropriate wig, sleep eyes with wire mechanism, bulgy paperweight eyes with tinting on upper eyelids, closed mouth, round face, pierced ears with tinted tips; jointed composition body with straight wrists and stubby fingers (sometimes with bisque hands); dressed; all in good condition. Sometimes with wire-operated sleep eyes. Sizes 4/0 (8in) to 8 (38in). Series "C" more easily found than "A."
Mark: (incised) $S^{IE} \ A \ O$

(red script)

J Steiner. Bte Sg. Bg. J Bourgin Ste

(incised) $S^{IE} \ C \ 4$

(red stamp)

J. STEINER B.S.G.D.G.

8in (20cm)	$ 3200 - 3500
10in (25cm)	3200 - 3500
15 - 16in (38 - 41cm)	4400 - 4900
21 - 24in (53 - 61cm)	6000 - 6600
28in (71cm)	8000 - 9000
33in (84cm) wire eyes at auction	13,500

Round face with open mouth: Ca. 1870s. Perfect very pale bisque socket head, appropriate wig, bulgy paperweight eyes, open mouth with pointed teeth, round face, pierced ears; jointed composition body; dressed; all in good condition.
Mark: None, but sometimes body has a label.
Two rows of teeth, 16 - 19in (41 - 48cm) $ 5000 - 6000**

Kicking, crying bébé, mechanical key-wind body with composition arms and lower legs **$2100 - 2300** Motschmann-type body with bisque shoulders, hips and lower arms and legs. (For photograph see *7th Blue Book*, page 361.)
18 - 21in (46 - 53cm) **$6500****
Bébé Chaise in stroller, cries, waves arms, moves head, 14in (36cm) doll, at auction **$6000**

**Not enough price samples to compute a reliable range.

Figure A or C Bébé: Ca. 1887 - on. Perfect bisque socket head, cardboard pate, appropriate wig, paperweight eyes, closed mouth, pierced ears; jointed composition body; dressed; all in good condition. Figure "A" more easily found than "C."
Mark: (incised) $J. \ STEINER$
$B^{TE} \ S.G.D.G.$
$PARIS$
$F^{I} \ ^{RE} \ A \ 15$

Body and/or head may be stamped:
"Le Petit Parisien
BEBE STEINER
MEDAILLE d'OR
PARIS 1889"
or paper label of doll carrying flag

8in (20cm)	$2600 - 3000
10in (25cm)	3000 - 3300
15 - 16in (38 - 41cm)	4200 - 4700
22 - 24in (56 - 61cm)	5500 - 6500
28 - 30in (71 - 76cm)	7500 - 8000
12in (31cm) original box, shift, shoes and socks	4000
Open mouth, 17in (43cm)	2500
22in (56cm)	2900

*Allow 20 - 30% more for Figure C.

Bébé Le Parisien: 1892 - on. Pefect bisque socket head, cardboard pate, appropriate wig, paperweight eyes, closed or open mouth, pierced ears; jointed composition

Jules Steiner continued

body; dressed; all in good condition. (For photograph see page 9.)
Mark: head (incised):   A -19
                            PARIS

(red stamp):
"LE PARISIEN"
body (purple stamp):
"BEBE 'LE PARISIEN'
MEDAILLE D'OR
PARIS"

Closed mouth:

13 - 15in (33 - 38cm)	**3500 - 4000**
18 - 20in (46 - 51cm)	**4500 - 5000**
23 - 25in (58 - 64cm)	**5500 - 6000**
30in (76cm)	**8000**
Open mouth, 20 - 22in (51 - 56cm)	
	2600 - 2800

Left: 24½in (62cm) Series C Bourgoin Steiner with wire eyes. *Private Collection.*

Bottom left: 16in (41cm) unmarked Steiner with two rows of teeth. *Richard Wright Antiques.*

Bottom right: 14in (36cm) Figure C Steiner. *Nancy A. Smith Collection.*

18in (46cm) Gigoteur mechanical Steiner. *H & J Foulke, Inc.*

18½ (47cm) Figure A Steiner. *H & J Foulke, Inc.*

342

Swaine & Co.

FACTS

Swaine & Co., porcelain factory, Hüttensteinach, Sonneberg, Thüringia, Germany. Ca. 1910 - on for doll heads. Bisque socket head, composition baby body.

Mark: Stamped in green:

Swaine Character Babies: Ca. 1910 - on. Perfect bisque head; composition baby body with bent limbs; dressed; all in good condition. (See previous *Blue Books* for photographs of specific models.)

Incised Lori, molded hair, glass eyes, open/closed mouth,

22 - 24in (56 - 61cm)	**$2800 - 3200**

#232, (open-mouth **Lori**):

12 - 14in (31 - 36cm)	**900 - 1000**
20 - 22in (51 - 56cm)	**1600 - 1800**

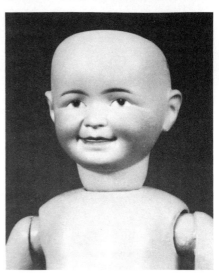

17in (43cm) B.P. character. *Richard Wright Antiques.*

DIP (wig, glass eyes, closed mouth):

11in (28cm)	**$ 800 - 900**
15in (38cm)	**1300 - 1450**
17 - 18in (43 - 46cm) toddler	**2000 - 2200**

DV (molded hair, glass eyes, open/closed mouth):

13in (33cm)	**1450**
16in (41cm)	**1650**

DI (molded hair, intaglio eyes, open/closed mouth):

12 - 13in (31 - 33cm)	**850 - 900**

B.P., B.O.: (smiling character):

16 - 18in (41 - 46cm)	**4000 - 5000****

F.P.:

8 - 9in (20 - 23cm)	**900 - 1250****

**Not enough price samples to compute a reliable range.

9in (23cm) DIP character baby. *H & J Foulke, Inc.*

FACTS

TERRI LEE Sales Corp., V. Gradwohl, Pres., U.S.A. 1946 - Lincoln, Neb.; then Apple Valley, Calif., from 1952 - Ca. 1962. First dolls, rubbery plastic composition; later, hard plastic. 16in (41cm) and 10in (25cm).
Mark: embossed across shoulders
First dolls:
           "TERRI LEE
           PAT. PENDING"
raised letters
Later dolls: "TERRI LEE"

Terri Lee Child Doll: Original wig, painted eyes; jointed at neck, shoulders and hips; all original tagged clothing and accessories; very good condition. 16in (41cm): (For photographs see *10th Blue Book*, pages 356 and 396.)

	$250 - 300*
Patty-Jo (black)	**500 - 600**
Jerri Lee, 16in (41cm)	**250 - 300***
Benjie (black)	**500 - 600**

Tiny Terri Lee, inset eyes. (For photograph see *8th Blue Book*, page 381.)

10in (25cm)	**150 - 175**
Tiny Jerri Lee, inset eyes, 10in (25cm)	**185 - 210**
Connie Lynn	**350 - 400**
Gene Autry	**1500****

Linda Baby. (For photograph see *8th Blue Book*, page 381.)

10in (25cm)	**185 - 195**
Ginger Girl Scout, 8in (20cm)	**110 - 125**

*Allow extra for special outfits or gowns.
**Not enough price samples to compute a reliable average.

16in (41cm) ***Benjie.*** *H & J Foulke, Inc.*

Thuillier

FACTS

A. Thuillier, Paris, France. Some heads by F. Gaultier. 1875 - 1893. Bisque socket head on wood, kid or composition body.

Mark:

A.8.T.

AT·N° 8

Marked A.T. Child: Perfect bisque head, cork pate, good wig, paperweight eyes, pierced ears, closed mouth; body of wood, kid or composition in good condition; appropriate old wig and clothes, excellent quality.

12 - 13in (31 - 33cm)	**$22,000 - 30,000**
16 - 18in (41 - 46cm)	**35,000 - 43,000**
22 - 24in (56 - 61cm)	**47,000 - 52,000**

Open mouth, two rows of teeth:

20 - 22in (51 - 56cm)	**$ 9000 - 12,000**
36in (91cm)	**25,000**

Approximate size chart:
1 = 9in (23cm)
3 = 12in (31cm)
7 = 15½in (39cm)
9 = 18in (46cm)
12 = 22 - 23in (56 - 58cm)
15 = 36 - 37in (91 - 93cm)

18in (46cm) A. 9 T. *Private Collection.*

FACTS

Société Française de Fabrication de Bébés et Jouets. (S.F.B.J.) of Paris and Montreuil-sous-Bois, France. 1922 - on. Bisque head, composition body. 5in (13cm) and larger.

Mark:

71 ⟨UNIS FRANCE⟩ 14?
301

Unis Child Doll: Perfect bisque head, wood and composition jointed body; good wig, sleep eyes, open mouth; pretty clothes; all in nice condition.

#301 or **60** (fully-jointed body):

8 - 10in (20 - 25cm)	$ 425 - 475
15 - 17in (38 - 43cm)	625 - 675
23 - 25in (58 - 64cm)	900 - 1000
28in (71cm)	1200
12in (31cm) all original, mint	750

Five-piece body:

5in (13cm) painted eyes	150 - 175
6½in (17cm) glass eyes	240 - 265
11 - 13in (28 - 33cm)	325 - 350

Black or brown bisque, 11 - 13in (28 - 33cm)

375 - 425

Bleuette, 10 - 11in (25 - 28cm)
$ 700 - 750

Princess (See page 226.):

#251 character toddler:

14 - 15in (36 - 38cm)	
	$1400 - 1500
28in (71cm)	2200 - 2400

Composition head 301 or **60:**

11 - 13in (28 - 33cm)	
	$ 150 - 175
20in (51cm)	350 - 400

Composition head #251 or **#247 toddler,** 22in (56cm)   650 - 750

Two views of 11½in (29cm) 301, Jumeau label, all original. *H & J Foulke, Inc.*

Vogue

FACTS

Vogue Dolls, Inc., Medford, Mass., U.S.A. 1937 - on. 1937 - 1948, composition; 1948 - 1962, hard plastic.
Creator: Jennie Graves.
Clothes Designer: Virginia Graves Carlson.
Clothes Label: "Vogue," "Vogue Dolls," or

VOGUE DOLLS, INC.
MEDFORD, MASS. USA
® REG U.S. PAT OFF

All-Composition Toddles: Jointed neck, shoulders and hips; molded hair or mohair wig, painted eyes looking to side; original clothes; all in good condition.
Mark: "VOGUE" on head
"DOLL CO." on back
"TODDLES" stamped on sole of shoe

7 - 8in (18 - 20cm)	**$200 - 225***
Mint condition	**250 - 275***

*Allow extra for unusual outfits.

Hard Plastic Ginny: All-hard plastic, jointed at neck, shoulders and hips (some have jointed knees and some walk); nice wig, sleep eyes (early ones have painted eyes, later dolls have molded eyelashes); original clothes; all in excellent condition with perfect hair and pretty coloring.
Mark: On strung dolls: "VOGUE DOLLS"
On walking dolls: "GINNY// VOGUE DOLLS"
7 - 8in (18 - 20cm):

1948 - 1949:

Painted eyes	**$225 - 325***
Separate outfits	**50 - 65**

1950 - 1953:

Painted eyelashes, strung	**$250 - 300***
Caracul wig	**325 - 350**
Separate outfits	**50 - 65**

1954:

Painted eyelashes, walks	**$175 - 225***
Separate outfits	**45 - 55**

1955 - 1957:

Molded eyelashes, walks	**$125 - 150***
Separate outfits	**40 - 50**

1957 - 1962:

Molded eyelashes, walks, jointed knees	**$100 - 125***
Separate outfits	**30 - 40**

*Allow extra for mint-in-box dolls.

Black *Ginny*, very rare. *Nancy A. Smith Collection.*

Black Ginny	700 up
Crib Crowd Baby, 1950	650*
Queen	700 up

*Allow extra for mint-in-box dolls.

Accessories:

Ginny's Pup	$150 - 175
Cardboard Suitcase with contents	
	40 - 45

Strung *Ginny* with painted lashes, all original. *Nancy A. Smith Collection.*

Ginny Queen. *Private Collection.*

Parasol	15 - 18
Gym Set	250 - 275
Dresser, Bed, Rocking Chair, Wardrobe	
	55 each
Shoe Bag with shoes	40 - 45
School Bag	75 - 85
"Hi I'm Ginny" Pin	50
Ginny's First Secret Book	125
Swag Bag, Hat Box, Auto Bag and	
Garment Bag	25 each

Vogue continued

All Composition Girl: Jointed neck, shoulders and hips; sleeping eyes, open or closed mouth, mohair wig; original clothes; all in good condition.
Mark: None on doll; round silver sticker on front of outfit.

    13in (33cm)   **$225 - 250**

13in (33cm) all-composition Vogue girl, all original. *H & J Foulke, Inc.*

Izannah Walker

FACTS

Izannah Walker, Central Falls, R.I., U.S.A. 1873, but probably made as early as 1840s. All-cloth. 15 - 30in (38 - 76cm).

Mark: Later dolls are marked:

Patented Nov. 4ᵗʰ 1873

Izannah Walker Doll: Stockinette, pressed head, features and hair painted with oils, applied ears, treated limbs; muslin body; appropriate clothes; in good condition.

17 - 19in (43 - 48cm)	**$16,000 - 18,000**
Fair condition, some touch-up	
	8500 - 9500
Poor condition	3000 - 4000

Izannah Walker doll with painted side curls. *Nancy A. Smith Collection.*

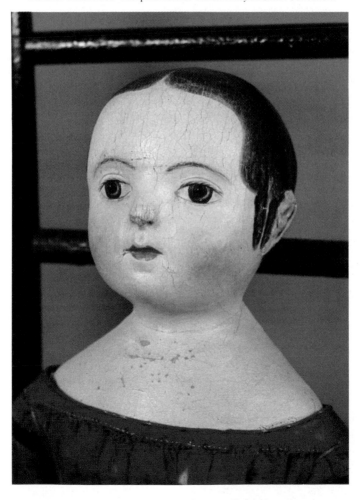

Wagner & Zetzsche

FACTS

Wagner & Zetzsche, doll factory, Ilmenau, Thüringia, Germany. Bisque heads by porcelain factories including Gebrüder Heubach and Alt, Beck & Gottschalck. 1875 - on. Bisque head, cloth, kid or composition body, celluloid-type heads.

Closed-mouth Child: Ca. 1880s. Perfect turned bisque shoulder head with solid dome (mold **639**) or open crown (mold **698**), sometimes with plaster dome, mohair wig, paperweight eyes (a few with sleep eyes), flat eyebrows, closed mouth, small ears; kid or cloth body with bisque hands; appropriate clothes; all in good condition. (For photograph see page Page 49.)

Mark: Blue paper label with "W Z" initials entwined in fancy scroll.

15 - 17in (38 - 43cm)	$ 750 - 850
20 - 22in (51 - 56cm)	1050 - 1250
26in (66cm)	1500

Character Baby or Child: Ca. 1910. Perfect bisque socket head, wig, sleep eyes, open mouth with upper teeth; dressed; all in good condition.

Mark: !0586
𝒲 u 𝒵
𝒥.
Germany
［EU/B♦N］

#10586 made by Gebrüder Heubach.
Baby body, 16 - 18in (41 - 46cm)
$ 700 - 800
Composition body, 14 - 16in (36 - 41cm)
550 - 650
#10585 (shoulder head, kid body),
16 - 18in (41 - 46cm) **375 - 425**

Portrait Children: 1915 - on. Celluloid-type head (**Haralit**) with molded hair, painted eyes. Portraits of the children of Max Zetzsche: **Harald, Hansi,** and **Inge**
Mark: "Harald
W.Z."
(or name of child)
Harald, 14in (36cm), fair condition
250 - 275**
Hansi, 8in (20cm) **125 - 150**
Inge, 1924, 14in (36cm). (For photograph see *8th Blue book*, page 279.) Excellent, all original **800 - 1000****
Barbele, 14in (36cm) all original, excellent, at auction **3250**

**Not enough price samples to compute a reliable range.

14in (36cm) G. Heubach 10586 for Wagner & Zetzsche. *H & J Foulke, Inc.*

Wax Doll, Poured

FACTS

Various firms in London, England, such as Montanari, Pierotti, Peck, Meech, Marsh, Morrell, Cremer and Edwards. 1850s through the early 1900s. Wax head, arms and legs, cloth body.
Mark: Sometimes stamped on body with maker or store.

Poured Wax Doll: Head, lower arms and legs of wax; cloth body; set-in hair, glass eyes; lovely elaborate original clothes or very well dressed; all in good condition.
Baby:

17 - 19in (43 - 48cm)	**$1350 - 1650***
24 - 26in (61 - 66cm)	**1900 - 2300***

Lady, 22 - 24in (56 - 61cm)

	2500 - 3500

Child, 17 - 18in (43 - 46cm)

	1500 - 1800*

Man, 18in (46cm) inset mustache

	1650 - 1750**

(For additional photograph see page 8.)
Baby or Child, lackluster ordinary face,

20 - 22in (51 - 56cm)	**800 - 1000**

*Greatly depending upon appeal of face.

27in (69cm) poured wax child. *Jensen's Antique Dolls.*

Wax (Reinforced)

FACTS

Various firms in Germany. 1860 - 1890. Poured wax shoulder head lined on the inside with plaster composition to give strength and durability, (not to be confused with wax-over-composition which simply has a wax coating), muslin body usually with wax-over-composition lower arms and legs.
Mark: None.

Reinforced Poured Wax Doll: Poured wax shoulder head lined on the inside with plaster composition, glass eyes (may sleep), closed mouth, open crown, pate, curly mohair or human hair wig nailed on (may be partially inset into the wax around the face); muslin body with wax-over-composition lower limbs (feet may have molded boots); appropriate clothes; all in good condition, but showing some nicks and scrapes.

11in (28cm)	**$ 250 - 300**
14 - 16in (36 - 41cm)	**375 - 425**
19 - 21in (48 - 53cm)	**550 - 650**
Lady, 23in (58cm)	**1000**
with molded shoulder plate	**2500****
with molded gloves, all original	
	2500**

Socket head on ball-jointed composition body (Kestner-type)

19in (48cm)	**1200 - 1300**

**Not enough price samples to compute a reliable range.

Wax-Over-Composition

FACTS

Numerous firms in England, Germany or France. During the 1800s. Wax-over-shoulder head of some type of composition or papier-mâché, cloth body, wax-over-composition or wooden limbs.
Mark: None.

English Slit-head Wax: Ca. 1830 - 1860. Wax-over-shoulder head with round face, not rewaxed; human hair wig, glass eyes (may open and close by a wire), faintly smiling; original cloth body with leather arms; original or suitable old clothing; all in fair condition, showing wear. (For photograph see *9th Blue Book*, page 387.)

14 - 15in (36 - 38cm)	$ 650 - 750
18 - 22in (46 - 56cm)	900 - 1100
26 - 28in (66 - 71cm)	1300 - 1500

Molded Hair Doll: Ca. 1860 - on. German wax-over-shoulder head, not rewaxed; molded hair sometimes with bow, glass sleep or set eyes; original cloth body; wax-over or wooden extremities with molded boots or bare feet; nice old clothes; all in good condition, good quality. (For photograph see *10th Blue Book*, page 404.)

14 - 16in (36 - 41cm)	**$275 - 375**
22 - 25in (56 - 64cm)	**500 - 600**

Alice hairdo, 16in (41cm), early model, squeaker torso   **550 - 650**

16in (41cm) Bartenstein double-face doll. *H & J Foulke, Inc.*

Wax-Over-Composition continued

Wax Doll with Wig: Ca. 1860s to 1900. German. Wax-over-shoulder head, not rewaxed; blonde or brown human hair or mohair wig, blue, brown or black glass eyes, sleep or set, open or closed mouth; original cloth body, any combination of extremities mentioned above, also arms may be made of china; original clothing or suitably dressed; entire doll in nice condition.
Standard quality:

11 - 12in (28 - 31cm)	**$125 - 150**
16 - 18in (41 - 46cm)	**300 - 325**
22 - 24in (56 - 61cm)	**400 - 450**

Superior quality (heavily waxed):

11 - 12in (28 - 31cm)	**225 - 250**
16 - 18in (41 - 46cm)	**400 - 450**
22 - 24in (56 - 61cm)	**600 - 650**
30in (76cm)	**750**
17in (43cm) all original and excellent	**575**

21in (53cm) wax over composition with sleep eyes. *Joanna Ott Collection.*

Bonnet Wax Doll: Ca. 1860 - 1880. Wax-over-shoulder head, with molded bonnet; molded hair may have some mohair or human hair attached, blue, brown or black set eyes; original cloth body and wooden extremities; nice old clothes; all in good condition.

16 - 17in (41 - 43cm) common model	**$ 350 - 450**
20in (51cm) boy with cap	**550 - 600**
28in (71cm) early round face with molded poke bonnet	**3000****
16in (41cm) molded hat perched on forehead	**2500****
24in (61cm) molded blue derby-type hat	**2000****

Double-Faced Doll: 1880 - on. Fritz Bartenstein. One face crying, one laughing, rotating on a vertical axis by pulling a string, one face hidden by a hood. Body stamped "Bartenstein."

15 - 16in (38 - 41cm)	**$ 850**

**Not enough price samples to compute a reliable average.

Norah Wellings

FACTS

Victoria Toy Works, Wellington, Shropshire, England, for Norah Wellings. 1926 - Ca. 1960. Fabric: felt, velvet and velour, and other material, stuffed.
Designer: Norah Wellings
Mark: On tag on foot: "Made in England by Norah Wellings."

Wellings Doll: All-fabric, stitch-jointed shoulders and hips; molded fabric face (also of papier-mâché, sometimes stockinette covered), painted features; all in excellent condition. Most commonly found are sailors, Canadian Mounties, Scots and Black Islanders.

Characters (floppy limbs):

8 - 10in (20 - 25cm)	$ 60 - 95
13 - 14in (33 - 36cm)	150 - 200
Glass eyes, 14in (36cm) black	200 - 250
Old Couple, 26in (66cm)	1200 pair

Children:

12 - 13in (31 - 33cm)	$ 400 - 500
16 - 18in (41 - 46cm)	600 - 700
23in (58cm)	1000 - 1200
Glass eyes, 16 - 18in (41 - 46cm)	700 - 800
Bobby, 16in (41cm) glass eyes	800 - 1000
Harry the Hawk, 10in (25cm)	200

10in (25cm) Wellings *Pixie*. *H & J Foulke, Inc.*

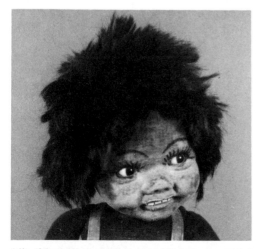

14in (36cm) Wellings black girl with glass eyes. *H & J Foulke, Inc.*

18in (46cm) Wellings girl, all original. *H & J Foulke, Inc.*

FACTS

English craftsmen. Late 17th to mid 19th century. All-wood or with leather or cloth arms.
Mark: None.

William & Mary Period: Ca. 1690. Carved wooden face, painted eyes, tiny lines comprising eyebrows and eyelashes, rouged cheeks, flax or hair wig; wood body, cloth arms, carved wood hands (fork shaped), wood-jointed legs. Appropriate clothes; all in fair condition. (For photograph see *9th Blue Book*, page 223.)

12 - 17in (31 - 43cm) **$50,000 up**

Queen Anne Period: Ca. early 1700s. Carved wooden face, dark glass eyes (sometimes painted), dotted eyebrows and eyelashes; jointed wood body, cloth upper arms; appropriate clothes; all in fair condition. (For photograph see page 8.)

24in (61cm) **$25,000 up**

Georgian Period: Mid to late 1700s. Round wooden head with gesso covering, inset glass eyes (later sometimes blue), dotted eyelashes and eyebrows, flax or hair wig; jointed wood body with pointed torso; appropriate clothes; all in fair condition.

12 - 13in (31 - 33cm)	**$2500 - 3000**
16 - 18in (41 - 46cm)	**4500 - 5000**
24in (61cm)	**6000 - 6500**

Early 19th Century: Wooden head, gessoed, painted eyes, pointed torso, flax or hair wig; old clothes (dress usually longer than legs); all in fair condition.

13in (33cm)	**$1300 - 1600**
16 - 21in (41 - 53cm)	**2000 - 3000**

17in (43cm) Georgian Period English Wood. *Richard Wright Antiques.*

Wood, German (Peg Woodens)

FACTS

Craftsmen of the Grodner Tal, Austria, and Sonneberg, Germany, such as Insam & Prinoth (1820 - 1830) Gorden Tirol and Nürnberg verlagers of pegwood dolls and wood doll heads. Late 18th to 20th century. All-wood, pegged or ball-jointed.
Mark: None.

Early to Mid 19th Century: Delicately carved head, varnished, carved and painted hair and features, with a yellow tuck comb in hair, painted spit curls, sometimes earrings; mortise and tenon peg joints; old clothes; all in fair condition.

6 - 7in (15 - 18cm)	$ 650 - 750
12 - 13in (31 - 33cm)	1350 - 1450
17 - 18in (43 - 46cm)	1800 - 2000
9in (23cm) exceptional all original condition	1700 - 1750
Fortune Tellers, 17 - 20in (43 - 51cm)	2500 - 3000

Late 19th Century: Wooden head with painted hair, carving not so elaborate as previously, sometimes earrings, spit curls; dressed; all in good condition.

4in (10cm)	$ 125 - 135
7 - 8in (18 - 20cm)	175 - 225
12in (31cm)	350 - 400

Wood shoulder head, carved bun hairdo, cloth body, wood limbs:

9in (23cm) all original	350 - 400
17in (43cm)	500 - 550
24in (61cm)	800 - 900
Turned red torso, 10in (25cm)	225 - 250

Early 20th Century: Turned wood head, carved nose, painted hair, peg-jointed, painted white lower legs, painted black shoes.

11 - 12in (28 - 31cm)	$ 60 - 80

13in (33cm) early 19th century German wood.
Richard Wright Antiques.

Wood, German (20th Century)

FACTS

Various companies, such as Rudolf Schneider and Schilling, Sonneberg, Thüringia, Germany. 1901 - 1914. All-wood, fully jointed or wood head and limbs, cloth body.
Mark: Usually none; sometimes Schilling "winged angel" trademark.

"Bébé Tout en Bois" (Doll All of Wood): All of wood, fully jointed; wig, inset glass eyes, open mouth with teeth; appropriate clothes; all in fair to good condition.

13in (33cm)	**$ 425 - 475**
17 - 19in (43 - 48cm)	**650 - 750**
22 - 24in (56 - 61cm)	**950**

14in (36cm) German all-wood doll. *H & J Foulke, Inc.*

Wood, Swiss

FACTS

Various Swiss firms. 20th century. All-wood or wood head and limbs on cloth body. Various sizes, but smaller sizes are more commonly found.
Mark: Usually a paper label on wrist or clothes.

Swiss Wooden Doll: Wooden head with hand-carved features and hair with good detail (males sometimes have carved hats); all carved wood jointed body; original, usually regional attire; excellent condition.

9 - 10in (23 - 25cm)	**$ 250 - 275**
12in (31cm)	**350 - 400**
17 - 18in (43 - 46cm)	**750 - 850**
12in (31cm) boy with carved hat	
	500

9in (23cm) Swiss wood boy. *H & J Foulke, Inc.*

Glossary

Applied Ears: Ears molded independently and affixed to the head. (On most dolls the ear is included as part of the head mold.)

Bald Head: Head with no crown opening, could be covered by a wig or have painted hair.

Ball-jointed Body: Usually a body of composition or papier-mâché with wooden balls at knees, elbows, hips and shoulders to make swivel joints; some parts of the limbs may be wood.

Bébé: French child doll with "dolly face."

Belton-type: A bald head with one, two or three small holes for attaching wig.

Bent-limb Baby Body: Composition body of five pieces with chubby torso and curved arms and legs.

Biscaloid: Ceramic or composition substance for making dolls; also called imitation bisque.

Biskoline: Celluloid-type substance for making dolls.

Bisque: Unglazed porcelain, usually flesh tinted, used for dolls' heads or all-bisque dolls.

Breather: Doll with an actual opening in each nostril; also called open nostrils.

Breveté (or Bté): Used on French dolls to indicate that the patent is registered.

Character Doll: Dolls with bisque or composition heads, modeled to look lifelike, such as infants, young or older children, young ladies and so on.

China: Glazed porcelain used for dolls' heads and *Frozen Charlottes*.

Child Dolls: Dolls with a typical "dolly face," which represents a child.

Composition: A material used for dolls' heads and bodies, consisting of such items as wood pulp, glue, sawdust, flower, rags and sundry other substances.

Contemporary Clothes: Clothes not original to the doll, but dating from the same period when the doll would have been a plaything.

Crown Opening: The cut-away part of a doll head.

DEP: Abbreviation used on German and French dolls claiming registration.

D.R.G.M.: Abbreviation used on German dolls indicating a registered design or patent.

Dolly Face: Typical face used on bisque dolls before 1910 when the character face was developed; "dolly faces" were used also after 1910.

Embossed Mark: Raised letters, numbers or names on the backs of heads or bodies.

Feathered Eyebrows: Eyebrows composed of many tiny painted brush strokes to give a realistic look.

Fixed Eyes: Glass eyes that do not move or sleep.

Flange Neck: A doll's head with a ridge at the base of the neck which contains holes for sewing the head to a cloth body.

Flapper Dolls: Dolls of the 1920s period with bobbed wig or molded hair and slender arms and legs.

Flirting Eyes: Eyes which move from side to side as doll's head is tilted.

Frozen Charlotte: Doll molded all in one piece including arms and legs.

Ges.(Gesch.): Used on German dolls to indicate design is registered or patented.

Googly Eyes: Large, often round eyes looking to the side; also called roguish or goo goo eyes.

Hard Plastic: Hard material used for making dolls after 1948.

Incised Mark: Letters, numbers or names impressed into the bisque on the back of the head or on the shoulder plate.

Intaglio Eyes: Painted eyes with sunken pupil and iris.

JCB: Jointed composition body. See *ball-jointed body*.

Kid Body: Body of white or pink leather.

Lady Dolls: Dolls with an adult face and a body with adult proportions.

Mohair: Goat's hair widely used in making doll wigs.

Molded Hair: Curls, waves and comb marks which are actually part of the mold and not merely painted onto the head.

Motschmann-type Body: Doll body with cloth midsection and upper limbs with floating joints; hard lower torso and lower limbs.

Open-Mouth: Lips parted with an actual opening in the bisque, usually has teeth either molded in the bisque or set in separately and sometimes a tongue.

Open/Closed Mouth: A mouth molded to appear open, but having no actual slit in the bisque.

Original Clothes: Clothes belonging to a doll during the childhood of the original owner, either commercially or homemade.

Painted Bisque: Bisque covered with a layer of flesh-colored paint which has not been baked in, so will easily rub or wash off.

Paperweight Eyes: Blown glass eyes which have depth and look real, usually found in French dolls.

Papier-mâché: A material used for dolls' heads and bodies, consisting of paper pulp, sizing, glue, clay or flour.

Pate: A shaped piece of plaster, cork, cardboard or other material which covers the crown opening.

Pierced Ears: Little holes through the doll's earlobes to accommodate earrings.

Pierced-in Ears: A hole at the doll's earlobe which goes into the head to accommodate earrings.

Pink Bisque: A later bisque of about 1920 which was pre-colored pink.

Pink-toned China: China which has been given a pink tint to look more like real flesh color; also call lustered china.

Rembrandt Hair: Hair style parted in center with bangs at front, straight down sides and back and curled at ends.

S.G.D.G.: Used on French dolls to indicate that the patent is registered "without guarantee of the government."

Shoulder Head: A doll's head and shoulders all in one piece.

Shoulder Plate: The actual shoulder portion sometimes molded in one with the head, sometimes a separate piece with a socket in which a head is inserted.

Socket Head: Head and neck which fit into an opening in the shoulder plate or the body.

Solid-dome Head: Head with no crown opening, could have painted hair or be covered by wig.

Stationary Eyes: Glass eyes which do not move or sleep.

Stone Bisque: Coarse white bisque of a lesser quality.

Toddler Body: Usually a chubby ball-jointed composition body with chunky, shorter thighs and a diagonal hip joint; sometimes has curved instead of jointed arms; sometimes is of five pieces with straight chubby legs.

Topsy-Turvy: Doll with two heads, one usually concealed beneath a skirt.

Turned Shoulder Head: Head and shoulders are one piece, but the head is molded at an angle so that the doll is not looking straight ahead.

Vinyl: Soft plastic material used for making dolls after 1950s.

Watermelon Mouth: Closed line-type mouth curved up at each side in an impish expression.

Wax Over: A doll with head and/or limbs of papier-mâché or composition covered with a layer of wax to give a natural, life-like finish.

Weighted Eyes: Eyes which can be made to sleep by means of a weight which is attached to the eyes.

Wire Eyes: Eyes that can be made to sleep by means of a wire which protrudes from doll's head.

Selected Bibliography

Anderton, Johana. *Twentieth Century Dolls.* North Kansas City, Missouri: Trojan Press, 1971.

_____. *More Twentieth Century Dolls.* North Kansas City, Missouri: Athena Publishing Co., 1974.

Angione, Genevieve. *All-Bisque & Half-Bisque Dolls.* Exton, Pennsylvania: Schiffer Publishing Ltd., 1969.

Borger, Mona. *Chinas, Dolls for Study and Admiration.* San Francisco: Borger Publications, 1983.

Cieslik, Jürgen and Marianne. *German Doll Encyclopedia 1800-1939.* Cumberland, Maryland: Hobby House Press, Inc., 1985.

Coleman, Dorothy S., Elizabeth Ann and Evelyn Jane. *The Collector's Book of Dolls' Clothes.* New York: Crown Publishers, Inc., 1975.

_____. *The Collector's Encyclopedia of Dolls, Vol. I & II.* New York: Crown Publishers, Inc., 1968 & 1986.

Corson, Carol. *Schoenhut Dolls, A Collector's Encyclopedia.* Cumberland, Maryland: Hobby House Press, Inc., 1993.

Foulke, Jan. *Blue Books of Dolls & Values, Vol. I-X.* Cumberland, Maryland: Hobby House Press, Inc., 1974-1991.

_____. *Doll Classics.* Cumberland, Maryland: Hobby House Press, Inc., 1987.

_____. *Focusing on Effanbee Composition Dolls.* Riverdale, Maryland: Hobby House Press, 1978.

_____. *Focusing on Gebrüder Heubach Dolls.* Cumberland, Maryland: Hobby House Press, Inc., 1980.

_____. *Kestner, King of Dollmakers.* Cumberland, Maryland: Hobby House Press, Inc., 1982.

_____. *Simon & Halbig Dolls, The Artful Aspect.* Cumberland, Maryland: Hobby House Press, Inc., 1984.

_____. *Treasury of Madame Alexander Dolls.* Riverdale, Maryland: Hobby House Press, 1979.

Gerken, Jo Elizabeth. *Wonderful Dolls of Papier-Mâché.* Lincoln, Nebraska: Doll Research Associates, 1970.

Hillier, Mary. *Dolls and Dollmakers.* New York: G. P. Putnam's Sons, 1968.

_____. *The History of Wax Dolls.* Cumberland, Maryland: Hobby House Press, Inc.; London: Justin Knowles, 1985.

King, Constance Eileen. *The Collector's History of Dolls.* London: Robert Hale, 1977; New York: St. Martin's Press, 1978.

Mathes, Ruth E. and Robert C. *Dolls, Toys and Childhood.* Cumberland, Maryland: Hobby House Press, Inc., 1987.

McGonagle, Dorothy A. *The Dolls of Jules Nicolas Steiner.* Cumberland, Maryland: Hobby House Press, Inc., 1988.

Merrill, Madeline O. *The Art of Dolls, 1700-1940.* Cumberland, Maryland: Hobby House Press, Inc., 1985.

Noble, John. *Treasury of Beautiful Dolls.* New York: Hawthorn Books, 1971.

Schoonmaker, Patricia N. *Effanbee Dolls: The Formative Years 1910-1929.* Cumberland, Maryland: Hobby House Press, Inc., 1984.

_____. *Patsy Doll Family Encyclopedia.* Cumberland, Maryland: Hobby House Press, Inc., 1992.

Tarnowska, Maree. *Fashion Dolls.* Cumberland, Maryland: Hobby House Press, Inc., 1986.

About the Author

The name Jan Foulke is synonymous with accurate information. As the author of the *Blue Book of Dolls & Values®*, she is the most quoted source on doll information and the most respected and recognized authority on dolls and doll prices in the world.

Born in Burlington, New Jersey, Jan Foulke has always had a fondness for dolls. She recalls, "Many happy hours of my childhood were spent with dolls as companions, since we lived on a quiet county road, and until I was ten, I was an only child." Jan received a B.A. from Columbia Union College, where she was named to the *Who's Who in American Colleges & Universities* and was graduated with high honors. Jan taught for twelve years in the Montgomery County school system in Maryland, and also supervised student teachers in English for the University of Maryland, where she did graduate work.

Jan and her husband, Howard, who photographs the dolls presented in the *Blue Book*, were both fond of antiquing as a hobby, and in 1972 they decided to open a small antique shop of their own. The interest of their daughter, Beth, in dolls sparked their curiosity about the history of old dolls—an interest that quite naturally grew out of their love of heirlooms. The stock in their antique shop gradually changed and evolved into an antique doll shop.

Early in the development of their antique doll shop, Jan and Howard realized that there was a critical need for an accurate and reliable doll identification and price guide resource. In the early 1970s, the Foulkes teamed up with Hobby House Press to produce (along with Thelma Bateman) the first *Blue Book of Dolls & Values*, originally published in 1974. Since that time, the Foulkes have exclusively authored and illustrated the ten successive editions, and today the *Blue Book* is regarded by collectors and dealers as the definitive source for doll prices and values.

Jan and Howard Foulke now dedicate all of their professional time to the world of dolls: writing and illustrating books and articles, appraising collections, lecturing on antique dolls, acting as consultants to museums, auction houses and major collectors, and selling dolls both by mail order and through exhibits at major shows throughout the United States. Mrs. Foulke is a member of the United Federation of Doll Clubs, Doll Collectors of America, and the International Doll Academy.

Mrs. Foulke has appeared on numerous television talk shows and is often quoted in newspaper and magazine articles as the ultimate source for doll pricing and trends in collecting. Both *USA Today* and *The Washington Post* have stated that the *Blue Book of Dolls & Values* is "the bible of doll collecting."

In addition to her work on the eleven editions of the *Blue Book of Dolls & Values*, Jan Foulke has also authored: *Focusing on Effanbee Composition Dolls; A Treasury of Madame Alexander Dolls; Kestner, King of Dollmakers; Simon & Halbig, The Artful Aspect; Focusing on Gebrüder Heubach Dolls; Doll Classics;* and *Focusing on Dolls*.

Index